Growth, Employment, and Equity

Growth, Employment, and Equity

The Impact of the Economic Reforms in Latin America and the Caribbean

Barbara Stallings
Wilson Peres

UNITED NATIONS
Economic Commission for Latin America and
the Caribbean

BROOKINGS INSTITUTION PRESS
Washington, D.C.

Growth, Employment, and Equity: The Impact of the Economic Reforms in Latin America and the Caribbean may be ordered from: BROOKINGS INSTITUTION PRESS, 1775 Massachusetts Avenue, N.W., Washington, DC 20036. Telephone: 800/275-1447 or 202/797-6258. Fax: 202/797-6004. Internet: www.brookings.edu.

Library of Congress Cataloging-in-Publication data

Stallings, Barbara.
    Growth, employment, and equity : the impact of the economic reforms in Latin America and the Caribbean / Barbara Stallings and Wilson Peres.
      p.   cm.
Includes bibliographical references and index.
    ISBN 0-8157-8087-7 (acid-free)
    1. Latin America—Economic policy. 2. Caribbean Area—Economic policy. 3. Latin America—Economic conditions—1982– 4. Caribbean Area—Economic conditions—1945– 5. Free enterprise—Latin America. 6. Free enterprise—Caribbean Area. I. Peres, Wilson. II. Title.
    HC123 .S83 2000   00-008633
    338.98—dc21   CIP

9 8 7 6 5 4 3 2 1

Typeset in Adobe Garamond

Composition by Cynthia Stock, Silver Spring, Maryland

Printed by R. R. Donnelley and Sons, Harrisonburg, Virginia

Contents

Foreword

The impact of the economic reforms undertaken by Latin American and Caribbean countries in the last two decades is at the core of the economic policy debate in the region as we enter the new decade. Trade opening, financial liberalization, and privatizations have radically changed the rules of the game under which business and labor operate. Changes in macroeconomic policy, which accompanied or preceded the reforms, sometimes reinforced their effects on special targets of structural reforms—particularly export growth—but sometimes ran in the opposite direction. The combined result was new market structures and changes in microeconomic behavior.

The evaluation of the effects of the reforms on economic growth, employment, and income distribution goes well beyond the interests of academic economists. Governments, political parties, and social actors are all demanding more in-depth evaluations of the results in order to design or propose policies that complement the reforms or correct their undesired effects. The Economic Commission for Latin America and the Caribbean (ECLAC) is actively participating in this process.

This book is the most important and comprehensive effort that ECLAC has undertaken to study the impact of the reforms. Although in recent years we have published several works that address this issue, their scope was much more limited, focusing on specific macroeconomic variables, such as growth or employment, or on specific productive sectors. The current endeavor constitutes a major effort to integrate analytical approaches and knowledge developed across ECLAC divisions, subregional headquarters, and country offices.

The evaluation of the impact of the reforms has been a difficult task. Data are poor, particularly for smaller economies. Even for larger countries, disaggregated information is seldom available. A three-year research project was necessary to produce new data and to analyze those data for nine countries in Latin America and the Caribbean. All large and most medium-size countries in the region were studied in the project, and small countries from all subregions (Central America, the Caribbean, and South America) were also included. We believe that the resulting analysis will provide important inputs for the policy debate.

The authors show that the reforms had a surprisingly small effect on growth and equity at the aggregate level. Although there are clear signs of recovery with respect to the 1980s, the changes in economic policy have not boosted performance in the ways that their proponents had predicted. While most countries have been successful in lowering inflation rates, the reforms may have made problems worse in other areas, especially employment. At the country level, substantial heterogeneity was found. One group of countries with especially problematic initial conditions became aggressive reformers, while others with a better record in the past were more cautious about embarking on profound changes. The fact that, on average, the former group has seen GDP expand more rapidly in the 1990s owes in large part to a catch-up process, once gross macroeconomic imbalances were corrected.

Unlike most other studies, this one did not stop at the aggregate or country levels. Indeed, one of the most important parts of the book is the sectoral and microeconomic analysis. These levels show evidence of more significant impacts of the reforms. Trade liberalization and privatization were instrumental in fostering market restructuring, which led to the entry of new actors and to new investment, particularly of foreign origin. Stronger competition from imports and from new actors in the domestic market led to widespread modernization, particularly in sectors undergoing rapid technological change, such as telecommunications. In other activities such as agriculture or manufacturing, the reforms fostered specialization and thus increased efficiency, but they also led to greater heterogeneity or even polarization between modern and traditional producers. Large firms, especially subsidiaries of transnational corporations, were the leaders in both investment and the incorporation of new technologies. Small domestic firms presented a very heterogeneous performance, but continued to produce mainly for the domestic markets. Consequently, they performed better when macroeconomic conditions were favorable.

The international economy has played an important, but contradictory, role in the reform process. Renewed access to international financial markets enabled countries of the region to break out of the foreign exchange constraint they faced during the 1980s. At the same time, the new flows have proved extremely volatile, causing substantial damage when they reversed course in 1994–95 and 1998–99. Latin American and Caribbean economies remain vulnerable to the trends in financial flows since exports have not grown as fast as imports, producing a widening trade gap that needs to be financed.

The book concludes that the reforms had favorable effects in several areas, but they were not sufficient to foster dynamic, stable economic growth in the region. Moreover, the region's problems in the areas of unemployment and inequality will not be resolved unless the reforms are complemented with policies to foster competitiveness, job creation, and a better income distribution. The final chapter of the book presents a set of policy proposals that are well integrated into current ECLAC efforts to develop a comprehensive policy strategy on growth, equity, and citizenship.

ECLAC could not have developed such a large project without the cooperation of an extensive network of researchers in each of the nine countries, who undertook field research, the production of new data, and country analyses. The creation of this network is another positive spillover of the project that resulted in this book. The coordination of a large number of consultants was handled through a two-tier organization of the project. Under the general guidelines of the project director, Dr. Barbara Stallings, four module coordinators and nine country coordinators supervised consultant work and undertook a significant part of the analysis included in this book. Four other books, including the detailed analysis and results developed in the modules on investment, technological progress, employment, and income distribution, will be published in both Spanish and English during the coming months. In addition, volumes are being published in the nine countries to present the analyses of each of the national reform processes. The basic working papers that provided much of the raw material for the project are available on the ECLAC website (www.eclac.cl).

External financing came from a number of international donors. First of all, we would like to acknowledge the central role of the Ministry of Development Cooperation of the Government of the Netherlands, which provided the basic grant for the project. The International Development

Research Centre of Canada (IDRC) also provided substantial funding, which enabled us to expand the scope of the project in important ways. These two sources were complemented by funds from the Ford Foundation and the Swedish International Development Agency. We are extremely grateful to all of these donors, without whose support the project could not have been undertaken.

José Antonio Ocampo
Executive Secretary
U.N. Economic Commission for
Latin America and the Caribbean

Preface

This book is the synthesis of a multi-year project to investigate the impact of the economic reforms in Latin America and the Caribbean. The project was a joint venture between the United Nations Economic Commission for Latin America and the Caribbean (ECLAC) and local researchers in the nine countries covered by the study: Argentina, Bolivia, Brazil, Chile, Colombia, Costa Rica, Jamaica, Mexico, and Peru.

The methodology of the project, which is presented in chapter 1, resulted from the long-term interaction between two ECLAC divisions: the Economic Development Division and the Division of Production, Productivity, and Management. This collaboration produced an innovative approach to the evaluation of the impact of the reforms, which focuses on the interaction of macroeconomic, sectoral, and microeconomic variables. Coordinating different research methodologies was not an easy task, but the learning process it implied was useful for our approach in this book and should lead to other research advances in the future.

The project produced a large amount of new data as well as new interpretations of the reform process. While much of the macroeconomic and social data came from existing ECLAC sources, we were also able to draw on a historical database of output and investment statistics. The sectoral information on investment was produced by the project, while information on productivity and firm performance derived from other closely related ECLAC research activities. Important sources for the analysis of employment and equity resulted from special processing of household surveys.

Obtaining new data was particularly difficult in the smallest countries. In several cases, especially in Jamaica, we could not get the type of information needed to undertake comparative sectoral analysis or time series long enough to allow significant quantitative analysis. These shortcomings sometimes resulted in the use of ad hoc subsets of countries when dealing with specific issues, which is apparent in the chapters that discuss investment, productivity, and employment at the country and sectoral levels. In a similar way, we did not have data on all variables for the full period through 1998. Had we insisted on always including all nine countries for the whole period, several crucial topics would have been omitted from the analysis. In the trade-off between comprehensiveness and relevance, we opted for the latter.

The project was organized along two axes: topics and countries. Five topical modules set the substantive agenda; each was directed by an ECLAC economist or consultant. The five included reforms and public policies, directed by Barbara Stallings; investment by Ricardo Bielschowsky and Graciela Moguillansky; technological change by Jorge Katz; employment by Jürgen Weller; and equity by Samuel Morley. The results of the modules provided basic inputs for various chapters of the book, as will be seen through specific acknowledgments. Volumes consisting of the analysis and conclusions of the investment, technology, employment, and equity modules will also be published separately. A list of these and all other project publications is included in a special section at the end of the book.

Country coordinators were in charge of the project in each of the nine countries. They identified consultants to carry out the studies, supervised the research in collaboration with the module coordinators, and produced edited volumes to analyze the particular characteristics of the reforms in each country. The country coordinators were as follows: in Argentina, Daniel Heymann, ECLAC-Buenos Aires; in Bolivia, Luis Carlos Jemio, Andean Development Corporation; in Brazil, Renato Baumann, ECLAC-Brasilia; in Chile, Ricardo Ffrench-Davis and Osvaldo Rosales, ECLAC-Santiago; in Colombia, Juan José Echavarría, Fedesarrollo; in Costa Rica, Anabelle Ulate, University of Costa Rica; in Jamaica, Damien King, University of the West Indies; in Mexico, Fernando Clavijo, Estrategia y Análisis Económico Consultores; and in Peru, Alberto Pasco-Font, Grupo de Análisis para el Desarrollo (GRADE).

An external advisory committee provided very useful advice on the project. It was constituted by six people who combine experience with both policymaking and research. Members were Nancy Birdsall, former executive vice president of the Inter-American Development Bank, now senior associate at the Carnegie Endowment for International Peace; René Cortázar, former minister of labor in Chile, former researcher at the Economic Research Corporation for Latin America (CIEPLAN), and currently executive director of Chilean National Television; Norman Hicks, senior economist in the Latin American and Caribbean Division of the World Bank; Juan Antonio Morales, president of the Central Bank of Bolivia and professor of economics at the Catholic University of Bolivia; Pitou van Dijck, professor of economics at the University of Amsterdam; and Dorothea Werneck, former minister of labor and industry in Brazil, former researcher at the Institute of Applied Economics Research (IPEA), and currently manager of the Brazilian Export Promotion Agency.

In addition to these colleagues, many other people were involved in the project. Over 70 individual researchers produced working papers that served as the basic inputs for the country and topic volumes as well as for this book. Two of them in particular, André Hofman of ECLAC and Stephany Griffith-Jones of the Institute for Development Studies at the University of Sussex, made extensive contributions throughout the project as well as writing key papers on economic growth and the international economy, respectively. An important collateral book on the impact of the reforms in agriculture was edited by Beatriz David and César Morales of ECLAC's Agricultural Development Unit. A second collateral project on the reforms and the environment was directed by Marianne Schaper of ECLAC's Environment Division and Claudia Schatán of ECLAC-Mexico. The environment project led to a number of working papers on this topic.

We are extremely grateful to all of the above individuals, both for their contributions to the project in general and for their comments on earlier versions of this book. We are indebted to a number of other people, as well. Gert Rosenthal, former executive secretary of ECLAC, made the project possible through various kinds of support. His successor, José Antonio Ocampo, read the entire manuscript twice and provided comments and advice that had an important impact on the book. In addition to those already mentioned, others who commented on parts of draft manuscripts or made special contributions to individual chapters include Oscar Altimir, Eduardo Antelo, Reynaldo Bajraj, Hubert Escaith, Peter Evans, Enrique Ganuza, Eric Hershberg, Rossana Mostajo, Joseph Ramos, Nola Reinhardt, Jaime Ros, Jaime Saavedra, Rogerio Studart, Anthony Tillett, and Vivianne Ventura Dias.

The project was financed by the Netherlands Ministry for Development Cooperation, the International Development Research Centre of Canada (IDRC), the Ford Foundation, and the Swedish International Development Agency (SIDA). Beyond the financial contributions of the various institutions, we would also like to thank several individuals who were especially helpful: Klaas van der Tempel and Menno Lenstra, former and current first secretaries of the Royal Netherlands Embassy in Santiago; Réal Lavergne, program officer for IDRC; Anthony Tillett, program officer for the Ford Foundation; and Torsten Wetterblad of SIDA.

Able assistance was provided by various people at ECLAC: Lucas Navarro and Claudio Pini as research assistants, Ximena Sánchez and María Eugenia Johnson in secretarial services, Dietrich von Graevenitz and Sofía Astete in project management, and Adriana Valdés in publications arrangements. Jennifer Hoover improved the manuscript substantially through her editorial skills. At the Brookings Institutution Press, we would like to thank Robert Faherty, Janet Walker, Larry Converse, Susan Woollen, and Becky Clark. The index was prepared by Mary Mortensen, and the proofreading was done by Erin Randall. Without the help of all of these people, this book would not exist. Of course, we remain responsible for its content.

Growth,
Employment,
and Equity

1 | *A New Approach to Analyzing Reforms: Macro-Micro Linkages*

In the last ten to fifteen years, the Latin American and Caribbean region has undergone the most significant transformation of economic policy since World War II. Through a series of structural reforms, an increasing number of countries have moved from the closed, state-dominated economies that characterized the import-substitution industrialization model to economies that are more market oriented and more open to the rest of the world. Complementary aspects of the process have accorded a new priority to macroeconomic stability, especially lower rates of inflation, and to increasing expenditure in the social area. Policymakers expected that these changes would speed up economic growth and increase productivity gains, at the same time that they would lead to the creation of more jobs and greater equity.

Have those expectations been fulfilled? It is impossible to make more than a preliminary analysis at this point, since in many cases the reforms are less than a decade old. Even tentative conclusions will be useful, however. Governments must decide whether the new policies are moving in the right direction and, even if they are, whether they would benefit from some mid-course corrections. This requires more data and analysis than were available when we began this project. Moreover, any conclusions that can be drawn will be relevant beyond the boundaries of the region itself. In

1

many parts of the world, including central and eastern Europe, the former Soviet Union, Africa, some parts of Asia, and even some industrialized countries with respect to specific policy areas, governments are experimenting with similar policy changes. Since Latin America has had a head start, others are interested in learning from its successes and failures.

The Literature on the Reforms

We are not, of course, the first to study the reforms and their impact. During the last decade, an extensive literature has developed on the topic.[1] Early works tend to express quite rigid views—albeit with little evidence to back them up—that the reforms would either resolve most of the socioeconomic problems in the region or that they would result in disaster. With time and experience, opinions have converged to a certain extent, and a more nuanced evaluation has emerged. Substantial differences of opinion still remain, however, on whether additional reforms are needed, what role the state should play, and what can be expected of the new economic model. These differing evaluations lead to variations in policy recommendations.

Most analysts have studied the reforms in terms of their impact on growth. While emphasizing that growth improved with respect to the 1980s, the majority holds that the impact was disappointing.[2] Post-reform growth was lower than the region's past performance, lower than in some other regions, and lower than necessary to deal with the region's social problems. Others, however, say that the growth rate was as good as could be expected or that growth would have been even slower without the reforms.[3] Most of this analysis concentrates on the aggregate level. An important exception is the United Nations Economic Commission for Latin America and the Caribbean (ECLAC), which points out that the lack of dynamism was accompanied by fundamental changes in sectoral and microeconomic mo-

1. Much of the debate was generated by two documents that were very influential in defining the new development model that Latin American and Caribbean governments began to implement. The World Bank (1991) introduced the concept of market-friendly policies, while Williamson (1990) coined the term Washington Consensus. Even earlier, in the mid-1980s, Bela Balassa and three prominent Latin American economists (1986) advocated many of the same reforms. Our review of the subsequent literature focuses on those works that are broadly comparative across countries and types of reforms. This leads to a concentration on studies produced by international organizations, which may bias our interpretation to some extent.

2. For examples, see the analyses in ECLAC (1996); IDB (1997); Burki and Perry (1997).

3. Easterly, Loayza, and Montiel (1997); Lora and Barrera (1997).

mentum; in particular, exports from the region had a good performance, although they were concentrated in a few sectors and generally incorporated low levels of technology.[4]

With respect to employment, the consensus is that job creation was generally insufficient, more because of relatively slow growth of the gross domestic product (GDP) than because of problems of employment elasticities.[5] The International Labour Organization (ILO) has taken the lead in stressing the problems in job quality. Thus Victor E. Tokman emphasizes that there was a strong expansion of employment during the economic recuperation of the first half of the 1990s, but these jobs were basically low paid and their productivity was low.[6] In addition, employment became increasingly precarious, both because jobs were concentrated in the informal sector, generally without social security, and because modern firms outsourced the labor process, transferring the cost of adjustment and instability to small firms and the self-employed.

Somewhat greater disagreement exists with respect to the impact of the reforms on equity. The Inter-American Development Bank (IDB) argues that the main deterioration in distribution occurred in the so-called lost decade of the 1980s and that the reforms helped to slow the tendencies of deteriorating income distribution and increasing poverty.[7] In particular, it identifies a positive effect of the trade opening on the real income of the first three quintiles of the income distribution, and a negative effect on the richest 20 percent. In contrast, Bulmer-Thomas, on the basis of empirical evidence for the period up to the early 1990s, suggests that the results of the so-called new economic model were basically regressive in terms of income distribution.[8] This was due to a decrease in real wages together with an increase in unemployment, real interest rates, the weight of the informal sector, and the concentration of wealth. The only element of the reform process that had a progressive role was fiscal reform, according to this analysis, in that it made possible the reduction of inflation. Similarly, Berry points to the negative role played by trade reform, which favored capital-intensive technology and subjected small firms to intense competitive pressures.[9]

4. ECLAC (1996).
5. See, for example, ECLAC (1997); Lora and Olivera (1998).
6. Tokman (1994). See also the ILO's annual *Panorama Laboral de América Latina y el Caribe.*
7. IDB (1997); see also Londoño and Székely (1997).
8. Bulmer-Thomas (1996).
9. Berry (1998).

Measuring the impact of the reforms on growth was very difficult since so many other things were happening simultaneously. In addition, the reforms themselves were a process, so it was hard to capture their impact at any particular point in time. This problem was even more acute in studying employment and equity than in analyzing growth, since data are more unreliable and the definition of relevant indicators is much more complex. Two main strategies have been used in the literature. ECLAC, Sebastian Edwards, and Shahid Javed Burki and Guillermo E. Perry, among others, describe the reform process and present indicators to capture their degree of implementation (such as the changing level of tariffs or number of privatized firms).[10] This approach then relies heavily on examples, qualitative indicators, and case studies of firms or countries to evaluate the progress of the reforms. A different approach was followed by the IDB, which developed an index of reforms to summarize the reform process in five areas (trade, taxes, finance, privatization, and the labor market).[11] The IDB designed these quantitative indicators to address the problem that there had been no systematic attempt to measure what had been reformed; without such a measure it was very difficult to evaluate the impact and to separate the reforms from other trends.

Efforts to quantify the reforms often confuse policy and performance variables. Given that it is frequently easier to devise measures of the results of an action than to measure the action itself, many studies mix the two types of indicators. Thus studies on trade reform might use indicators like the ratio of exports plus imports to GDP, while attempts to measure fiscal reform might rely on measures like taxes as a share of GDP. In this context, despite its limitations, the IDB's reform index is a contribution in that it helps to concentrate attention on the reforms themselves.

An author's approach to characterizing the reforms is linked to the methodology used for analyzing their effects. Authors who explicitly or implicitly reject the possibility of measuring the reforms tend to stress the richness and complexity of the processes and to make evaluations that are mainly historical. They make attempts to attribute results to individual elements of the new policy package. A particular variant of this approach is found in an analysis by the World Bank, which says: "[our] analysis . . . of economic performance fulfills the dual purpose of assessing the state of reform and evaluating general economic development, *under the hypothesis*

---

10. ECLAC (1996 and 1998a); Edwards (1995); Burki and Perry (1997).
11. See especially IDB (1996); Lora (1997).

that in the recent experience of Latin American countries, economic development is largely a reflection of macroeconomic and structural reforms."[12]

In contrast to the historical approach are the authors who try to quantify the reforms; they then use their measures as independent variables in regression equations to "explain" economic growth or other variables of interest. Thus, for example, growth equations of the type popularized by Robert Barro tend to incorporate an additional variable.[13] The IDB index serves this purpose for many analysts, but other ad hoc proxies have also been used. In principle, analysis of this type makes it possible to separate the influence of the reforms from that of other simultaneous events, especially macroeconomic policies; in practice, the variables are so interrelated that the results are questionable.

Indeed, many problems exist with this literature, which is extremely diverse in coverage as well as methodology. The quantitative analyses of the IDB, in particular, have been criticized, both for the oversimplifications necessary to construct the reform indexes and for the attempt to draw conclusions about the effects that go well beyond what the data and the (sometimes debatable) econometric analysis will bear. Nonetheless, these criticisms should not obscure the advance that these efforts at quantification and methodological precision signify. Neither should they minimize the problems of alternative methodologies based almost exclusively on historical analysis that uses ad hoc examples, circumstantial evidence, and expert opinion.

In addition to methodological problems of various sorts, four substantive limitations appear in the studies reviewed.

(1) Failure to disaggregate the variables. The tendency of the analysis to focus exclusively on variables and processes at the aggregate level makes it difficult to capture the differences between countries, sectors, and socioeconomic actors with respect to the adoption, implementation, and impact of the reforms. If a possible result of the reform process is the growing heterogeneity of the productive structure and its performance, failure to disaggregate makes it impossible to recognize this, much less explain it. This problem is important at two levels.

First, the lack of attention to processes and variables at the sectoral level hinders comprehension of the processes of specialization within the productive system, which may affect the growth capacity of the new struc-

---

12. Burki and Perry (1997, p.27), emphasis added.
13. Barro and Sala-i-Martin (1995).

tures generated by the reforms. These factors may also weaken domestic supplier chains, reducing the impact of investment and technological modernization.

Second, the absence of analysis and evaluation at the microeconomic level makes it impossible to trace a key objective of the reforms: to modify the behavior of microeconomic actors, in particular, of firms. Moreover, no one has explored changes in entrepreneurial behavior in the areas of investment and the incorporation of technical progress across a wide range of countries, which would be a crucial indicator of the success or failure of the reform process.

(2) Failure to emphasize the mechanisms of articulation between national economies and the international context. This problem is seen in the scarce attention that is paid to phenomena associated with the external financial opening and to the dynamics of foreign direct investment and the assimilation of technological progress. It is paradoxical because the preoccupation with an efficient integration into an increasingly globalized world economy is at the center of the new model of growth. Beyond a general recognition of the importance of the trade opening, however, the noncommercial dimensions of that integration do not receive adequate attention. Nor is much attention paid to the links between the reforms, macroeconomic policies, and the international context.

(3) Failure to consider that the package of reforms and policies may be internally inconsistent. Although the framework of a market-friendly development model informed the design of the reforms and the policy instruments they engendered, detailed analysis of the internal consistency of the reform package and associated policy variables is lacking. This concerns relations among the reforms themselves, between the reforms and the macroeconomic and social policies that accompanied them, and between both the reforms and policies and the international environment in which the new economic model has to function. The assumption of coherence has led to the persistence of some serious problems.

(4) Scant attention to the articulation of the dynamics of employment and the distribution of income with the rest of the model. Employment and equity, as well as their relation to investment, productivity, and growth, are absent from the original formulations of the Washington Consensus and the market-friendly development model. There was a subsequent attempt to link the reforms to employment and equity, but the mechanisms of transmission among the various components have yet to be adequately conceptualized.

A New Conceptual Framework

This book builds on the literature, but it also presents significant innovations to deal with the four problems identified above. The main characteristic that distinguishes it from other comparative studies of economic reforms is the focus on the interaction between macroeconomic and microeconomic processes. To make significant advances at this time, it is crucial to focus less exclusively on the macroeconomic and regional levels and more on countries and the microeconomic behavior of firms, grouped by sector, size, and ownership characteristics. Different countries and groups of firms are affected quite differently by government policies, including structural reforms, and by the increasingly globalized world economy. Some have been able to take advantage of the new opportunities created, while others have seen their situations become ever more precarious. The sum of these behaviors produces the aggregate trends that others have observed and measured. Knowing what lies behind the aggregates is essential for designing policy measures to improve future economic performance.

Another way to characterize our approach is that it insists on the need to make economic actors central to the analysis and to try to understand their reactions to government policies in order to explain, predict, and (if necessary) modify their behavior. In particular, we focus on entrepreneurs' decisions on whether to invest and to incorporate new technologies. Under what domestic and international conditions will they make positive decisions? What will be the time frame for implementing investment decisions? Without a positive response on investment, and without increased productivity through technical progress and better skills for workers, medium- and long-term growth cannot take place, although economic recovery can occur.

A disaggregated approach is also necessary for analyzing outcomes other than growth, especially the generation of employment and any change in the patterns of income distribution. Job-creation capacities vary widely for large and small firms and for firms in labor-intensive or capital-intensive or natural resource–intensive sectors. The skill differential that characterizes jobs in different categories of firms is then a crucial factor in determining patterns of income distribution.

Given the centrality of economic actors for our approach, we start by considering the reforms as a set of signals in the form of government policy decisions. When governments want to change the way their economies (and societies) operate, they make policy decisions and transmit them to the relevant actors; these decisions constitute our signals. The governmental decisions are essential for creating a new environment in which the private sector can operate more dynamically. The environment is also influenced, both positively and negatively, by international forces that are generally beyond the control of most governments, including capital flows, interest rates, expansion of output in importing countries, and trade regimes. These will have to be taken into consideration as well.

In addition to the signals and the environment they help to create, we need to be concerned about the reception of the policy signals at the microeconomic level in decentralized economies. A first issue with respect to reception obviously involves information. Do the actors know that policies have changed and what the government is trying to signal through its policy decisions? In the real world of imperfect information, not all actors have access to the same formal channels, and informal channels are even more skewed to favor some groups over others. We must therefore assume that information will be unequally distributed, and that less powerful actors will have less access.

Information alone, however, is not sufficient. A second question concerns the credibility of the information and signals. Do the actors believe what the government says at any given moment, and do they believe that the new policies will remain in force for the foreseeable future? If they have doubts, they will not be willing to take the risks involved in making the new investments that are necessary to incorporate new technology and, ultimately, to pave the way for a new growth path.[14]

Lack of credibility with respect to economic reforms arises from three possible sources. First, the various components of the policy package may be inconsistent. If the reforms and policies are inconsistent among themselves, they create mixed signals, and the recipients are confused about what they should do. In an extreme situation, inconsistency may lead to a crisis that precipitates a change in policy stance. Second, key sectors of the population may not support the policies. Lack of support or, more important, active opposition may cause the relevant actors to surmise that the policies will be abandoned sooner or later. Third, the reforms may exist within an

14. A substantial literature has developed around the concept of credibility. Until recently, it has focused almost exclusively on domestic factors that might affect the government's incentives to maintain or change its policy stance. See, for example, Calvo (1986); Rogoff (1987); Persson (1988); Persson and Tabellini (1989); Rodrik (1989). Recently, however, Drazen (1997) has expanded the scope of the discussion to include international factors, which is especially relevant for our purposes.

unfavorable international environment. Even with consistent policies and a reasonable degree of domestic support, an unfavorable international environment, such as a lack of external finance or a sharp deterioration in the terms of trade, will pose credibility problems. This is especially the case with a policy package that increases the openness of the economy and thus the dependence on external factors.

These three sources of credibility problems are closely interrelated. A negative international environment can lead to, or increase, inconsistency among policies. Ironically, even a positive external context (such as abundant international finance) can create policy inconsistency. Either policy inconsistency or an unfavorable environment can undermine support for policies. Insofar as key economic actors perceive the presence of one or more of these problems, they are likely to draw the conclusion that the policies will be changed and will make their own decisions accordingly.

Finally, beyond information and its credibility, the economic actors must be able to take advantage of the new circumstances. For example, they must have access to domestic or international financial resources that enable them to invest; they must have knowledge of the technological advances in their area; they must have access to the appropriate equipment that embodies the new technology; and they must have workers with the necessary training to use the new equipment they have acquired. Again, the resources at the disposal of different actors vary substantially across sizes and sectors of firms.

To study the processes of signaling, response, and the resulting outcomes, we have worked with the conceptual framework shown in figure 1-1.[15] Our analytical framework begins with the external context, which we model as variables related to international finance and the demand for Latin American exports. The past performance of these and other international variables has helped to determine the initial domestic conditions (economic, social, and political) in each country. In the present, the external context has a strong impact on government policy, making certain policy choices more likely than others. Beyond its impact in the policy arena, external finance facilitates investment and technical change processes, while international demand and the vagaries of financial flows have an impact on the dependent variables, especially growth rates.

15. For this framework, we owe a debt to the authors of the World Bank's *The East Asian Miracle* (1993), despite a number of differences in the two approaches. In the early days of our thinking about this project, when *The East Asian Miracle* had recently been published, it gave us a number of ideas about how to conceptualize a vast array of variables and processes.

Figure 1-1. *Conceptual Framework*

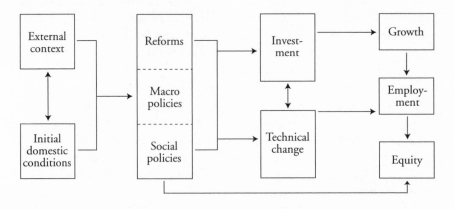

Initial conditions within each of the countries are mostly determined by domestic developments, although they are also influenced by external factors. We take these initial conditions as given, rather than trying to explain them, but they are crucial in determining both policy choice and response. From the perspective of policy choice, we are particularly interested in several economic variables, including growth and inflation rates, the structure of output and employment, and links with the world economy. Social characteristics of the population and the ability of governments to make and implement policy decisions are also important. At the firm level, the accumulated learning and productive capacity are elements that governments must take into account.

Based on the initial conditions in each country and on external influence, governments make decisions on reforms (such as import liberalization, domestic financial liberalization, opening of the capital account, privatization, and tax reform), macroeconomic policies (including fiscal, monetary, and exchange rate measures), and social policies (especially with respect to education and health). Although the nine countries for this study had undertaken substantial reforms and changes in macroeconomic and social policies, policy decisions on individual items were not necessarily the same. On the contrary, one of the things we want to investigate is the difference in the choice and implementation of reforms and policies and how this affected the outcomes.

The study analyzes investment and technical change at both the aggregate and sectoral levels to see what determines the response to the reforms.

At the aggregate level, the response is related to the interaction of the reforms with macroeconomic policy and the international context. The uncertainty created by changes in the rules of the game and the volatility of key macroeconomic variables merit particular attention. The behavior of these variables, and the uncertainty they generate, may lead to a delayed response in investment and technological change. At the sectoral level, we study the transmission mechanisms between these same variables and the process of investment and the incorporation of new technologies. These operate through shifts in market structure, corporate strategy, and the entry of new actors into specific markets.

The three dependent variables of the model are growth, employment, and equity. Growth in the post-reform period is compared with that of the 1950–80 base period, and its components (that is, capital accumulation, labor accumulation, and productivity) are analyzed in a growth-accounting framework. The characteristics of the growth process (in particular, the types of firms that are expanding output dynamically or lagging behind) and the decisions on the type of technology to be incorporated will determine employment generation; the latter is disaggregated by productive sectors and size of firm. Employment characteristics, especially the salary differential between skilled and unskilled workers, are important in determining the distribution of income, although this may be offset by other economic and social trends.

Six Propositions

We use this framework to explore a set of six propositions. They take as a point of departure the previous judgment on the impact of the reforms: growth has been modest; employment has grown slowly and with problems in job quality; and inequality has not improved and may even have gotten worse. The propositions, then, are directed toward answering the question of why the impact has not been more favorable.

First, the initial conditions in the various countries were quite diverse and affected the extent to which reforms were adopted. Variables of particular importance include macroeconomic stability, economic distortions, past growth rates, and the degree of governability. The greater such problems in the recent past, the more willing countries are to undertake large-scale reforms in the hope of improving future economic performance. At the same time, a history of past turbulence and failed reform or stabilization attempts will increase the credibility problems of governments intent on changing policy course. Countries that have done well in the past have much less reason to undertake risky reforms, and there is likely to be less support for doing so.

Second, governments frequently introduced reforms that were inconsistent with their macroeconomic and social policies. The most obvious case is when high rates of inflation and deficits continued, thus leading to uncertainty for economic actors. Even if stability is attained, however, other contradictions may exist. For example, exchange rate appreciation, stimulated by newly liberalized capital flows, prevents firms from taking full advantage of the new export opportunities presented by trade liberalization. The way in which budget deficits are controlled may also generate contradictions: cutting expenditures for social policies limits growth potential as well as possibly increasing inequality, while reducing public investment limits the expansion of essential infrastructure.

Third, the reforms were slow to produce an impact at the microeconomic level because of the great uncertainty they generated, especially if they were combined with macroeconomic instability. This led to a hesitation on the part of investors to engage in large-scale projects, as they preferred to defer irreversible decisions. One possibility is that the timing of the response is arbitrary, depending on particular country conditions. It is also possible that a pattern can be found across countries, geared to the level of uncertainty and its impact on investors' risk-return calculations.

Fourth, the uneven response of actors helped to explain both the less-than-hoped-for performance to date in most countries in the region, as well as the differential performance across countries. We may expect a heterogeneous reception of the signals—creating leading and lagging sectors—and thus the average response for the economies of the region would be modest. The percentage of actors receiving and responding positively to the signals also varies across countries (and across sectors and firms by size), so that country averages vary quite substantially. Within countries and sectors, economic actors' past experience results in a heterogeneous reception of, and response to, the signals from the reforms. The effects have implications for all three of our dependent variables: growth rates, employment, and equity.

Fifth, the positive effects of reforms were frequently undermined by unfavorable trends in the international economy. Capital flows, for example, helped to sustain high growth, despite contributing to distortions such as overvalued exchange rates. However, sharp declines or reversals of—and great volatility in—private capital flows can overwhelm the positive effects. On the trade side, external demand can also contribute to economic growth, but volatility in export prices and sudden declines in demand can undermine the positive impact. The reforms have exacerbated both the positive and negative effects by increasing the openness of the economies to international flows.

Sixth, the reforms were incomplete in that they lacked the proper institutional support typically found in the industrial world. A key example relates to the development of factor markets—namely, capital, technology, and labor. Although these markets are imperfect in all parts of the world, they are especially deficient in developing countries, including Latin America and the Caribbean. Capital markets lack long-term segments, labor markets lack training opportunities for unskilled or low-skilled workers, and technological progress is frequently limited to the largest firms. Another way in which the reforms were incomplete refers to the lack of a proper regulatory framework to complement privatization and liberalization reforms. For example, banking crises have been frequent in Latin American and Caribbean countries in recent years, since local governments have failed to establish and enforce adequate rules on reserves and lending practices.

Methodological Considerations

The focus of our approach on macro-micro relations and the centrality of actors has clear implications for methodology. Specifically, we must go beyond the econometric or formal modeling techniques that typify most of today's economic research. We do use quantitative methods whenever this is possible. For example, we engage in econometric analysis to explain investment and growth outcomes as well as employment and equity patterns. Many parts of the following chapters, however, require qualitative, historical analysis. In particular, the complex interrelation of variables leads to the use of such methodology in the sectoral analysis of investment.

The post-reform period covers a relatively short time span, and pooling data before and after involves some important statistical assumptions that may or may not be valid. Like others, we have engaged in such analysis, but the results must be read with a substantial amount of caution. Our concentration on nine countries also limits the number of possible observations, although it enables us to go into more detail on the policy and institutional framework. In some particular cases, especially the chapter on equity, the analysis draws on a larger set of countries, thus making econometric analysis more feasible.

The issue of timing goes beyond problems with numbers of observations. Much of the literature on reforms centers on comparisons between the 1980s and 1990s. This clearly creates a bias in the results, since the 1980s were characterized by very low growth and the deterioration of a variety of social indicators. A comparative analysis of the 1980s and 1990s thus attributes to the reforms results that are merely the consequence of recovery. To avoid this particular problem, some authors have turned to comparisons with the 1970s. This type of comparison is also problematic since the 1970s were a period of unusual dynamism based on borrowed resources, which eventually led to the crisis of the 1980s. In other words, the economic situation was not sustainable. Obviously the best possible comparison would be with a similar economic situation in which no reforms had been implemented. Since this kind of counterfactual analysis is of dubious value, our solution is to draw whenever possible on a data set that uses as a base the 1950–80 period, which provides a better measure of previous economic performance.[16]

As implied above, the focus on nine countries has both advantages and disadvantages. It limits the range of methodologies that can be employed, and in some cases precludes the use of powerful quantitative techniques, but it gives a much better understanding of the interaction of variables that are difficult, if not impossible, to measure precisely. Since these latter variables may well provide the key to understanding the mechanisms behind the quantitative results found by other researchers, the sacrifice may be considered worthwhile.

The nine countries were selected because they had the longest history of implementing economic reforms in the region. Given that the aim of the project was to study the impact of the reforms, this was the most obvious way to select the sample.[17] Four of the countries—Bolivia, Chile, Costa Rica, and Mexico—have reforms that date to the mid-1980s or, in the case of Chile, to the mid-1970s with a reinvigorated period beginning in the mid-1980s. Four others—Argentina, Brazil, Colombia, and Peru—began

16. Such a methodology is being used in a joint project by the United Nations Development Program (UNDP), ECLAC, and the IDB. See Vos and others (forthcoming).

17. The alternative would have been a sample that mixed reformers and non-reformers, using the latter as a type of control group. Our main reason for not using this alternative research design was that two of the countries that would enter the sample as non-reformers (Ecuador and Venezuela) were in such difficulties that reaching meaningful conclusions would have been impossible. Macroeconomic instability and lack of consensus on the need for reforms gave rise to extremely volatile economic conditions, under which long-term trends on investment, productivity, and other variables could not have been detected.

Table 1-1. *Weight of Nine Countries in Latin America and the Caribbean, 1998*

Country	Population (millions)	GDP (billions of 1995 dollars)	GDP per capita (1995 dollars)	Exports (billions of 1998 dollars)	Imports (billions of 1998 dollars)
Argentina	36.1	304.8	8,438	25.3	31.0
Bolivia	8.0	7.6	959	1.3	2.3
Brazil	166.3	711.9	4,281	51.1	60.8
Chile	14.8	76.9	5,187	14.8	17.1
Colombia	40.8	83.9	2,056	10.9	14.6
Costa Rica	3.8	9.8	2,550	5.4	6.2
Jamaica[a]	2.5	4.7	1,869	1.4	3.1
Mexico	95.8	428.1	4,467	117.3	125.3
Peru	24.8	65.5	2,642	5.7	8.2
Subtotal	392.9	1,693.2	3,605	233.2	268.6
Total Latin America[b]	485.5	1,876.1	3,865	263.4	307.2
Share of nine (percent)	80.9	90.3	111.5[c]	88.5	87.4

Source: Project database, on the basis of ECLAC statistics.

a. Data for Jamaica are for 1997.

b. Total Latin America includes twenty countries for population, GDP, and GDP per capita; seventeen countries are included for exports and imports.

c. Ratio of the weighted average GDP per capita of the nine countries to the weighted average GDP per capita of the twenty countries.

their reforms in the early 1990s.[18] Jamaica is frequently considered to be an example of the group of earlier reformers, but our own analysis puts it in with the latter group, indicating that the reforms are best dated as beginning around 1990. Given the much longer history of the Chilean reforms, some added weight is given to this country in the chapters that follow.

Although the countries were selected for their reform history, they also represent the vast majority of the population, economic output, and international trade of the Latin American and Caribbean region. As can be seen in table 1-1, the nine countries account for 81 percent of total population, 90 percent of aggregate GDP, and 88 percent of international trade (the average of exports plus imports). In terms of per capita GDP, they are slightly above the regional average. Finally, other characteristics of the nine coun-

18. Argentina actually had a brief experience with reforms at the end of the 1970s, but the process was aborted and not resumed until the Menem government took office in 1989.

economies

tries are relatively diverse. They include the three largest countries in the region (Argentina, Brazil, and Mexico), three medium-size economies (Chile, Colombia, and Peru), and three smaller ones (Bolivia, Costa Rica, and Jamaica). They also have substantial geographic diversity within the hemisphere.

Building on an in-depth analysis of this group of countries, we can arrive at a better comprehension of the processes stimulated by the economic reforms. We can see which countries did better and why, which types of firms did better and why, and how the diversity affected the distribution of benefits. Only with this kind of understanding will we be in a position to propose a set of policy recommendations in the final chapter of the book.

The book is organized in the following manner. Chapter 2 analyzes the international context in which the reforms took place, with emphasis on trade and capital flows. Chapter 3 discusses the reforms, macroeconomic policies, and social policies, together with their interrelations. Chapter 4 is the first of two chapters that focus on the aggregate level of analysis, in this case analyzing trends in investment, productivity, and growth. Chapter 5, then, follows with an aggregate-level analysis of employment generation (incorporating both quantity and quality dimensions) and equity. Chapter 6 turns to the sectoral and microeconomic levels, to examine questions that could not be answered at the aggregate level. In particular, the chapter focuses on whether the reforms have changed the structure of output, investment, and productivity so as to provide faster, more sustainable growth as well as adequate employment opportunities. Chapter 7 concludes with a summary of the findings and a set of policy recommendations.

2 | The International Context: Trade and Capital Flows

The reform process in Latin America and the Caribbean is taking place in the context of an increas-
ingly integrated international economy.[1] While there is a growing realiza-
tion that the current globalization process has important historical
precedents, especially in the late nineteenth and early twentieth centuries,
there is also a consensus that this wave of integration is exceptional. The
globalization of capital markets is very extensive, while the integration of
markets for goods and services, technology, and information is creating a
gradual convergence in patterns of production and consumption around
the globe.

Globalization is viewed either as a process of multilateral lowering of
policy constraints to the free movement of goods and services across national and regional borders, or as a microeconomic phenomenon led by
the strategies and behavior of corporations.[2] These strategies have caused
intense international processes of economic restructuring at both the sectoral and firm levels, which has resulted in the largest wave of mergers and

1. An important input for the discussion of capital flows in this chapter was Griffith-Jones (2000);
Vivianne Ventura Dias contributed to the analysis of trade. Neither is responsible for the conclusions
drawn.
2. Oman (1994).

17

acquisitions in economic history. Behind these microeconomic processes, we find a technological revolution, particularly in the fields of communications, information technology, and transportation. Those changes have reduced production costs, time, and complexity, thereby strengthening the advantages of spreading technology costs on large production runs, marketing global brands, and operating at a world scale.[3] All these changes had an impact on Latin American economic performance in the last decades. This chapter, however, focuses on the globalization of trade and capital flows to and from the region, since a detailed analysis of the microeconomic dimensions of globalization, particularly the technological revolution, is beyond the scope of the book.

The basic argument of the chapter is that trends in the international economy have had highly contradictory effects on the reform process and the performance of the region's economies. The reforms in general, especially privatization and the liberalization of trade and capital accounts, provided incentives for a large increase in private capital flows to the region in the early 1990s. Those flows helped sustain the higher growth rates being encouraged by the reforms themselves, even though they generated distortions such as overvalued exchange rates. At the same time, the contraction or reversals of the flows led to crises that were very costly in terms of growth and investment. Likewise, trade liberalization permitted the increase in imports of equipment and inputs required by the modernization effort, but it also contributed to enlarged trade deficits that had to be financed by volatile capital inflows. In summary, Latin American economies are still vulnerable to balance-of-payments problems.

The chapter primarily focuses on Latin American and Caribbean countries' participation in the globalization process since 1980. The second section discusses changes in trade patterns and the impact of commodity prices on foreign earnings. It also reviews the importance of international and regional markets in the global integration of Latin America and the institutional constraints of the new international trade regime. The third section characterizes capital flows by volume and composition, paying special attention to the volatility of different types of flows and to the relation between capital flows and economic growth patterns. The chapter finishes with some conclusions about the links between the global economy and the reform process and about their joint impact on Latin American and Caribbean economic performance.

3. Turner and Hodges (1992).

Latin American Trade Relations

The value of world trade was characterized by a dramatic upward trend in the postwar period. According to the World Trade Organization (WTO), world merchandise exports ballooned from $58 billion in 1948 to $5.3 trillion in 1997.[4] In real terms, the expansion of trade over the fifty years exceeded the expansion of output by a large margin. The value of Latin America's trade also rose rapidly, although it grew more slowly than the world average. Total Latin American merchandise exports in 1948 were about $7 billion, rising to $230 billion in 1997. The increase in export volume in Latin America was much lower than the world average in the 1960s and 1970s, and it was also lower than growth of the region's gross domestic product (GDP) (see table 2-1). In other words, exports were becoming less important as a share of output in Latin America, while the opposite was happening elsewhere.[5] Trade policies in industrialized countries bore some responsibility for this trend, but it was basically due to the decision of Latin American governments to industrialize through an inward-oriented strategy.

This pattern changed beginning in the early 1980s. Export volume expanded faster than the region's GDP throughout this period and faster than export volume for the world as a whole in 1990–98. Initially, this shift could be attributed to the onset of the debt crisis, when Latin America had to produce trade surpluses to meet its debt service in the absence of capital inflows. The reform process may have been important in continuing the strong performance of exports, however, even after capital flows resumed. An additional factor in the 1990s was the opening of Latin American regional markets for trade in higher value added goods, as will be discussed below.

The rapid growth of export volume during the 1980s and 1990s was frequently offset by negative price trends, particularly in 1980–85. Thereafter, export prices improved, although some groups of products showed poorer performance. Prices of nonfuel primary commodities enjoyed a very favorable situation from late 1993 until mid-1997, when the financial cri-

---

4. WTO (1998).

5. The statistics on Latin American trade in the 1960s and 1970s were strongly influenced by the behavior of Brazil and Venezuela. For example, a simple average of growth rates of export volume, excluding Venezuela, exceeded GDP growth in 1955–65 and was roughly similar in 1965–73. See Cárdenas, Ocampo, and Thorp (forthcoming, Introduction).

Table 2-1. *Trade and Output Growth Rates, 1960–98*
Percent

Region	Component	1960–70	1970–80	1980–85	1985–90	1990–98
World	GDP	5.2	3.7	2.0	3.3	2.3
	Exports (volume)	7.4	5.1	2.5	6.4	6.7
	Exports (value)	9.3	20.3	−0.6	12.1	6.3
	Imports (volume)	8.6	5.4	2.7	7.1	7.0
	Imports (value)	9.2	20.2	−0.4	12.0	6.3
Latin America	GDP	5.5	5.6	0.6	1.9	3.4
	Exports (volume)	3.1	2.2	5.5	5.1	9.3
	Exports (value)	5.7	20.6	0.8	5.8	9.8
	Imports (volume)	4.9	7.4	−5.9	6.4	14.3
	Imports (value)	6.3	21.7	−8.1	9.7	14.3

Source: ECLAC (1998a) for 1960–95; United Nations (1999) for 1996–98.

sis in Asia stalled a booming demand there for all primary products. Figure 2-1 shows that the terms of trade deteriorated for the region as a whole during the 1980s, remained flat during the early 1990s, and improved slightly from 1994 to 1997 before falling again.

Table 2-1 and figure 2-1 also show trends for Latin American imports. With the single exception of the period 1980–85, the volume of imports grew faster than that of exports; the difference was especially large in the 1970s. After 1985, the increase in the value of imports also far exceeded that of exports, leading to increasing trade deficits. The very rapid growth of imports was partly due to the pent-up demand for foreign goods of all kinds (consumer items as well as capital and intermediate goods) after nearly a decade of foreign exchange constraints. It was also due to the so-called wealth effect following stabilization, and it was facilitated by the lowering of tariffs and nontariff barriers and by overvalued exchange rates in many countries of the region.

The product composition of Latin American and Caribbean merchandise exports reflected the pattern for global trade as a whole, whereby primary goods had a declining share. While primary products still accounted for more than half of the value of Latin American exports in 1980, they had fallen to less than a quarter in 1998 (see table 2-2). These averages hide sharp differences across countries, especially between Mexico and the rest. In particular, the strong performance of manufactured exports in Mexico,

Figure 2-1. *Trade Indicators, 1980–98*

Index, 1995 = 100

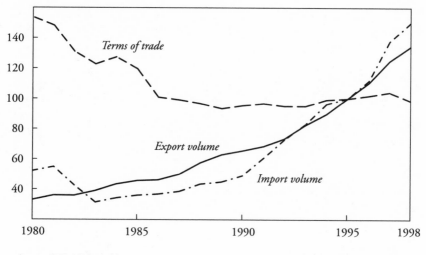

Source: ECLAC (1999b).

combined with the fact that Mexico accounted for nearly 40 percent of all Latin American and Caribbean exports by the late 1990s, boosted the total regional share of manufactured exports substantially. (See chapter 6 on the comparison between Mexico and other countries.)

The geographic focus of Latin American trade flows also changed substantially in recent decades, especially in the 1990s. Two main developments helped to account for the changes, both linked to processes of regional integration. First, the implementation of the North American Free Trade Agreement (NAFTA) led to an impressive increase in the U.S. share in Mexican exports and imports. Whereas the United States bought 63 to 70 percent of Mexican exports between 1965 and 1990, by the late 1990s it purchased nearly 85 percent. As was the case for product composition, the magnitude of Mexican trade also tends to bias regional averages toward its geographic composition. Mexico accounted for 70 percent of all the Latin American Integration Association (LAIA)[6] exports to the United States

6. Eleven countries are members of LAIA: Argentina, Bolivia, Brazil, Chile, Colombia, Ecuador, Mexico, Paraguay, Peru, Uruguay, and Venezuela.

Table 2-2. *Structure of Merchandise Exports, 1970–98*[a]
Percent

Type of export	1970	1980	1990	1998[b]
Commodities	56.9	54.5	38.9	22.7
Agriculture	33.0	18.6	15.0	12.1
Mining	8.0	5.4	4.8	2.9
Energy	15.9	30.5	19.1	7.7
Semi-manufactures	34.3	30.1	30.9	19.8
Manufactures	8.3	15.1	29.0	55.9
Traditional	2.2	4.5	6.5	9.2
Basic inputs	1.9	2.4	7.3	5.5
New industries, labor intensive	2.7	4.7	8.0	24.5
New industries, capital intensive	1.5	3.5	7.2	16.7
Other	0.5	0.3	1.2	1.6
Total	100.0	100.0	100.0	100.0
Amount (billions of dollars)	13.1	81.2	113.7	255.7

Source: Project database, on the basis of ECLAC statistics.

a. Countries include Argentina, Bolivia, Brazil, Chile, Colombia, Costa Rica, Ecuador, Jamaica, Mexico, Peru, Uruguay, and Venezuela.

b. Data for Jamaica are for 1997.

during the 1990s. The share of the United States as a destination of Latin American exports, with Mexico included, thus increased from 33 percent in 1965 to almost 50 percent in 1997. When Mexico is excluded, the U.S. share actually fell, from 30 in 1965 to 25 percent in 1997. A similar picture emerges for imports.[7]

Second, integration was proceeding at a rapid pace among two groups of countries in South America: the Southern Common Market (Mercosur), which includes Argentina, Brazil, Paraguay, and Uruguay, with Bolivia and Chile as associate members, and the Andean Community, which includes Bolivia, Colombia, Ecuador, Peru, and Venezuela. These developments led to a growing share of intra-regional trade, especially among the former group; intra-Mercosur trade represented 7 percent of the group's total international trade in 1992 and 20 percent in 1998. The parallel increase for the Andean Community was from 8 to 11 percent. Similar developments were underway in Central America and the Caribbean, although these coun-

7. ECLAC (1999b).

tries were also becoming more integrated into the U.S. economic space. Trade within the Central American Common Market rose from 22 to 25 percent between 1992 and 1998, while that of the Caribbean Community (Caricom) grew from 6 to 19 percent between 1992 and 1997.[8]

In contrast with the dynamic changes occurring in trade relations with the United States and within the region, trade between Europe and Latin America was flat in recent decades. Latin American and Caribbean exports to the European Union fell from 22 to 14 percent of the total between 1990 and 1998. Trade with Japan and developing Asia currently represents only a small share for the region as a whole (less than 6 percent of total regional exports in 1998), but it has become a significant market for several countries, especially Chile and Peru. By 1998, Chile was exporting 30 percent of all its goods to Asia, and Peru 23 percent.[9]

Combining the data on export composition and geographic destination generates some important conclusions. Latin American trade with Europe and Asia continues to be mainly of the inter-industry type, whereby the region exports primary products (including processed raw materials) and imports industrial goods. The Mexico-dominated trade with the United States is more of the intra-industry kind, with manufactured goods exchanged on both sides of the ledger, although the Latin American manufactured exports tend to be less sophisticated. It is mainly within the region itself that trade not only involves manufactures, but also consists of products that are intensive in technology and skilled labor. The challenge, then, is to use the intra-regional trade as a building block to move toward higher value added exports to other parts of the world.

The importance of this challenge becomes apparent if we examine trends in Latin American competitiveness in the recent past. Regional exports lost market share in the industrialized countries as a whole. Between 1985 and 1990, the share fell from 6.2 to 4.8 percent; between 1990 and 1996 it grew somewhat to 5.3 percent. Although part of the lost ground was recovered, the region remains far behind the performance of the very dynamic East Asian exporters,[10] which increased their share from 6.3 to 9.0 percent

8. Relations within the Latin American and Caribbean regional integration groups are not limited to trade. Investment flows across borders are also important, as are political relations among the countries. For an extensive analysis of these topics, see ECLAC's annual publication, *Latin America and the Caribbean in the World Economy.*

9. ECLAC (1999b).

10. China, Hong Kong, Indonesia, Malaysia, Republic of Korea, Singapore, Taiwan (Province of China), and Thailand.

Table 2-3. *Latin American and Asian Exports to Industrialized Countries,*
1985 and 1996
Percent

Region (year)	Rising stars[a]	Falling stars[a]	Lost oppor-tunities[a]	Retreat[a]	Total
Latin America (1985)	13.4	16.5	11.5	58.6	100.0
Latin America (1996)	37.6	29.5	13.1	29.8	100.0
Latin America, excluding Mexico (1985)	8.1	32.4	11.1	48.3	100.0
Latin America, excluding Mexico (1996)	21.3	38.4	11.3	29.1	100.0
Hong Kong, Korea, Singapore, and Taiwan (China) (1996)	53.6	7.4	33.4	5.5	100.0
China, Indonesia, Malaysia, and Thailand (1996)	62.2	28.4	5.5	3.9	100.0

Source: Authors' calculations, on the basis of software and database described in ECLAC/World Bank (1999).

a. See text for definitions.

in the 1985–96 period.[11] Among industrialized countries, as we have already seen, a small gain was made in the U.S. market while a decline occurred in Europe. This was in sharp contrast to the Asian exporters who more than doubled their share in the latter, suggesting that the poor performance of the region's exports to Europe has more to do with the types of goods exported than with market access.

Another competitiveness indicator classifies export specialization in dynamic versus lagging sectors in industrialized country markets. The software used to make the above calculations can also sort a country or region's exports into four groups: those for which an exporter gains market share in dynamic sectors (rising stars), gains share in lagging sectors (falling stars), loses share in dynamic sectors (lost opportunities), or loses share in lagging sectors (retreat). Table 2-3 shows that Latin America increased its exports in dynamic sectors from 13 percent in 1985 to 38 percent in 1996, while significantly reducing its exports in lagging sectors. About half of that gain, however, was due to Mexico. Moreover, the Asian exporters did much bet-

11. Authors' calculations, using the database and software described in ECLAC/World Bank (1999).

ter in the same period. The difference is due to the type of exports: natural resource–based manufactured goods (typical of Latin America) are less dynamic than others, such as higher value added manufactures (typical of East Asia).

If Latin American and Caribbean countries want to promote exports in the future, they must do so within the constraints of the new rules of the game. The Uruguay Round of the General Agreement on Tariffs and Trade (GATT, now the WTO) limited options in this sense. In particular, subsidies contingent upon export performance and the use of domestic rather than imported goods are explicitly prohibited. Nonetheless, more room for maneuver remains than is generally realized. While direct subsidies of exports can no longer be used, other options are still open. A variety of macroeconomic policies are completely compatible with the new rules; for example, exchange rates can be set to stimulate exports. Measures to support national competitiveness may also be used, as long as they are across the board and not mainly oriented toward exports. These include policies geared toward human resource development, technology promotion, infrastructure construction, market information, and the promotion of small enterprises. Finally, business facilitation measures can be used to promote foreign direct investment, which may prove useful for expanding a country's exports. [12]

Capital Flows to Latin America

The behavior of capital flows to Latin America in the last two decades was much more variable than the behavior of trade flows. There were major reversals: after a significant surge between 1975 and 1981, the region experienced a net outflow of capital from 1983 to 1990 before a new surge occurred in the 1990s. A good deal of short-term volatility also characterized the large inflows of the last decade. As will be discussed later, one reason for the current volatility has to do with the changing composition of capital flows. Figure 2-2 summarizes the pattern of net private capital flows to Latin America from 1975 through 1998.

The significant increase in the volume of private flows to Latin America in the 1990s can be explained by both domestic and international factors. The extensive structural reforms carried out by the majority of countries in the region did much to encourage the return of private capital. More bal-

12. Kuwayama (1999); see also Tussie (1997).

Figure 2-2. *Net Capital Inflows, 1975–98*

Billions of 1990 dollars[a]

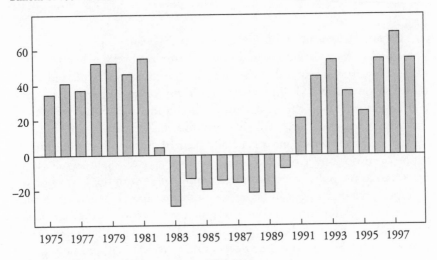

Source: Griffith-Jones (2000), on the basis of ECLAC data.
a. Data were deflated by the U.S. consumer price index.

anced macroeconomic policies, such as the elimination of budget deficits and tighter monetary policies, were also crucial to the process. The reforms served to both ease the entry of foreign capital and increase the creditworthiness of Latin American borrowers.

External factors were also extremely important. In the early 1990s, the recession in the industrialized countries and the reduction of U.S. interest rates contributed to the influx of foreign funds to Latin America. This implied that any change in this situation, such as a rise in U.S. interest rates, could cause a reduction of capital flows to the region, as happened in 1994–95. Financial liberalization in industrialized countries and the growing international diversification of the portfolios of institutional investors also served to encourage the flow of capital to emerging markets generally, including Latin America.[13]

The rise in flows to Latin America in the 1990s was accompanied by increased volatility of those flows. Not only was the pattern of surges and reversals repeated over time, but it also became more frequent in recent

13. See Griffith-Jones (1998) for a discussion of these factors.

Table 2-4. *Capital Flows to Latin America, 1975–98*

Period	Mean (billions of 1990 dollars)	Standard deviation (billions of 1990 dollars)	Coefficient of variation (percent)
1975–81	45.6	8.1	17.8
1982–90	–15.4	9.6	–62.3
1991–98	44.9	16.7	37.1

Source: Griffith-Jones (2000), on the basis of ECLAC data.

years. The two recent crises, namely, the Mexican peso crisis of 1994–95 and the international financial crisis of 1997–99, brought violent swings in the levels of capital flows to Latin America. The peso crisis led to a significant but fairly brief reversal of portfolio flows to the region in 1995, while the international financial crisis that began in Asia caused major declines in capital flows to Latin America and a currency crisis in Brazil.

Table 2-4 shows the mean, standard deviation, and coefficient of variation for each of the three sub-periods mentioned above. These calculations show that the average volume of capital flows to Latin America in the 1990s (in constant dollars) was approximately the same as the period before the debt crisis, but that flows have become much more volatile. Furthermore, the cycles of surges and declines have been far more frequent in the 1990s than they were in the 1970s and 1980s. On the positive side, the recoveries also seem quicker.

In comparison with trade flows, the pattern of capital inflows is more closely linked to that of economic growth, as can be seen in figure 2-3. During the period 1976–81, the region grew at an average of around 4.5 percent per year, while receiving capital flows at a similar share of GDP. During the period of capital scarcity between 1982 and 1990, growth fell to around 1.3 percent per year, while net capital flows to the region became negative. Growth and capital inflows continued to follow a similar pattern in the 1990s. After 1994, fluctuations of GDP growth were larger than fluctuations in net capital movements as a share of GDP, whereas the opposite pattern was found previously.

Fluctuations of growth in Latin America result from a number of domestic and external factors; volatile capital flows are only one of these factors, albeit a very important one. Moreover, the causality between flows and growth runs both ways, since high growth rates are one of the factors that attract foreign finance to developing economies. It is safe to conclude,

Figure 2-3. *GDP Growth Rates and Net Capital Inflows, 1976–98*[a]

Percent

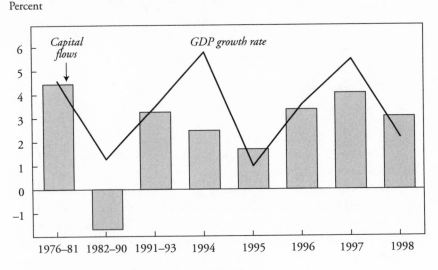

Source: Griffith-Jones (2000), on the basis of ECLAC data.

a. Net capital flows as a share of GDP.

however, that capital inflows contribute to higher levels of growth in Latin America, and sharp reductions or reversals in flows have a strong contractionary impact on the region's economies, especially if they lead to financial crises.

The effect of changes in levels of net capital flows on GDP growth occurs in the first instance via the impact of flows on imports, although a number of other mechanisms, such as variation in levels of bank lending, are also important. Large inflows permit higher imports, which reduces the external constraint to an increased use of productive capacity. Higher aggregate demand then facilitates growth of output and employment. If capital flows continue, spare productive capacity is used up, and the confidence of private actors increases. Flows may then increase levels of investment, which would increase the likelihood of more sustainable growth. In this scenario of sustained growth, positive effects of the capital flows could interact with positive impacts from the reforms; these include the transfer of more efficient technology that increases productivity, as well as more dynamic responses from entrepreneurs, who see their efforts at investing and innovating rewarded by higher profits and growth.

Figure 2-4. *Composition of Net Private Capital Inflows, 1990–98*

Billions of dollars

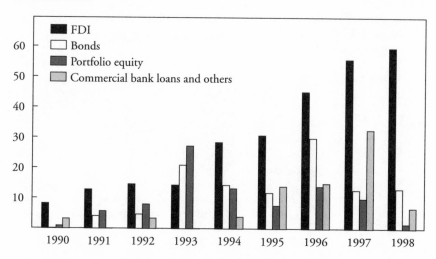

Source: Griffith-Jones (2000), on the basis of World Bank data.

A less rosy scenario is, unfortunately, more common. When capital flows decline or are totally reversed, this leads in the first instance to a sharp contraction of imports, as exports are slower to respond; the contraction in imports then leads to a fall in growth. These links clearly operated for Latin America in the 1983–89 period, when the reversal of capital flows and the large increase in debt servicing were major factors in the dramatic fall in imports (of around 40 percent in the first instance); this fall, in turn, was a major factor in Latin America's poor growth performance during those years. Sharp declines or reversals of flows led to lower imports and lower growth in the 1990s as well. In addition, large surges of capital flows contributed to overvalued exchange rates, regardless of the exchange rate regime adopted. This overvaluation discouraged investment in tradables and especially in exports, which were meant to be one of the most dynamic elements in reformed economies.

An important determinant of capital flow volatility is the term structure of net inflows. Figure 2-4 shows the breakdown of private capital flows to Latin America between 1990 and 1998 into foreign direct investment (FDI), bonds, portfolio equity, and commercial bank loans. Bonds and

Figure 2-5. *Net Foreign Direct Investment Inflows, 1990–98*

Billions of dollars

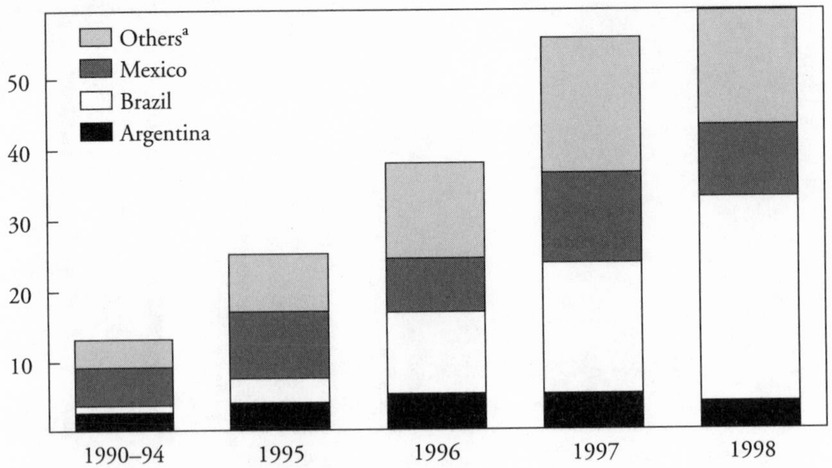

Source: Griffith-Jones (2000), on the basis of ECLAC data.
a. Bolivia, Chile, Colombia, Costa Rica, Dominican Republic, Ecuador, El Salvador, Guatemala, Haiti, Honduras, Nicaragua, Panama, Paraguay, Peru, Uruguay, and Venezuela.

equity (which tend to be more liquid) and bank lending (around 50 percent of which was short-term in this period) have been more volatile than FDI in the 1990s.

Figure 2-5 examines the behavior of FDI in more detail. Latin America and the Caribbean received FDI flows of around $60 billion in 1998, a significant increase over earlier years. Indeed, FDI flows to Latin America boomed in the 1990s. Foreign direct investment to LAIA member countries surged from $5 billion in 1985–89 to $12 billion in 1990–94, reaching $48 billion in 1995–98. Investment undertaken in 1990–97 accounted for 45 percent of the accumulated stock of FDI, which exceeded $300 billion at the end of the period. Brazil received the largest volume of FDI, but its share of total FDI stock in the region fell from 62 to 39 percent during the decade, while Mexico's rose from 21 to 26 percent.[14]

Although privatization was an important force behind FDI flows, the acquisition of private assets was also relevant, particularly in the second half of the decade when large private domestic enterprises in manufactur-

14. ECLAC (1998c).

ing, electricity, and oil were taken over by foreign investors.[15] This process resulted in an important increase in the share of transnational corporation (TNC) subsidiaries in the sales of the largest corporations in the region. Among the 500 largest firms in all economic sectors, TNCs increased their share in total sales from 27 percent in 1990–92 to 39 percent in 1998, capturing 12 of the 16 percentage points that state-owned enterprises lost as a result of privatization. A similar evolution took place among the 200 largest exporters, where TNCs increased their share from 31 to 45 percent, and among the largest manufacturing firms (see chapter 6).[16] In this context, greenfield investment played a less important role during the decade, although the expansion and modernization of privatized firms attracted relatively large inflows in 1994–96. Data suggest that a similar process took place in 1998–99.[17]

Other kinds of capital also became increasingly important in Latin America in the 1990s, especially international bond issues. Before 1989, Latin America and the Caribbean had only limited access to the international bond market. Since then, the region has enjoyed extensive access, and the importance of bond financing as a source of external finance has risen significantly. Figure 2-6 shows that the volume of international bond issues in Latin America and the Caribbean rose from less than $3 billion in 1990 to a peak of $54 billion in 1997. Bond issues by Latin American countries fell during the Mexican peso crisis in 1994–95, recovered rapidly, but then fell again in 1998. Bond financing is relatively expensive for Latin America, since margins have been high. Moreover, spreads, which had been falling since the peso crisis, rose sharply as a result of the international financial crisis that began in mid-1997. The crisis also reversed the previous improvement in the average maturity of Latin American bond issues.[18]

---

15. In 1994–96 foreign investors focused on the creation of new assets related to large investment projects and the modernization of firms they had already established in the region or acquired through privatizations. In 1996–97, in contrast, investment was fundamentally oriented toward the acquisition of existing firms, as it had been during the first part of the decade. Estimates for 1997 indicate that 71 percent of FDI ($41.7 billion of a total of $58.5 billion) in LAIA member countries involved the acquisition of existing assets. Of this total, net purchases of assets from the private sector amounted to $24.3 billion, or 58 percent of total asset acquisitions and 42 percent of total FDI (ECLAC, 1998c.).

16. ECLAC (2000b).

17. ECLAC (1998c) and (2000b).

18. It is important to note that the trend toward rising maturities before the crisis was offset by the increasing share of bonds issued with options. Because options allow the lender to pull out before the official maturity date, the apparent improvement may have been an illusion. See Griffith-Jones (2000).

Figure 2-6. *International Bond Issues, 1990–98*

Billions of dollars

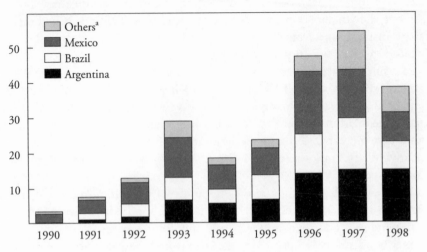

Source: Griffith-Jones (2000), on the basis of IMF data.
a. Bahamas, Bolivia, Chile, Colombia, Costa Rica, Dominican Republic, Ecuador, Guatemala, Jamaica, Panama, Peru, Trinidad and Tobago, Uruguay, and Venezuela.

International stock issues were another important source of capital for Latin American countries in the 1990s, although to a much lesser extent than bond issues. Stock issues fell sharply as a result of the Mexican peso crisis; unlike bonds, they recovered only gradually in 1996–98, failing to reach precrisis levels. The share of bank lending in total private capital flows to Latin America was significantly less important in the 1990s than it was in the 1970s. Banks that report to the Bank for International Settlements (BIS) showed steady growth in outstanding claims to Latin America, from around $200 billion in 1993–94 to nearly $300 billion in mid-1999. The share of short-term claims (up to one year) on Latin American borrowers increased during the 1990s, from around 37 percent in 1991 to around 52 percent in the first half of 1999. Nonetheless, the share of short-term claims in Latin America compares relatively favorably to that in Asia, where the figure remained at over 60 percent between 1992 and 1997.[19]

19. BIS (1999).

Conclusions

A number of key elements in the international environment have greatly influenced the impact of the reforms on economic performance. With respect to world trade, the value of Latin American exports in the postwar period experienced a clear rising trend, although the region's share in total world exports fell until some recovery occurred in the 1990s. The acceleration in the growth of exports in the recent decade is partly explained by the economic reforms. Nonetheless, the increased growth of exports (in volume as well as value) did not lead to a comparable growth of output. It is this divergence of trends that needs to be remedied.

Global capital flows also increased rapidly, and in this case Latin America's share grew. These trends are found with both portfolio flows and FDI, although the former grew more than the latter. A key feature of capital flows to Latin America was their volatility, and the cycles of surges and steep declines became more frequent in the 1990s. Crises were also more frequent, and higher volatility led to uncertainty, which discouraged investment that is crucial for allowing reforms to bear fruit and lead to higher growth in the future. Far more clearly than in the case of trade, levels of capital flows and growth seem to be closely correlated in Latin America. When capital flows increase, economic growth accelerates; when they fall significantly or are reversed, growth (or even output) falls.

There is an important relation between trends in trade and capital flows. One of the reasons that Latin America exhibits a weak link between exports and growth of GDP is that the creation of such a link requires a fair amount of time for the development of supplier networks. That is, investment must occur in many sectors and firms of different sizes, including small and medium-size suppliers as well as assembly plants, in order for large exporting firms to transmit growth to other parts of the economy. If the volatility of capital flows is such that the investment process is frequently interrupted, the necessary incentives for investment will be absent. Of course, perfect conditions will never exist, but the volatility in the 1990s may have been exceptional. The highly problematic experience with capital flows in the 1990s, and much of the recent literature on the subject, raises the possibility that large surges of easily reversible capital flows may have net negative effects on long-term growth and development.[20] This is

20. See, for example, Bhagwati (1998); Radelet and Sachs (1998); Rodrik (1998).

in contrast with growing empirical evidence that FDI and, potentially, trade contribute to long-term growth.[21] In the final chapter, we recommend policy measures for maximizing the benefits, while minimizing the problems, with trade and capital flows.

21. See, for example, Borensztein, de Gregorio, and Lee (1995); Ffrench-Davis and Reisen (1998).

3 | Structural Reforms and Public Policies

The package of structural reforms has altered the context in which the Latin American and Caribbean economies operate, increasing the role of market mechanisms over that of administrative controls, the role of the private sector at the expense of the state, and regional integration into the global economy. The objectives of macroeconomic policy, including fiscal, monetary, and exchange rate policies, have also shifted, giving renewed priority to establishing and maintaining balanced accounts. Both the reforms and macroeconomic policies are aimed at creating improved conditions for rapid growth via increased investment and technological change. Social policy has also witnessed important advances during the current decade as all governments have increased social expenditure, reflecting the view that this area can complement other efforts to achieve economic progress while simultaneously increasing equity in the societies. Nonetheless, problems remain because of lack of consensus on the role of the public and private sectors and the inherent difficulties in increasing the quality of social services.

The goal of this chapter is to provide systematic information on what has happened in these policy spheres and to analyze the interrelations among them in order to lay the basis for understanding the response of private sector actors to the new policy initiatives. With respect to the reforms themselves and macroeconomic policies, the countries essentially behaved in two different ways, depending on their initial conditions. One group, for which initial conditions were unusually difficult, became aggressive reformers and implemented many changes in rapid order. A second group enjoyed more favorable initial conditions, and these countries were more cautious about undertaking profound structural reforms. Social policies appear to have followed a different logic, based mainly on history. Countries with a strong tradition of social expenditure maintained this posture, while others made special efforts to catch up. The interactions among the reforms and policies were too often inconsistent, leading to less than optimal responses by economic actors. This area will need attention in the future.

The chapter first examines the reform process: the reasons for the changes, the reforms that were most important, a set of indicators to measure the reforms, and differences among countries with respect to their implementation. Next, it shifts to macroeconomic accomplishments and the interactions between reforms and macroeconomic policies. Social policy trends are also examined, with a special focus on expenditure in education and health areas. A concluding section looks at the implications for topics covered in other chapters, namely, investment, growth, employment, and equity.

First Generation Structural Reforms

The structural reforms undertaken by Latin America and the Caribbean marked the most significant change in development strategy since the initiation of the so-called import substitution industrialization (ISI) model. As has been extensively documented, the ISI model rested on two main pillars: a strong role for the state (that is, government expenditure as a large share of gross domestic product (GDP), extensive regulations, and an increasing presence of state-owned firms) and a relatively closed economy (that is, high tariff barriers, quotas, and exchange controls).[1]

Despite the *ex post* criticisms of these policies, they were quite successful in increasing the sophistication and growth performance of a number

---

1. In an important work on this period, Cárdenas, Ocampo, and Thorp (forthcoming) argue that the term ISI is inappropriate. They suggest that "state-led industrialization" or "accelerated industrialization" is more accurate. They also stress that governments changed their policies during the period rather than following a constant model throughout.

of economies in the region. In the 1970s, for example, Brazil and Mexico were frequently compared with Korea and Taiwan as newly industrializing economies (NIEs). Average annual growth rates in Brazil and Mexico between 1950 and 1980 were 7.0 and 6.5 percent, respectively, while their industrial sectors became powerful engines of growth and employment. Their export baskets came to include a substantial role for industrial products, although the onset of oil exports in Mexico in the late 1970s lowered the share in that country. Smaller economies also experienced successful growth under the ISI model. Among project countries, Colombia and Costa Rica grew more than 5 percent per year during the 1950–80 period.[2]

In the 1960s and 1970s, the Asian NIEs adopted an explicit export orientation that built on their prior experience with ISI. The Latin American countries, in contrast, chose a more mixed approach: Peru moved deeper into import substitution; others, such as Argentina, Chile, Colombia, and Costa Rica, began to promote exports; and Mexico and especially Brazil relied on a combination of both. Almost all the countries in the region sought to finance trade deficits, increase investment—and, in some cases, consumption—through greater access to foreign capital, particularly loans from international commercial banks with their new glut of petrodollars. In Argentina and Chile, the borrowers were mainly from the private sector; in other cases, public sector borrowing was dominant. Colombia alone did not participate heavily in the borrowing spree, although it began to seek more funds at the end of the 1970s.

Initially, the alliance between the banks—in need of new borrowers—and the Latin Americans—in need of capital for domestic purposes—appeared to be advantageous for all. The negative side was the buildup of a large debt, which approached $350 billion in 1982. This debt might have been manageable had international prices and interest rates continued on the path that most observers expected, but significant changes occurred at the beginning of the 1980s. Prices for commodities, except oil, fell sharply, leading to large trade deficits. At the same time international interest rates more than doubled. Since most of the new loans had been contracted at floating interest rates and, increasingly, on a short-term basis, the conditions were created for the debt crisis that began with the Mexican moratorium in August 1982.

In the early years after the debt crisis began, it was usually assumed that stabilization programs would be sufficient to get through the crisis until

2. Data are from Hofman (2000).

another credit cycle began. A new mood swept the region in the second half of the decade, however, as it gradually became clear that this viewpoint was unrealistic. A number of factors converged to push government leaders toward more far-reaching decisions on economic policy.[3]

One such factor was that as private capital sources dried up, the international financial institutions, especially the International Monetary Fund (IMF) and the World Bank, began to assume a more important role in international finance. For a number of years these institutions had been pushing for policies known as structural adjustment (namely, greater openness and deregulation); they were now in a position to require policy changes along these lines in return for refinancing and new loans. At the same time that these international actors acquired new influence in Latin America, a group of local technocrats who had been advocating similar policies began to obtain important posts in economic ministries and central banks.

Reinforcing trends were underway at the international political level. In the leading industrialized countries, a set of conservative leaders (especially Reagan and Thatcher) were advocating policies in their own countries that were similar to those pushed by the World Bank and the IMF in Latin America. Even more significant changes were taking place in Europe with the fall of the Soviet Union and the end of communism in central and eastern Europe. These changes undermined support for state-led development strategies among local groups in Latin America and the Caribbean.

A final set of factors involved economic trends in developing countries. In the 1980s, the mainstream interpretation attributed the success of the East Asian countries to their supposedly open and unregulated economies. While this interpretation was later altered substantially, at a crucial moment many Latin American leaders believed that the main explanation for Asian success, and their own relative failure, lay in these variables. Examples in the region reinforced this view. Chile, which provided the earliest case of a structural reformer in Latin America, emerged from the debt crisis relatively quickly; its neighbor Peru, in contrast, sank ever deeper into chaos under Alan García's state-centered policies. Moreover, attempts at heterodox stabilization, not only in Peru but also in Argentina and Brazil, failed and led to hyperinflation.

All of these factors helped push Latin American governments to make a major overhaul of their economic approach, moving in the direction of

---

3. See Stallings (1992) and Edwards (1995) for a similar analysis of causes behind the new development strategy.

the open economies and private sector leadership that characterized the structural reform package. Expectations for the new development model were initially very high. Their proponents thought that the policies would not only speed up economic growth, but also lead to the generation of more jobs and increased equality. A key mechanism was to lift regulations and give more rein to the private sector, which was believed to be much more efficient than its public sector counterpart, such that the former would take the lead in the production process by investing more and increasing productivity. The opening of the economies would reinforce this process: competition from abroad would require greater efficiency and also provide increased access to finance and technology.

The result of these two processes would be higher growth, based on a shift in the direction of the region's comparative advantage. The opening of the economies would not only involve imports, but would also increase exports, in particular, labor-intensive exports. This was a key link to faster job creation, since it was believed that Latin American and Caribbean countries had a comparative advantage in labor-intensive products. The greater volume of employment would, in turn, help to lower both the poverty that had climbed to new levels during the 1980s and the inequality that was higher in Latin America than in any other part of the world. Later in the book we will identify where some of these initial assumptions may have been erroneous, as we attempt to evaluate the new development model.

The Reform Content

The structural reforms can be defined in a variety of ways. We have chosen to concentrate on a package of five basic reforms that were prevalent across the region, while acknowledging that others could be added to the general list and that some additional reforms were quite important in individual countries. Our five are as follows: liberalization of imports, liberalization of the domestic financial system, opening the capital account of the balance of payments, privatization, and tax reform. The common element among them is greater reliance on market mechanisms, both domestically and internationally. In describing the reforms below, we emphasize the views of the reformers themselves; our analysis of the policies follows in later chapters.

IMPORT LIBERALIZATION. At the beginning of the reform period, Latin American markets were protected from international competition in a variety of ways. The two most important were high tariffs and import quotas on industrial and agricultural products. Both forms of protection tended to vary widely across sectors and even individual products, such that some were heavily protected while others were not. The different levels of protection were exacerbated if effective protection was taken into account.

Advocates of reform voiced a number of arguments against protection. First, it lowered the efficiency of the economy by closing it off from external competition and by limiting exposure to new technologies. Second, it led countries to stray from their comparative advantage and produce a broad array of products, again with low levels of efficiency. Third, the resulting high prices hurt consumers as well as exporters by making them pay the cost of protecting local producers. Fourth, protection established the basis for rent-seeking behavior, whereby bureaucrats accepted bribes and firms devoted resources to gaining advantages in the system rather than increasing their efficiency. Finally, while the legitimacy of the infant industry argument was generally acknowledged, it was argued that once high tariffs were put into place, it was very hard to eliminate them.

One of the most pervasive reforms, then, was the dismantling of the old protective structure. Quotas were eliminated; tariff rates were lowered; and tariff dispersion was limited, with a few countries moving toward a single flat rate. This process was not completely irreversible, however, as external crises led to some temporary backtracking. In addition, while the integration process in Latin America and the Caribbean generally supported trade liberalization, it led to higher tariffs for a few individual items.

DOMESTIC FINANCIAL REFORM. The domestic financial system during the ISI period was an important instrument of government control of the economy. First, interest rates on both deposits and loans were set by the government. The real rates were often negative, at least *ex post*, as inflation exceeded nominal rates. Second, reserve requirements were very high, so the commercial banks had little freedom to expand their portfolios. Third, the government issued administrative directives for the allocation of a substantial share of commercial bank credit. Fourth, government-owned banks were responsible for a large amount of the lending that took place, often intermediating between external sources of credit and local borrowers. Together, these processes led to a situation typically referred to as financial repression.

According to the critics, the results of financial repression were low saving rates, since depositors frequently received negative interest on their funds; low monetization of the economies; low access to credit, especially for small and medium-size enterprises; and credit directed to borrowers on the basis of political connections, not the profitability of their projects. The main changes in this area, then, were to free interest rates to be set by market forces, to lower reserve requirements, to limit or end directed credit, and to privatize or close government-owned banks. A related institutional reform was the tendency toward making central banks autonomous of finance ministries. In this way, reference interest rates and reserve policies were increasingly controlled by an independent entity whose main (or only) goal was to control inflation. More will be said later on the consequence of this reform for macroeconomic policy.

OPENING THE CAPITAL ACCOUNT. Capital controls were usually a complement to trade protectionism and financial repression in the pre-reform period. Exchange controls enabled governments to regulate the amount of foreign currency that could be taken out of a country, and they required economic actors to buy local currency through official channels at lower-than-market rates. More specific restrictions concerned particular types of capital flows. Foreign direct investment (FDI) was often a target, with respect to the sectors in which it could be invested and capital repatriation.[4]

Reformers charged that capital controls led to black markets in foreign currency, taking many functions out of government hands and leading to the same type of rent-seeking behavior described earlier. They were also said to limit local firms' access to foreign capital and the complementary resources of technology and markets. The main reforms with respect to the capital account were the elimination of exchange controls and the end to restrictions on FDI and other types of flows. Most of these reforms were aimed at limiting controls on capital outflows, but the surge of foreign capital in the first half of the 1990s led a few governments to impose controls on capital inflows (especially short-term flows) to limit their impact on macroeconomic policy. The latter controls involved reserve requirements on capital during a certain period (as in Chile and Colombia) or a tax on capital inflows (as in Brazil).

4. It is interesting to note that FDI was regarded as the most negative kind of foreign capital in the 1970s, which explains the wave of nationalizations as well as controls. By the 1990s, in contrast, FDI had become highly valued, not only for its links to export markets and technology, but also for its long-term stability relative to volatile short-term portfolio flows.

PRIVATIZATION. State-owned enterprises became especially common in Latin America and the Caribbean during the 1970s, although some dated back much earlier. Many of these enterprises were giant natural resource firms that accounted for a large percentage of export receipts and government revenues. They had been brought under government control because ownership by transnational corporations (TNCs) seriously limited the governments' ability to manage their economies. Public utility monopolies were also typically in the public sector from an early date. Other sectors were later brought under government control for a variety of reasons.

Despite their similar ownership structure, the state enterprises were managed in different ways. Some were treated as semi-autonomous entities and were expected to make profits like any private firm; others served as an instrument of diverse government aims, such as providing cheap inputs to favored sectors or jobs to unionized workers. The latter type of firms typically ran large deficits, not necessarily because they were inefficient but because of government pricing and employment policies. These deficits had to be covered by general government revenues, which increased central government disequilibria. Moreover, these firms typically did not have access to sufficient capital for investment, so they tended to use technology that was below the international state of the art.

The most common reform in this area was to sell the firms to the private sector, whether domestic or foreign. Nonetheless, they were sold under different conditions that had a strong impact on their later functioning. As will be seen in chapter 6, important variants included the price paid, the buyer's experience in the sector, the degree of competition, and the regulatory framework. Bolivia developed a particularly interesting variation of privatization, known as capitalization. Under the rules of capitalization, the buyer had to commit itself to a future investment program.

TAX REFORM. During the ISI period, many Latin American governments imposed very high marginal tax rates on corporations and wealthy individuals. Royalties and taxes on foreign corporations were especially attractive targets. Taxes on international trade were an important source of revenue for some countries, as were excise taxes on particular items. From the reformers' viewpoint, this tax system was inefficient for at least three reasons: it led to intricate schemes for tax evasion; it undermined incentives to invest and to export; and it impinged on other economic decisions by distorting the price structure.

The reform package included several changes in the tax structure to correct the problems identified. The lowering of taxes on trade was discussed above in connection with import liberalization. Taxes on exports were also lowered or eliminated altogether. In addition, the maximum rates were lowered on individuals and corporations, and some of the ad hoc taxes were rescinded. To make up for the loss of revenue, a value added tax (VAT) was instituted or increased, becoming the main source of tax income in many countries. The VAT was both easier to collect and considered more neutral than other taxes, thus having less impact on decisionmaking by economic agents.

OTHER REFORMS. In addition to these five, a number of other important structural reforms have been implemented in some countries. Most notably, labor reform sought to create more flexible rules by eliminating practices such as lifetime employment and very high costs for dismissal; social security reform transformed traditional "pay as you go" systems into private "capitalization" schemes; and decentralization moved revenues and responsibilities from the central government to provinces or municipalities. These reforms were not as widespread as the five summarized above, however.

The Reform Indexes

To study the five reforms, project economists created a set of indexes for analyzing and comparing the implementation process.[5] The quantitative indexes also give us the capacity to study the impact of the reforms through econometric and other kinds of analysis.[6] Box 3-1 outlines the components of the indexes. In general, the indexes measure the degree to which the economy is more open and more market-led, with scores ranging from 0 to 1. While a score of 1 indicates the greatest degree of openness or market orientation, relative to other countries, it is crucial to note that a

5. Morley, Machado, and Pettinato (1999). The indexes were based on seventeen countries, rather than only on the nine project countries.

6. Of course, cross-country quantitative indicators have disadvantages as well as advantages. They obviously cannot include many important qualitative details. Likewise, when sources that include a large number of countries are used, doubts arise on the reliability of individual observations.

Box 3-1. *Structural Reform Indexes*

The basic structural reform index consists of five subindexes. They, in turn, generally have several components.

Components

Import liberalization: (1) average level of tariffs and (2) dispersion of tariffs.

Domestic financial liberalization: (1) control of bank lending rates (0 if controlled, 1 if market determined); (2) control of bank deposit rates; and (3) reserves-to-deposits ratio.

Capital account opening: indexes of (1) controls on foreign direct investment; (2) limits on profit repatriation and interest payments ; (3) controls on external credits by national borrowers; and (4) controls on capital flows.

Tax reform: (1) maximum marginal rate on corporate income; (2) maximum marginal rate on personal income; (3) value added tax rate; and (4) efficiency of value added tax (ratio of VAT rate to the receipts from this tax as share of GDP).

Privatization: One minus the ratio of value added in state-owned enterprises to nonagricultural GDP.

Data sources

The indexes are a modification and extension of those prepared by Eduardo Lora of the Inter-American Development Bank.[a] For import liberalization, domestic financial liberalization, and tax reform, the Lora indexes for 1985–95 were extended backward to 1970 and, in the case of financial liberalization, corrections

---

score of 1 is not necessarily ideal; it may well be that a somewhat lower score would lead to better performance, at least on some variables.[7]

Figure 3-1 shows the pattern of the five individual reforms as well as the overall index for the 1970–95 period. The discussion in Morley,

---

7. Not surprisingly, there was a relatively high correlation between some of the pairs of indexes, which leads to difficulties in econometric estimations. The correlation matrix among the five indexes for the nine countries in the period 1970–95 is the following:

	Trade reform	Financial reform	Capital account	Privatization	Tax reform
Trade reform	1.00	0.66	0.47	−0.10	0.59
Financial reform	0.66	1.00	0.26	0.10	0.66
Capital account	0.47	0.26	1.00	−0.15	0.27
Privatization	−0.10	0.10	−0.15	1.00	0.15
Tax reform	0.59	0.66	0.27	0.15	1.00

of errors on interest rates were made. For privatization, a new index was developed, with the basic information coming from World Bank.[b] The index on capital account opening was also created by the project since Lora did not have an index on this topic. The main source was the IMF's annual publication, *Balance of Payments Arrangements*.

Construction

Each index is normalized to fall between zero and one, with one being the most reformed or free from distortion or government intervention. The difference between each country's raw index and the least liberalized country observation is expressed as a percentage of the difference between the maximum and minimum observations for all the countries over the entire period. Note that this implies that the maximum value of any index is the level actually attained in some country between 1970 and 1995.

In formal terms, the index value for country i at time t is:

$$I_{it} = (IR_{it} - Min) / (Max - Min)$$

I_{it} is the index value for country i in year t
IR_{it} is the raw value of the reform measure for country i in year t
Max is the maximum value of the reform measure for all countries in all years
Min is the minimum value of the reform measure for all countries in all years

Source: Morley, Machado, and Pettinato (1999).
a. IDB (1996); see also Lora (1997).
b. World Bank (1995a).

Machado, and Pettinato stresses that the reform process has not been uniform across time or subject area.[8] In three of the five areas—namely, import liberalization, financial liberalization, and tax reform—change started in the 1970s in Argentina, Chile, and Colombia among the nine project countries, as well as in Uruguay. These early reformers were responsible for virtually all of the rise in the trade and financial reform indexes during the 1970s. The tax reform index also rose in this period, reflecting the adoption of value added tax systems in a large number of countries. Capital account controls were tightened in the early 1970s, due principally to policy

8. Morley, Machado, and Pettinato (1999).

Figure 3-1. *Reform Indexes, 1970–95*[a]

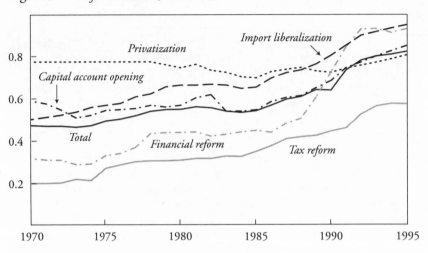

Source: Morley, Machado, and Pettinato (1999).
a. Sample includes the nine project countries plus Dominican Republic, Ecuador, El Salvador, Guatemala, Honduras, Paraguay, Uruguay, and Venezuela.

changes under the second Perón government in Argentina and the military government in Peru; this process was subsequently reversed with liberalization under military governments in Argentina and Chile. In this early period, the only privatizations were the sales of a large number of relatively small state enterprises in Chile.

After 1982, the Latin American debt crisis not only stopped the reform process, but also reversed it in several of the early reforming countries. In response to the debt crisis, Argentina, Bolivia, and Chile imposed temporary controls on capital account transactions. Many countries (among them Argentina, Brazil, Chile, Colombia, Mexico, and Peru) increased tariff and nontariff restrictions on imports. The process of financial liberalization was either halted or reversed, and no further progress was made in either tax reform or the opening of the capital account during this period.

A far more general and widespread adoption of the structural reform package started around 1985 and accelerated significantly in the 1990s. Countries such as Chile and Argentina, which had been leaders in the first round, continued to extend their reforms. Most other countries in the region followed the early reformers by lowering tariffs and reforming their tax systems. Moreover, almost all countries decontrolled their interest rates and made efforts to integrate domestic and international capital markets more closely.

On examining the reform process across the region, one important pattern that emerges is the degree of convergence over time. Countries that had relatively liberalized economies in 1985 tended to introduce fewer additional reforms, while the others made a significant effort to catch up over the subsequent decade. The success of the early reformers, particularly Chile, was presumably an incentive for others to accelerate their own reform processes. By 1995, the main elements of the reform package had been adopted across almost all the countries of the region.[9]

Aggressive versus Cautious Reformers

Despite the eventual convergence, the process started out quite differently. It is possible to identify a set of "aggressive" reformers versus others who were more "cautious" on the basis of the speed and scope of the reforms. The former group undertook many reforms in a relatively short period of time, while the latter implemented reforms more gradually. These differences were closely correlated with initial conditions in the period preceding the reforms. Four elements, in particular, influenced later policy choice: growth performance, inflation, degree of economic distortion (here measured by the reform index), and level of governability.

These elements tended to cluster. At one extreme, Argentina, Bolivia, Chile, and Peru scored poorly on all four elements (see table 3-1). On average, the four had annual inflation rates of over 1,200 percent in the five years preceding the initiation of the reform process. GDP in those same periods contracted by an average of 0.7 percent. The reform index averaged .477, indicating a high level of economic distortion, and governability had broken down substantially. This included near civil war in Chile during the Popular Unity government, a disintegrating state in Bolivia, the inability of President Alfonsín to even complete his term in Argentina, and the Sendero Luminoso guerrilla war in Peru.

9. Unfortunately, the reform index used in the project ends in 1995. More recent calculations using the same indicators for the nine project countries show that privatization is the area where most reform occurred in 1996–98. Bolivia, Brazil, Colombia, and Peru did the most in this area, followed by Argentina and Chile. Activity was quite modest in the other four reform areas. The country that carried out the most reforms was Brazil (see Paunovic, 2000).

Table 3-1. *Initial Conditions among Aggressive and Cautious Reformers*

Country	Year[a]	Inflation[b]	Growth[c]	Reform index[d]	Governability[e]
Aggressive reformers					
Argentina	1989	1,191 (4,924)[f]	−1.3	.664	Low
Bolivia	1985	1,100 (8,171)[f]	−1.9	.445	Low
Chile	1974	228 (609)[f]	1.8	.316	Low
Peru	1990	2,465 (7,650)[f]	−1.5	.484	Low
Simple average	. . .	1,246	−0.7	.477	Low
Cautious reformers					
Brazil	1990	708	4.4	.696	Medium
Colombia	1990	26	4.6	.689	Medium/high
Costa Rica	1986	27	2.0	.524	High
Jamaica	1989	14	1.9	.560	Medium
Mexico	1985	66	2.0	.578	Medium/high
Simple average	. . .	168	3.0	.609	Medium/high

Source: Authors' calculations, on the basis of project data.

a. Year reforms began.

b. Consumer price indexes, December-December, averaged for five years preceding reforms.

c. Average annual growth rate of GDP, measured in constant 1980 dollars, for five years preceding reforms.

d. Index reported in Morley, Machado, and Pettinato (1999) for year reforms began.

e. Authors' evaluation of governments' ability to make and carry out policy decisions at the end of the pre-reform period.

f. Inflation in the year of highest price rises near the beginning of the reform period.

The same pattern is found in each of the countries individually, with two exceptions. One is Argentina's relatively high score on the reform index. This resulted from Argentina's earlier period of reforms in the late 1970s when a number of changes were made, especially in the trade and financial areas and opening the capital account. The reforms were then suspended until the early 1990s. The other difference that stands out in the table is the relatively low inflation rate in Chile, which averaged 228 percent in the five years preceding the reforms and 609 percent in the single highest year. This rate appears low in comparison with the other countries in the group, but in the context of the times before the hyperinflations of the 1980s, it was considered an extremely high rate as, of course, it is today.

The consequence of these traumatic experiences was to create an environment in which governments and other important actors were willing to experiment with drastic changes in economic policy, since the existing situation was considered unacceptable and unlikely to respond adequately to modest policy shifts. The changes came about when a new government came to power through a military coup in Chile but through elected governments in the other three countries. The new governments increased the capacity to govern, thus making policy change possible. In addition, the very negative economic conditions led to the heavy involvement of the international financial institutions, especially the IMF and the World Bank. These institutions were strong advocates of the economic reforms, which reinforced the new governments' own inclinations toward extensive change.

The four countries responded to the multiple domestic and international pressures by implementing a number of reforms in very rapid order. In a process sometimes referred to as shock treatment, tariffs were lowered, other taxes were cut, financial systems were liberalized, capital accounts were opened, and public sector firms were sold.[10] All of these changes were new when Chile undertook reform in the early 1970s, such that the country had little guidance to go by. For the other three, especially Argentina and Peru in the 1990s, the Chilean experience offered both a positive model and a source of lessons.

Table 3-1 also delineates the initial conditions of the cautious reformers: Brazil, Colombia, Costa Rica, Jamaica, and Mexico. The contrast with the aggressive reformers is quite stark. Average inflation among the five countries in the preceding period was much lower at 168 percent, while the previous growth rate was much higher at 3.0 percent. The level of economic distortion was lower, with an index of .609, and problems of governability did not match those among the aggressive reformers.

Another way of viewing the difference between the two groups is that among the cautious reformers, the central actors believed the countries

10. Williamson provides a vivid example of the concept of aggressive reformers in describing the Bolivian reforms of 1985. "[President] Paz's advisors planned the equivalent of about five GATT rounds, six Gramm-Rudmans, and more deregulation than had been accomplished by the Carter and Reagan administrations together, all overnight" (1990, p. 356).

were basically sound and had much worth preserving. The particular source of pride varied across cases. For Brazil and Mexico, it was a powerful industrial sector and economies among the dozen largest in the world. For Colombia, it was a historical reputation for sensible policy decisions and a stable economy. For Costa Rica, it was a popular set of social benefits that underpinned a vibrant democracy. Jamaica fits marginally within this second group. It experienced serious conflicts in the 1970s but never the society-wide convulsions that characterized the aggressive reformers. Moreover, although growth in Jamaica was quite weak, its economy was never disrupted to the extent that the aggressive reformers' had been.

In contrast to the aggressive reformers, the cautious reformers were more gradual and selective in their changes, in part because domestic opposition was more widespread. The international financial institutions were an important force in overcoming domestic opposition, especially in the two smaller countries, Costa Rica and Jamaica. The authors of project case studies on those two countries report that reforms were "imposed" on Costa Rica by the World Bank's structural adjustment loans and "foisted on the people [of Jamaica] by . . . an unwilling administration and, later, by an unfocused one merely following to a limited extent world economic fashion."[11]

As noted above, the average inflation rate among the cautious reformers was quite high at 168 percent. This figure provides the basis for subdividing this group of countries. Brazil and Mexico had serious inflation problems, with price rises that were high either in absolute terms (Brazil had an average of 708 percent in the five years preceding the reforms) or in comparison to historical averages (Mexico's average of 66 percent in the five pre-reform years contrasted with the 16 percent average for the 1970s and single-digit inflation earlier). The second subgroup (Colombia, Costa Rica, and Jamaica) had inflation rates that averaged 22 percent per year, suggesting that their macroeconomic conditions were basically sound, according to the judgment of the times.

This categorization—the aggressive reformers, the cautious reformers with macroeconomic problems, and the cautious reformers with stable macroeconomic conditions—is useful for analyzing other topics in the book, especially investment and growth patterns. The three groups also took somewhat different approaches to macroeconomic policy.

11. Villasuso (2000); King (2000).

Macroeconomic Policies and Outcomes

The structural reform process in Latin America and the Caribbean did not take place in a vacuum. The most important factors determining the impact of the reforms, beyond the content of the reforms themselves, were the international context and the macroeconomic policies of the respective governments. While the literature makes some attempt to decide which of these three factors was the most important in determining outcomes, our focus in this chapter is on understanding the connections among them.[12]

The change in macroeconomic policy stance in the region over the last fifteen years has been as important as the change in development model. The 1970s (or, more precisely, the decade between the first oil shock and the onset of the debt crisis) marked a peak of loose macroeconomic policy, as fiscal and current account deficits reached major proportions. Thus, six of seventeen countries in the region for which data are available had fiscal deficits that exceeded 3 percent of GDP in the period 1974–82, while ten of nineteen had current account deficits over 5 percent of GDP in the same years.[13] Current account deficits generally shrank during the remainder of the 1980s, but fiscal deficits increased and inflation rose dramatically, reaching four or even five digits in a number of countries. The association of these excesses with the debt crisis and the high costs it entailed led to a major shift in opinion among the region's governments, which came to revalue macroeconomic equilibrium.

Stabilization

In some cases stabilization preceded the reforms, in some cases the two were simultaneous, and in one instance (Brazil) stabilization actually came later. Even given this diversity, however, a set of stylized facts generally characterized the macroeconomic policies that accompanied the structural reforms. First, there was a narrow focus on lowering inflation to the one-digit level or even to the average of the industrialized countries. The tendency toward a single target for macroeconomic policy was reinforced

---

12. Some analysts try to distinguish among the various factors through use of an econometric model (for example, Lora and Barrera, 1997); others simply argue that one or the other was more important (for example, Rodrik, 1996).

13. Calculated on the basis of IMF, *Government Finance Statistics Yearbook* (various years), and ECLAC data.

Table 3-2. *Inflation Trends, 1991–98*[a]

Percent

Country	Highest inflation rate (year)[b]	1991	1992	1993	1994	1995	1996	1997	1998
Argentina	4,924 (1989)	84.0	17.6	7.4	3.9	1.6	0.1	0.3	0.7
Bolivia	8,171 (1985)	14.0	10.5	9.3	8.5	12.6	7.9	6.7	4.4
Brazil	1,864 (1989)	475.0	1,149.0	2,489.0	929.0	22.0	9.1	4.3	2.5
Chile I[c]	609 (1973)	369.2[d]	343.3[d]	198.0[d]	84.2[d]	37.2[d]	38.9[d]	31.2[d]	9.5[d]
Chile II[c]	27 (1990)	18.7	12.7	12.2	8.9	8.2	6.6	6.0	4.7
Colombia	32 (1990)	26.8	25.1	22.6	22.6	19.5	21.6	17.7	16.7
Costa Rica	15 (1986)	25.3	17.0	9.0	19.9	22.6	13.9	11.2	12.4
Jamaica	17 (1989)	80.2	40.2	30.1	26.9	25.5	15.8	9.2	7.9
Mexico	159 (1987)	18.8	11.9	8.0	7.1	52.1	27.7	15.7	18.6
Peru	7,650 (1990)	139.0	56.7	39.5	15.4	10.2	11.8	6.5	6.0
Simple average[e]	...	98.0	149.0	291.9	115.8	19.4	12.7	8.6	8.2
Simple average, excluding Brazil[e]	...	50.9	24.0	17.3	14.2	19.0	13.2	9.2	8.9

Source: Project database, on the basis of ECLAC statistics; Corbo and Fischer (1994: 32–33) for Chile I.

a. Variation in consumer price index, December–December.

b. In year near beginning of reforms.

c. Chile is listed twice to distinguish two phases of reforms.

d. 1974–81.

e. Excluding Chile I.

by the move toward independent central banks that themselves had a single target. Second, fiscal policy supported the fight against inflation by shrinking deficits; this was done primarily by cutting expenditure rather than by raising taxes or other revenues. Third, monetary policy was also geared toward stabilization, although it could be expansionary if the demand for real money balances rose. High interest rates were a key instrument of stabilization, in combination with both floating exchange rates and fixed or semi-fixed schemes. Finally, much less consensus prevailed on exchange rate policy. In some countries and in some periods, the exchange rate was used primarily to lower inflation; in an increasing number of cases, it was set in order to maintain international competitiveness and stimulate growth. The shift from the former to the latter approach usually proved to be traumatic.

With respect to the inflation goal, the nine project countries were quite successful, as were most other countries in the region. Table 3-2 shows the declining rate of increase of consumer prices from the beginning of the reform and stabilization period through 1998.[14] Every case demonstrates improvement over the initial level, although those cases with the highest initial inflation obviously saw the most dramatic declines. The patterns were not always linear: a reversal sometimes occurred, but then the declining path was resumed.

Argentina, Bolivia, and Peru dropped rapidly from hyperinflation in the 1980s to two-digit inflation and then continued to the single-digit level; Chile did the same in the 1970s, as did Brazil in the 1990s. The policy mix to produce stabilization varied, with some countries using exchange rate policy while others relied mainly on monetary or fiscal policy. Costa Rica, Jamaica, and Mexico suffered temporary reversals in their stabilization efforts; Colombia had double-digit inflation that only declined moderately over the period.

Low and Volatile Growth

While stabilization policies had an undeniably positive impact on inflation, they also contributed to restraining growth rates in the short and

14. Several tables in this section include data for Chile in the 1970s and early 1980s as well as the 1990s. Given the longer time period covered by the Chilean experience, this provides some additional data for the reader. For the sake of clarification, the table references are to Chile I (1974–81) and Chile II (1990–98).

Table 3-3. *GDP Growth Rates, 1991–98*[a]

Percent

Country	1991	1992	1993	1994	1995	1996	1997	1998
Argentina	10.6	9.6	5.7	8.0	–4.0	4.8	8.6	4.2
Bolivia	5.3	1.6	4.3	4.7	4.7	4.4	4.4	4.7
Brazil	1.0	–0.9	4.2	4.5	1.6	1.7	2.2	0.0
Chile	8.0	12.3	7.0	5.7	10.6	7.4	7.6	3.4
Colombia	2.0	4.0	5.2	6.0	5.8	2.1	3.1	0.6
Costa Rica	2.3	7.7	6.3	4.5	2.4	–0.6	3.7	6.2
Jamaica	0.7	1.5	1.5	1.1	0.5	–1.7	–2.4	–0.7
Mexico	4.2	3.6	2.0	4.4	–6.1	5.2	6.8	4.9
Peru	2.8	–1.4	6.4	13.1	7.3	2.4	6.9	0.3
Simple average	4.1	4.2	4.7	5.8	2.5	2.8	4.5	2.6
Weighted average	3.5	2.8	3.9	5.3	-0.6	3.5	5.0	2.4

Source: Project database.

a. Based on constant 1980 dollars.

medium run. Moreover, they were procyclical, as interest rates were raised and fiscal expenditure was cut to slow price increases, protect the exchange rate, or deal with balance-of-payments problems. Expansion of output thus displayed a stop-go pattern in the 1990s, both for the project countries as a group and for many of them individually. As table 3-3 shows, growth rates peaked twice in the decade, in 1994 and 1997, and each peak was followed by a sharp decline. Attempts to control inflation and retain or regain investor confidence were important causes of both declines, which were centered in Mexico in 1995 and in Brazil in 1998. Stabilization policies were also associated with temporary recessions in individual countries (for example, Peru in 1990–91, Costa Rica in 1996, and Jamaica throughout much of the decade). Similar experiences, although not shown in the table, occurred in Chile in 1975, Costa Rica in 1982–83, Bolivia in 1985, and Argentina in 1989–90. As discussed in chapter 4, when these stabilization episodes coincided with the initiation of the reforms, the resulting slowdown or contraction in growth contributed to a delay in investor response.

The Twin Deficits

Tables 3-4 and 3-5 present the fiscal and current account deficits: the so-called twin deficits. Here we see a more mixed picture than in the case of the successful inflation results. The change in fiscal stance is perhaps the best-known example of the more general shift in macroeconomic policy in the region. The deficits of the nine project countries averaged 3.5 percent of GDP in 1973–82, 4.4 percent in 1983–90, and an average of 1.4 percent in 1991–98. The figure fell dramatically through 1994, when the average deficit was only 0.1 percent of GDP. It then began to expand again, reaching 3.1 percent in 1998.[15] The decline in deficits was generally the result of cuts in spending rather than increases in revenue, which caused problems that will be discussed in the section on social policy.

These averages, of course, mask differences in the individual countries. Only Chile maintained a surplus throughout the 1990s, while Argentina, Mexico, and Peru alternated between surpluses and small deficits (less than 2 percent of GDP). In other cases, a significant shift occurred at some point during the decade. Although deficits remained low in Colombia until 1996, the expansion of demand earlier in the decade had set the stage for later problems. An inflexion point occurred in Costa Rica in 1994, Brazil in 1995, and Jamaica in 1996. Bolivia had fiscal problems throughout the decade. The earlier Chilean period saw a rapid reduction of the fiscal deficit from 16.1 percent of GDP in 1971–73 to a surplus by 1976.

Current account deficits were also reduced in the 1990s compared to the two previous decades, although the decline was less than that seen in the fiscal area. The average current account deficit among the project countries was 4.6 percent of GDP in the period 1973–82 and 4.0 percent in 1983–90. This fell to 3.7 percent in 1991–98. As with the fiscal deficit, the current account deficits were fairly small at the beginning of the 1990s (averaging 1.9 percent of GDP in 1991). The smallest average deficits in the 1990s have been in Brazil and Argentina. By the end of the decade, most countries had substantially higher deficits. The average in 1998 was 5.5 percent, with deficits in five of the nine countries exceeding 5 percent. In the case of Chile in 1973–81, a very large current account deficit developed, reaching a massive 14.5 percent of GDP by 1981.

Comparing tables 3-4 and 3-5 in terms of standard accounting identities leads to some interesting conclusions about the 1980s versus the 1990s. In the former period, the average fiscal deficit across countries and years exceeded the current account deficit, meaning that the private sector accounts (savings minus investment) were in surplus. In the latter period, the average fiscal deficit was less than half the size of the current account defi-

---

15. These numbers are not completely comparable across periods or across countries, since the definition of the government sector varies to some extent and the data source changes in the 1990s.

Table 3-4. *Fiscal Balance as Percent of GDP, 1983–98*[a]

Percent

| Country | Average | | 1991 | 1992 | 1993 | 1994 | 1995 | 1996 | 1997 | 1998 |
	1983–90	1991–98								
Argentina	-3.6	-0.7	-1.6	-0.1	1.4	-0.2	-0.6	-1.8	-1.4	-1.2
Bolivia	-5.2	-3.6	-4.3	-4.4	-6.1	-3.0	-1.8	-2.0	-3.4	-4.0
Brazil	-10.8	-3.3	-0.2	-1.8	-0.8	1.1	-4.9	-5.9	-6.1	-8.0
Chile I[b]	-16.1[c]	0.8[d]	-3.5[d]	-0.9[d]	0.6[d]	0.1[d]	1.5[d]	3.3[d]	4.5[d]	0.8[d]
Chile II[b]	-0.4	1.9	1.5	2.3	2.0	1.7	2.6	2.3	2.0	0.4
Colombia	-1.5	-0.8	0.0	-0.1	0.3	2.6	-0.5	-2.0	-3.1	-3.4
Costa Rica	-2.1	-3.9	-3.1	-1.9	-1.9	-6.9	-4.4	-5.2	-3.9	-3.3
Jamaica	-2.5	-1.3	2.4	2.2	3.3	1.3	2.2	-6.7	-8.3	-6.9
Mexico	-8.3	-0.3	-0.4	1.6	0.7	-0.3	-0.2	-0.1	-0.6	-1.2
Peru	-5.1	-0.2	-0.9	-1.5	-1.2	3.0	-0.1	-1.0	0.0	-0.6
Simple average[e]	-4.4	-1.4	-0.7	-0.4	-0.3	-0.1	-0.9	-2.5	-2.8	-3.1

Source: Project database, on the basis of ECLAC and IMF statistics; Corbo and Fischer (1994: 32–33) for Chile I.

a. Nonfinancial public sector except Chile and Costa Rica (central government only).

b. Chile is listed twice to distinguish two phases of reforms.

c. 1971–73.

d. 1974–81.

e. Simple average excluding Chile I.

Table 3-5. *Current Account Balance as Percent of GDP, 1983–98*
Percent

Country	Average		1991	1992	1993	1994	1995	1996	1997	1998
	1983–90	1991–98								
Argentina	-1.5	-2.5	-0.3	-2.4	-3.0	-3.6	-1.0	-1.3	-3.7	-4.5
Bolivia	-9.4	-5.8	-5.3	-7.3	-7.2	-1.2	-4.9	-5.6	-6.9	-7.9
Brazil	-0.7	-1.7	-0.4	1.6	0.0	-0.2	-2.6	-3.1	-4.2	-4.5
Chile I[a]	-2.9[b]	-5.0[c]	-0.4[c]	-5.2[c]	1.7[c]	-3.7[c]	-5.2[c]	-5.4[c]	-7.1[c]	-14.5[c]
Chile II[a]	-5.2	-3.4	-0.3	-2.2	-5.6	-3.0	-2.1	-5.2	-5.4	-6.2
Colombia	-1.9	-3.2	5.7	2.0	-4.4	-4.5	-5.4	-5.8	-6.2	-6.6
Costa Rica	-7.5	-3.5	-1.8	-5.6	-8.2	-2.9	-3.4	-1.2	-2.2	-2.8
Jamaica	-6.7	-3.7	-6.4	0.8	-4.3	0.2	-3.5	-4.0	-5.3	-7.0
Mexico	0.2	-3.9	-4.7	-6.7	-5.8	-7.0	-0.5	-0.7	-1.9	-3.8
Peru	-3.3	-5.5	-3.5	-5.0	-5.7	-5.4	-7.3	-5.9	-5.3	-6.1
Average[d]	-4.0	-3.7	-1.9	-2.8	-4.9	-3.1	-3.4	-3.6	-4.6	-5.5

Source: Project database, on the basis of ECLAC and IMF statistics; Corbo and Fischer (1994: 32–33) for Chile I.

a. Chile is listed twice to distinguish two phases of reforms.
b. 1971–73.
c. 1974–81.
d. Simple average excluding Chile I.

cit, so the private sector was the main source of deficit spending. An important exception to this generalization was Brazil, where the fiscal deficit in the 1990s was larger than the current account deficit, while in Costa Rica the two were approximately the same size. These results reflect the general trend during the period of governments retreating in favor of the private sector.

Real Interest and Exchange Rates

Real interest and exchange rates, shown in tables 3-6 and 3-7, are closely connected to the twin deficits and have other impacts on the economies as well. As an integral part of monetary policy, interest rates were used to buttress fiscal policy in the 1990s, especially as fiscal deficits began to rise. They were also used to support the exchange rate in those cases in which an exchange rate anchor was part of the stabilization strategy. High lending rates thus typified most countries in the current decade.[16] Only Argentina, Chile, and Mexico had real lending rates in the 10 percent range for any substantial part of the 1990s. In Colombia and Costa Rica, rates averaged in the 10-20 percent range, while in Bolivia, Brazil, Jamaica, and Peru, as well as Chile in the 1970s, real rates were even higher[17] (see table 3-6).

High real interest rates had at least two negative impacts on the region's economies. First, they expanded fiscal deficits since they increased the amounts governments had to pay in interest. This problem was especially serious for those countries with large internal debts resulting from previous deficits. Second, high domestic interest rates had a negative impact on investment—especially for small firms, since large firms have access to international credit markets—and thus on the expansion of output and employment. This further increased fiscal deficits, since low growth reduces tax revenues and increases government transfer payments.

Real exchange rates followed equally problematic trends. Real depreciation was typical of many Latin American and Caribbean countries in the 1980s, because of both the lack of capital inflows and the resulting necessity to increase exports. Real appreciation was the pattern during much

---

16. Even for countries with low rates in the Latin American context, the cost of capital was high compared to the Group of Seven nations, where similar rates in the 1990s were around 6–8 percent.

17. In Argentina, Bolivia, and Peru, a large percentage of bank loans were made in dollars rather than local currency. In the case of Peru and especially Bolivia, the dollar rates were substantially lower than those shown in table 3-6.

Table 3-6. *Real Interest Rates, 1988–98*[a]

Percent

Country	Average 1988–90	1991	1992	1993	1994	1995	1996	1997	1998
Argentina	n.a.	n.a.	n.a.	n.a.	5.7	14.0	10.3	8.8	9.6
Bolivia	21.1	16.2	29.8	41.8	44.3	37.0	38.6	43.3	29.4
Brazil	214.8	76.9	138.5	157.6	-0.4	18.7	26.3	37.7	50.7
Chile I[b]	n.a.	n.a.[c]	n.a.[c]	n.a.[c]	16.3[c]	18.9[c]	15.6[c]	10.1[c]	14.7[c]
Chile II[b]	15.6	5.7	7.4	10.3	8.0	9.2	9.3	9.0	14.5
Colombia	14.3	12.9	8.1	11.0	14.4	18.2	17.8	13.3	19.8
Costa Rica	10.3	7.8	5.2	18.4	17.2	11.0	7.5	8.3	9.6
Jamaica	10.7	-13.0	-18.3	17.7	10.6	19.7	14.1	24.3	24.0
Mexico	n.a.	n.a.	n.a.	11.2	12.5	17.4	1.9	11.6	11.1
Peru	716.7	67.2	57.7	32.8	24.2	14.5	13.0	19.7	21.9
Average[d]	143.4	24.8	32.6	37.6	15.2	17.7	15.4	19.6	21.2

Source: IMF (2000); ECLAC, on the basis of official statistics, for Brazil; Corbo and Fischer (1994: 32–33) for Chile I.

a. Rates are average annual short-term lending rates to businesses, deflated by the consumer price index.

b. Chile is listed twice to distinguish two phases of reforms.

c. 1974–81.

d. Simple average excluding Chile I.

Table 3-7. *Real Effective Exchange Rates, 1987–98*[a]
(1990 = 100)

Country	Average 1987–90	1991	1992	1993	1994	1995	1996	1997	1998
Argentina	126.9	71.0	62.8	57.6	57.2	61.0	62.1	60.3	59.0
Bolivia	86.7	99.7	104.2	110.4	116.2	119.0	111.1	108.4	104.0
Brazil	125.0	131.7	141.2	136.7	137.9	121.4	114.3	113.1	118.5
Chile I[b]	80.3[c]	164.9[d]	197.7[d]	166.8[d]	134.4[d]	149.7[d]	150.8[d]	130.6[d]	113.5[d]
Chile II[b]	97.1	99.7	96.2	98.2	94.8	89.2	86.0	80.2	82.4
Colombia	91.1	101.0	89.4	85.7	74.7	74.8	69.4	65.0	69.3
Costa Rica	102.2	109.8	104.6	104.5	105.0	101.4	100.4	102.6	103.9
Jamaica	84.2	116.4	135.3	126.8	130.0	125.4	105.6	90.7	85.1
Mexico	113.1	90.9	83.9	80.0	82.2	121.6	108.3	93.9	94.0
Peru	140.4	83.1	83.7	93.1	87.9	87.7	86.4	86.8	88.1
Average[e]	107.4	100.4	100.1	99.2	98.4	100.2	93.7	89.0	89.4

Source: Project database, on the basis of ECLAC statistics; Corbo and Fischer (1994: 32–33) for Chile I.

a. The average of the indexes for the real exchange rate for the currency of each country against the currencies of its main trading partners, weighted according to the relative magnitude of imports from those countries in the period 1992–96. Consumer price indexes were used to deflate the indexes.

b. Chile is listed twice to distinguish two phases of reforms.

c. Average 1970–73.

d. 1974–81; 1973 = 100.

e. Simple average excluding Chile I.

of the 1990s. In some cases, the appreciation stemmed from government policy that employed an exchange rate "nominal anchor" to fight inflation. In other cases, it was simply very difficult to avoid appreciation in the face of the massive capital inflows described in chapter 2. The result was a tendency toward larger trade and current account deficits as exports became more expensive and imports cheaper. In response to the large current account deficits, governments felt compelled to restrain growth, often by raising interest rates. The alternative was perceived to be a foreign exchange crisis.

The amount of appreciation varied, of course, depending on the particular range of years selected. Table 3-7 shows the average for the period 1987–90 and the yearly variation between 1991 and 1998. The countries with the largest appreciation in this period were Argentina (66 percent between 1989 and 1993, but stable thereafter), Mexico (40 percent between 1987 and 1994, followed by a large devaluation), and Colombia and Jamaica (33 percent in 1991–98 and 1992–98, respectively). Chile and Brazil had lesser appreciation in the 1990s, while Bolivia, Costa Rica, and Peru (since 1991) generally managed to maintain the real value of their exchange rates. Chile also had a large appreciation in 1979–82 when the local currency was pegged to the dollar.

If we combine the information in tables 3-2 through 3-7, we can compare patterns of macroeconomic policy and outcomes across project countries and relate them to the three types of reformers (that is, aggressive, cautious but unstable, and cautious and stable). The four aggressive reformers put strong emphasis on reducing large fiscal deficits and inflation, but they were less concerned about other aspects of macroeconomic policy, especially large current account deficits. The rationale, whether explicit or implicit, was that any deficits originating in the private sector would be self-correcting. Nevertheless, a current account deficit led to a crisis in Chile in the early 1980s.

Both of the cautious but unstable reformers continued to have macroeconomic problems, which eventually resulted in foreign exchange crises. In the case of Mexico, the manifestation was a very large current account deficit; in Brazil the use of higher interest rates to protect the currency both exacerbated existing fiscal problems and created a major recession. Following the 1994–95 peso crisis, Mexico's macroeconomic policy became much more orderly: the devaluation cut the external deficit and interest rates came down, while the fiscal deficit remained small. Moreover, growth resumed, but inflation was slow to fall, and real wages suffered as a consequence. It is too early to tell if Brazil will follow a similar path after the 1999 devaluation, although growth seems to be picking up.

Among the cautious and stable reformers, the pattern diverged somewhat after the beginning of the reform process. Costa Rica maintained macroeconomic equilibrium in relative terms, despite fiscal problems deriving from the failure of an important bank. Colombia and Jamaica encountered more generalized disequilibria with appreciated exchange rates, high interest rates, and rising fiscal deficits. Colombia also had a large current account deficit, while growth rates in Jamaica were low or negative. Nonetheless, no country in this group faced macroeconomic problems as serious as those of Mexico and Brazil.

Links between Reforms and Macroeconomic Policy

An important question to ask about the reforms themselves as well as about the relation between the reforms and macroeconomic policies is whether they have been consistent and mutually reinforcing, or whether they have been so contradictory as to undermine the effectiveness and credibility of the package as a whole. Not surprisingly, the evidence seems to support an ambivalent conclusion, across both countries and time periods and also across reform and policy areas.

Consistencies

At the most general level, the trend toward a more equilibrated macroeconomic policy stance, together with a set of reforms that opened new opportunities to the domestic and foreign private sectors, gave an important psychological boost to entrepreneurs; in Keynesian terms, it raised animal spirits. The reforms-cum-macroeconomic stability also ended the external financial constraint that had crippled the region during most of the 1980s.[18] In particular, the new context attracted substantial amounts of foreign direct investment. The overall result in some cases was new investment, the incorporation of new technology, and ultimately better growth opportunities. Nonetheless, as discussed in chapter 4, this process was subject to significant lags as firms waited to see if the reforms would continue. Other conditions at the microeconomic level were also necessary to supple-

---

18. This, of course, was in the context of substantial international liquidity and low interest rates in the industrialized countries.

ment the initial reforms and the new stability in order for investment to occur in more than a few favored sectors.

At a more specific level, the most successful mix of reforms and macroeconomic policy occurred in the area of inflation. Governments generally targeted macroeconomic policy at taming inflation, as seen earlier. Trade liberalization supported these efforts in two important ways. First, inputs could be imported at lower prices, thus making it possible for local companies to produce cheaper goods. Second, competition with foreign products constrained the ability of local business to raise prices, even if all their inputs were local. Privatization also helped to lower inflation through a positive impact on fiscal deficits. When loss-making firms were privatized, subsidies were eliminated and fiscal accounts improved permanently. In addition, privatization brought in one-time revenues that helped lower deficits in the short run; in the longer run, other arrangements had to be sought to replace revenues generated by selling state firms. For governments that used such revenues to pay down debt, the lower interest payments helped to perpetuate lower deficits; those that used them to increase spending tended to run into trouble later on.

Inconsistency Syndromes

Other areas displayed significant contradictions among reforms and macroeconomic policies that undermined governments' growth-with-equity goals. Our case studies point to three principal inconsistency syndromes. The first, which affected all countries except Bolivia and Costa Rica, involved opening the capital account, which produced a rush of short-term capital into the countries and led to appreciation of the local currency. The appreciation, in turn, made imports cheaper and exports more expensive, thus increasing the trade deficit. It also sent mixed signals to firms that had been encouraged by the trade reforms to begin selling abroad and to invest in new capacity oriented toward exports. While the trade deficit could be covered in the short run by the very capital inflows that caused the appreciation, the flows were reversible and could leave the country as quickly as they entered in response to domestic problems or international financial trends. In the best of cases, the capital outflows caused disruptions in the local economy; in the extreme, they resulted in currency crises that were extraordinarily costly and took years to overcome.

A second syndrome centered on financial liberalization and monetary policy, which became more difficult to manage if accompanied by capital account opening. Financial liberalization was designed to end financial repression, so it is not surprising that domestic interest rates rose following the reforms. Our evidence suggests that overshooting was quite typical in such situations, leading to local interest rates substantially higher than international rates. This was especially problematic for small firms that did not have access to the international markets. Even more important for the economies as a whole were problems that financial liberalization caused for the banking sector. Local banks frequently were not adept at evaluating long-term credit risks because of government influence over interest rates and credit allocation before the reforms. When large amounts of foreign capital entered countries, thereby increasing the availability of credit, the banks became overextended. Particular problems resulted if they had borrowed in foreign currency, since their debts then ballooned when the reversal of capital inflows forced a devaluation. In this way, banking crises merged with currency crises.

The third syndrome involved fiscal policy. All governments in our study sought to lower or eliminate their fiscal deficits, but several of the reforms made this more difficult. One was tax reform, which lowered rates on individuals and corporations. At least in the short run, there is no evidence in our cases to support the idea that lowered tax rates have increased revenues as supply-side theorists have argued in the industrialized countries. Another reform that interfered with lowering fiscal deficits was import liberalization. This was especially important for the smaller and less-developed countries that relied heavily on tariffs as a source of government revenue. For them, import liberalization caused problems in the short run that might or might not be offset in the longer run by a trade version of the supply-side argument (that is, lower tariffs stimulate economic growth, which leads to other sources of revenue). The behavior of the exchange rate was an important element in determining the ultimate outcome. A third reform, decentralization, exacerbated the fiscal deficits of the central governments by transferring revenues to provinces and municipalities without always transferring the counterpart obligations. As mentioned above, privatization could help fiscal policy in the short run, but it created its own trap later on.

Social Policy and Social Expenditure

Social policy was an integral part of the reform process from the beginning, at least in principle. The basic idea was to get the government out of productive activities, where the private sector could do a better job, thus freeing public resources for social expenditure. Among the blueprints for reform, both the World Bank's market-friendly model and the Washington Consensus embodied this idea.[19] One of the World Bank's main elements was "investment in people," including education, health care, nutrition, and family planning. Likewise, one of the ten items in the Washington Consensus was adjusting fiscal priorities to give greater importance to health and education. These policies were widely perceived as having double value: they would lead to higher productivity and thus better economic performance at the same time that they increased equity and mobility in very unequal societies.

Social policy, broadly speaking, is a rather vague concept referring to all government interventions to improve the welfare of the population and to incorporate excluded groups. In practice, its meaning varies from country to country in terms of both the areas covered and types of activities involved. While all would include health and education, others would also include programs oriented toward particular groups (for example, labor, the elderly, women, the handicapped, and minorities) or to solve particular problems (such as poverty alleviation, urban reconstruction, or agrarian reform). Cutting across these activities, we focus on social expenditure, which is a central component of almost all of them.

The overall category of social expenditure, in turn, includes a variety of activities that have different effects on economic performance and on the distribution of income and welfare. Latin American statistics typically divide social spending into four categories: education, health, social security, and other (including housing subsidies). The first two, which are often referred to as human capital, are valued because they are useful in promoting economic development and are progressive in terms of distribution. (Funding for university education is a partial exception, in that it is not a progressive expenditure but is important in promoting growth.) Social security and housing subsidies, in contrast, normally have a regressive impact. As will be discussed further in chapter 5, public spending on primary and secondary schooling as well as on health care are concentrated on the lower part of the income distribution structure, while social security and housing subsidies provide disproportionate benefits to the middle income strata.[20]

---

19. World Bank (1991); Williamson (1990).
20. ECLAC (1999c, chapter 4).

Table 3-8. *Changes in Social Expenditure, 1980–97*
1997 dollars and percent

Country	Per capita social expenditure			Social expenditure as share of total public expenditure			Social expenditure as share of GDP		
	1980–81	1990–91	1996–97	1980–81	1990–91	1996–97	1980–81	1990–91	1996–97
High spending									
Argentina	1378	1222	1570	50.1	62.2	65.1	16.7	17.7	17.9
Brazil	368	476	566	44.4	51.0	54.2	9.7	11.0	11.8
Chile	558	451	725	62.4	60.8	65.9	18.4	13.0	14.1
Costa Rica	487	445	550[a]	66.0	64.4	65.1[a]	19.5	18.2	20.8[a]
Medium spending									
Colombia	156	181	391	27.2	29.7	38.2	7.8	8.1	15.3
Jamaica	194[b]	234	244[a]	22.8[b]	26.8	19.2[a]	n.a.	9.2	9.7[a]
Mexico	333	283	352	28.8	41.6	52.9	7.9	6.5	7.8
Low spending									
Bolivia	60	55	119	34.6	25.8	44.2	5.6	6.0	12.0
Peru	133[c]	41	76[a]	23.6[c]	14.3	37.5[a]	4.6[c]	2.0	6.0[a]
Simple average	407	376	510	40.0	41.8	49.1	11.3	10.2	12.8

Source: ECLAC (1999c) and Mostajo (2000), on the basis of the ECLAC Social Development Division database.
a. Only 1996.
b. 1985.
c. 1980.

Social expenditure declined in most Latin American and Caribbean countries in the 1980s (see table 3-8). This reflected the urgent need to cut fiscal deficits, which we have seen were large during that decade. In the process, a low priority was accorded to social spending in comparison with other sectors, such as general administration, defense, and debt service. One study that examined fiscal trends during the 1980s found that social spending was markedly procyclical, except in Chile and Colombia. That is, when economic activity contracted, social spending fell by even more, with a decline in the share of social spending in GDP, and when economic activity expanded, social spending increased.[21]

To differing degrees and with differing emphases, countries gave greater priority to the social area in the 1990s. All nine project countries increased per capita social expenditure in that decade; except for Peru, the increase more than made up for the decline of the 1980s. After taking account of inflation, the average rise in social expenditure per capita between 1980–81 and 1996–97 was 25 percent. With the exception of Brazil, Jamaica, and Colombia, the overall figures represented a decline during the 1980s and a sizable rise in the 1990s.[22] Social expenditure as a share of total public expenditure followed a similar pattern, with an average increase of 23 percent over the seventeen year period. The share in 1996–97 was generally higher than 1980–81, but the intraperiod pattern was more mixed. The most common situation involved modest change during the 1980s followed by a large rise in the 1990s. Finally, social expenditure as a share of GDP also rose in most countries, but at a slower pace (13 percent) than for the other two indicators.

At the country level, two differing trends seem to have been at work. Four countries already had relatively high levels of social expenditure by a combination of the three indicators shown in table 3-8. These countries (Argentina, Brazil, Chile, and Costa Rica) improved their performance modestly, but there was little room to make big increases, especially in terms of social spending within total spending. Chile was a partial exception to this generalization, since social spending rose by an average of 7 percent per year and the share of total expenditure increased from 61 to 66 percent in the 1990s. Another group of countries had much lower social

21. Cominetti and di Gropello (1995); see also Cominetti and Ruiz (1998).
22. Our data on social expenditure for Brazil include only spending by the federal government. These data underestimate social expenditure by the public sector because they do not include spending at the state and municipal levels (ECLAC, 1999c, Box 4.1).

spending at the beginning of the decade (Bolivia, Colombia, Jamaica, Mexico, and Peru); they put a high priority on catching up in the 1990s. Bolivia and Peru made especially dramatic improvements, although from very low initial levels, while Colombia also made an important effort from a higher starting point.

Beyond the issue of the quantity of social services, Latin American countries at the beginning of the 1990s had serious problems with the quality of those services. With respect to education, issues included poor training of teachers, high student-teacher ratios, poor quality of textbooks, lack of other equipment, and an emphasis on rote learning rather than problem solving. In the health area, indicators of poor quality were long waits for treatment, poor training of doctors, high patient-doctor ratios, and lack of medicines and new treatments. The poor quality of public housing was as common in Latin America as in other parts of the world. The pension systems frequently reached only a small percent of the population, and high inflation rates eroded their value.

To deal with the quality problems, many Latin American and Caribbean governments began reforms in the social area. While some of the new policies were parallel to the economic reforms that were identified earlier in the chapter, others embodied quite different approaches. In practice, most countries tried a combination. One type of reform involved improving the central government's delivery of services in education, health, housing, and social security through better training of personnel, better facilities, more participation of beneficiaries, and so on. A second, which had substantial overlap with the first in terms of goals, focused on the decentralization of social services to municipal and provincial levels of government, especially with respect to education and health. The idea behind this process was that if the administration of services were moved to the local level, it would be both more efficient and more equitable. The third approach was the one most closely related to the economic reforms since it involved privatizing certain aspects of the delivery of social services. Specifically, a number of countries encouraged the establishment of private schools, health care, and pension systems for those who could afford to pay, leaving the rest of the population in the public system.[23]

While all of these reforms have their critics, the privatization approach

23. Reform of the central government system is discussed in ECLAC (1997, chapter 5), decentralization in di Gropello and Cominetti (1998), and privatization of the health and pension system in ECLAC (1998b, chapter 7).

is especially controversial because it infringes on the principle that all citizens have an equal right to social services. The privatized system offers first-class services to those who can afford to pay, while the public sector usually provides services of much lower quality. Thus students in private schools perform better on standardized tests and are more likely to go on to secondary and university education and to get good jobs. People who receive treatment from doctors in the private health system have access to preventive care, the latest international treatments, and good hospital facilities, while those who must rely on the public system must wait in very long lines to receive inadequate care. The new pension systems, following the Chilean example, involve individual workers paying into private pension funds, which will later be responsible for providing pensions to retirees.

These social policy trends are not independent of the economic reforms and macroeconomic policies that were examined earlier in the chapter. The 1980s manifested clear contradictions between macroeconomic and social policies. The need to reduce fiscal deficits to cut inflation rates collided with the need to expend resources to achieve social and economic goals. The macroeconomic priority usually won out. This had a negative impact on public welfare in the short run; it is also likely to have created longer-run problems that are more difficult to measure in terms of economic growth and productivity. In the 1990s, the contradiction between macroeconomic stabilization and social policy was less severe as governments became more aware of the benefits of social spending, especially on education. It was the reduction of fiscal deficits in the 1980s, however, that permitted higher social spending in the 1990s. The economic reforms contributed through the sale of loss-making state firms and additional revenues from privatizations.

Whether social policies will continue to coexist harmoniously with reforms and macroeconomic policies remains to be seen. Per capita social expenditures can be increased in three ways: growth of GDP, increased public expenditure as a share of GDP, and increased priority of social expenditure as a share of total public expenditure. In addition, the impact of a given amount of money can be increased by raising the efficiency and productivity of the expenditure.[24] This list serves as an indicator of the areas to watch. If growth slows, the rate of increase of social expenditure may also slow or even fall. Macroeconomic prudence currently limits public expenditure as a share of GDP (since high taxes are considered to dis-

---

24. For a discussion of the efficiency of social expenditure see ECLAC (1998b, chapters 1 and 6).

courage investment), and some countries are approaching their maximum social spending as a share of total public spending. Rapid growth may therefore be the only way to avoid a contradiction among these policy areas. Later chapters of this book discuss whether the reforms and macroeconomic policies being followed are likely to lead to high growth rates in the future, thus preventing the resurgence of this contradiction.

Conclusions

The reform process led to the adoption of a series of changes in economic policy in Latin America and the Caribbean that reflected mainstream economists' critiques of the import substitution model. The reforms were adopted to varying degrees across the region. Among the nine project countries, four engaged in rapid, comprehensive reforms, while the other five were more gradual and selective. We argued that the difference had to do with initial conditions, whereby those with especially grave problems were willing to experiment with deeper reforms. Later chapters examine whether the differences in speed and scope affected outcomes.

Macroeconomic policy change was more homogeneous, with all nine countries making substantial progress in lowering inflation. Fiscal deficits, which are crucial determinants of inflation rates, fell in the 1990s with respect to the two previous decades, but they began to rise again in the mid-1990s. Interest rate and exchange rate policies diverged more than fiscal policy. With a few exceptions, however, real interest rates remained relatively high, in part to protect exchange rates. The real exchange rates, in turn, generally tended to appreciate, either as an explicit government policy to combat inflation or as a result of large inflows of foreign exchange. The relation between the reforms and macroeconomic policy was sometimes mutually reinforcing, especially with respect to inflation, but in other cases inconsistencies dominated. We identified three inconsistency syndromes, involving capital account opening, trade reform, and the exchange rate; domestic financial reform, banking regulation, and interest rates; and tax reform, privatization, and fiscal policy.

Social policy, operationalized as social spending, became a more important component of the policy package in the 1990s. In the 1980s, social expenditure was one of the first items to be cut to lower deficits. In the following decade, however, governments appeared to come to the conclusion that better social conditions could make a positive contribution to economic growth. In addition, they would help to deal with the high levels of inequality that characterized the region. Thus social spending increased in all project countries in the 1990s, accompanying the return to higher growth rates.

A major conclusion of the chapter is that the structural reforms must not be viewed in isolation but rather as part of a policy package that includes the macroeconomic and social areas. These three elements can work together to create a propitious environment that encourages private sector actors to invest and increase output, or they can be contradictory, thus sending mixed signals and undermining incentives for the private sector. In addition, international economic trends will have an impact on all three, and they must be taken into account as well.

These policies are relevant for all of the remaining topics of the study—investment, growth, employment, and equity—but several particularly strong links can be identified. The reforms and macroeconomic policies, together with the international context, are the dominant factors influencing investment decisions and the incorporation of new technology. A properly educated labor force is a necessary complement, especially with respect to new technology and higher productivity. Since growth is heavily determined by investment and technological trends, these same policies are indirectly relevant for analyzing growth. Social expenditure is also a key factor in the analysis of employment generation, quality of employment, and equity.

4

Investment, Productivity, and Growth: Recovery and Modest Advances

Having reviewed the process of economic reforms, together with the public policies that accompanied them and the international context in which they took place, we can now turn to the main task of the book—analyzing the impact of the reforms first at the aggregate level and then at the sectoral and microeconomic levels. This chapter, then, uses an aggregate, economy-wide approach to focus on investment, productivity, and growth.[1]

Most of the literature on the impact of the reforms is concerned with their effect on the growth rate of gross domestic product (GDP), and the analysis concentrates on macroeconomic variables. This is hardly surprising, since the principal reason for undertaking the reforms in the first place was to increase the efficiency of Latin American and Caribbean economies in order to raise growth rates. Illustrative of this approach is the title of one of the early reform manifestos: "Toward renewed economic growth in Latin America."[2] Other benefits, especially employment generation, were expected to follow from more dynamic growth.

---

1. Major inputs for this chapter include Hofman (2000), Moguillansky and Bielschowsky (2000), and Katz (2000). These authors are not responsible for the conclusions reached on the basis of their data.

2. Balassa and others (1986).

The early literature advocating the reforms as a way of raising growth rates stressed the need to move from production that was overwhelmingly oriented toward the domestic market to a greater emphasis on exports. Three economic arguments were presented to support the benefits of export-led growth: greater efficiency at the microeconomic level as a result of more competition; better exploitation of economies of scale, especially for small and medium-size countries; and moderation of stop-go cycles deriving from foreign exchange shortages or recurring crises in agricultural production.[3] The most important instrument for achieving export-led growth was argued to be a competitive exchange rate, although this was considered a necessary but not sufficient condition. Eliminating the special privileges enjoyed by import-substitution firms and providing positive incentives for exports were also required, together with credibility for the policies from the point of view of investors. Many of these same issues are still on the agenda more than two decades later.

The more recent literature on the link between growth and reforms aims to determine whether the predicted positive relation actually came about. A surprising degree of consensus has been reached on the topic. The dominant conclusion is that while growth obviously improved in comparison with the lost decade of the 1980s, it was quite modest. ECLAC, in a statement that is representative of others in the literature, says: "Most of the region's economies have grown at moderate rates, which, while respectable, are lower than in the past and insufficient to redress technological and social lags."[4] In a somewhat more positive vein, experts at the IDB indicate that growth in the 1990s was well above what it would have been in the absence of the reforms. Nonetheless, they agree that growth rates were unsatisfactory, below historical rates, and much lower than in the high-growth countries of East Asia.[5] The questions that now need to be addressed are why growth rates were disappointing, compared to expectations, and how to improve performance.

Some of the literature trying to measure the impact of the reforms on growth links the two directly, in the presence of certain control variables. In a typical example, Eduardo Fernández Arias and Peter Montiel regress per capita GDP on various structural reform proxies and macroeconomic

3. See, for example, Krueger (1978); Bhagwati (1978). Krueger says that while in theory incentives for exports and import substitutes should be equated at the margin, in practice countries with a positive export bias did better. She cites Brazil and South Korea as examples (pp. 282-83).

4. ECLAC (1996, p.11).

5. IDB (1996).

variables, while controlling for initial GDP, education, terms of trade, and external demand. They find that the reform variables had a highly significant positive effect on growth. While investment and productivity are implicitly assumed to be important, they are not explicitly incorporated into the analysis.[6]

Others examine investment directly, either as an end in itself or as part of a two-step analysis of growth.[7] Lora and Barrera argue that the reforms' main contribution to economic growth was the turnaround in total factor productivity growth in the 1990s compared to the 1980s. (It was negative in the 1980s.) An increase in the investment coefficient was also important, but of lesser magnitude.[8] Rodrik, in contrast, says that while the relation between investment and growth is erratic in the short run, "in the long run, investment is key."[9] He adds that policymakers and analysts have neglected the central role of investment for growth in developing countries, suggesting the need to focus on investment incentives if performance is to improve.

Our approach in this chapter assumes that it is essential to study the behavior of all three variables: investment, productivity, and growth. It is necessary to understand the relative importance of investment and productivity behavior in explaining growth rates, in comparison to other factors that also have an impact. Moreover, the three variables provide different kinds of information: investment and productivity trends give us some leverage in forecasting future growth rates.[10]

We proceed in the following way. The next section examines data on long-term trends in investment and productivity. We then discuss the impact of the reforms in these areas, differentiating transitory versus permanent effects as well as three resulting phases in investment and the incorporation of technical progress. We also provide an econometric model of the determinants of investment, including the structural reforms. This is followed by an examination of growth patterns, using growth-accounting techniques to link the various factors and to illuminate differences among countries. We then discuss the impact of the reforms on growth, again

6. Fernández Arias and Montiel (1997).

7. ECLAC (1996) is an example of the former, Lora and Barrera (1997) of the latter.

8. Lora and Barrera (1997).

9. Rodrik (1999, p.15). De Gregorio and Lee (1999) argue that the importance of investment declines as a determinant of growth when other variables are added to the equation. When those variables are not included, investment incorporates their effect, and the coefficient for investment is larger.

10. Of course, these issues are complicated since there is a reverse causation between growth and investment, via the accelerator relation.

presenting econometric evidence. A final empirical section returns to the issue of exports and their contribution to growth. The conclusions emphasize what can and cannot be learned at the aggregate level, establishing the basis for the subsequent analysis of sectors and types of agents.

Long-term Trends in Investment and Productivity

Investment and productivity in the post-reform period need to be seen in the long-term perspective of the behavior of these variables during the postwar period as a whole. A very simple representation of these trends is depicted in table 4-1, which shows four benchmark years: 1950 (the beginning of the period), 1980 (at or near the peak of investment resulting from the ISI model), 1990 (at or near the trough following the debt crisis), and 1998 (the latest available year).[11]

A clear pattern emerges from the table, as reflected in both the simple averages and the majority of the individual countries. Investment as a share of GDP rose significantly in the three decades between 1950 and 1980, from 16 to 21 percent (an average annual increase of 1 percent). That improvement in investment performance was practically wiped out by the crisis of the 1980s, during which time the average investment coefficient fell back to only 17 percent (an average annual drop of 2.2 percent during the decade). Half the countries (Argentina, Brazil, Colombia, and Peru) had lower investment coefficients in 1990 than they had had in 1950. Between 1990 and 1998, however, the average investment coefficient rose by 3.8 percent a year, to 23 percent, more than recovering its 1980 peak.[12] By 1998, Bolivia and Chile were far above their previous highs. Mexico, in contrast, was still substantially below its 1980 level, while Brazil was below its 1950 level. The explanations for these different outcomes are quite complex; no single factor can account for them.[13]

The data on investment raise two main questions: is the investment sustainable, and is it sufficient? The issue of sustainability, in turn, involves

11. Due to lack of information, Jamaica could not be included in most of the analysis in this chapter.

12. Note that this result—investment at a new peak—is based on simple averages. Data based on weighted averages show investment still below previous peaks because of the poor performance of Mexico and especially Brazil, which account for a very large share of any weighted average for Latin America and the Caribbean.

13. As would be expected, public sector investment fell as a share of GDP in most countries during the 1970–98 period, while private sector investment rose. See Moguillansky and Bielschowsky (2000, appendix A-6).

Table 4-1. *Gross Fixed Investment as a Share of GDP, 1950–98*[a]
Percent

Country	1950	1980	1990	1998
Argentina	15.5	25.1	12.5	23.5
Bolivia	9.1	14.2	13.9	26.5
Brazil	18.8	23.6	15.5	16.9
Chile	19.1	18.6	21.6	28.9
Colombia	16.0	16.8	14.0	15.4
Costa Rica	16.0	23.9	23.1	26.6
Mexico	14.8	24.8	18.4	20.8
Peru	18.3	23.5	17.5	25.2
Simple average	16.0	21.3	17.1	23.0

Source: Project database.
a. Based on constant 1980 dollars.

two subpoints. First, we need to know if investment rates will remain at their current levels or if they will rise or fall in the coming years. As explained in the next section, the answer is that we still cannot predict. With the single exception of Chile, the reforms and other new features of the regional economies are not yet consolidated. They still depend on both positive and negative transitory factors that derive from the vast changes the economies have undergone. Future results will depend on whether governments and the private actors in the various countries can work together so as to adequately balance the risk and return factors that stimulate investment. In practice, this implies finding ways—within the new rules of the game—to compensate for the absence of the old incentives that firms received during the import substitution period.

Second, sustainability also depends on how investment is being financed. The relative contribution of national versus external savings is particularly important. Figure 4-1 provides a set of indicators on the relation between savings and investment in the project countries.[14] Little external savings occurred during the 1980s; investment had to be financed by na-

14. The data in figure 4-1 are not totally comparable with others in the book since they are based on total investment (including inventory movements), while elsewhere we work with fixed investment. Another difference is in base years for constant dollar calculations (1995 in figure 4-1, compared to 1980 for the rest of the book).

Figure 4-1. *Investment and Its Financing, 1990–98* [a]

Percent of GDP in 1995 dollars

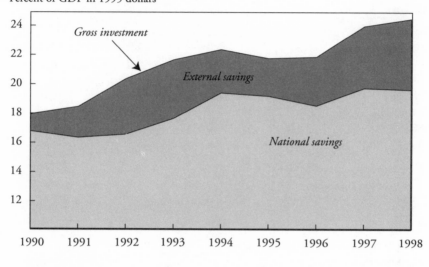

Source: Project database.
a. Based on simple averages for eight project countries (excluding Jamaica).

tional savings. In the 1990s, the return of foreign capital flows changed that pattern substantially. By 1998, external savings had risen to account for over 5 percent of GDP, compared to nearly 19 percent for national savings. The 5 percent figure for foreign savings, which is the same as the current account deficit, is about the limit of what investors seem willing to finance, even in a period of substantial liquidity. Higher national savings would be advisable, but at the same time there are serious doubts about whether policies to stimulate savings are effective (as opposed to savings increasing as a function of higher growth).

As to whether investment has been sufficient, the answer depends in the first instance on the growth rate that has been adopted as a target. Several years ago, ECLAC suggested that a 6 percent growth rate is needed to tackle the social issues pending in the region (poverty, unemployment, and others).[15] There seemed to be substantial agreement around a figure of this magnitude. The next step was to estimate the investment coefficient

15. ECLAC (1996).

Table 4-2. *GDP per Worker, 1950–98*
Thousands of 1980 dollars

Country	1950	1980	1990	1998
Argentina	6.9	14.1	10.6	15.2
Bolivia	3.2	5.3	4.2	4.4
Brazil	3.1	9.5	8.5	8.6
Chile	5.9	10.9	11.1	16.1
Colombia	4.0	8.1	8.9	10.0
Costa Rica	3.7	9.2	8.2	8.8
Mexico	5.8	17.0	16.0	16.1
Peru	3.9	8.4	5.5	6.2
Simple average	4.6	10.3	9.1	10.7

Source: Project database.

needed to achieve this rate of growth. Here, more controversy arose. Based on capital-output ratios for a number of countries, the hypothesized investment rate of 28 percent of GDP (in 1980 dollars, but with the structural characteristics of the 1990s) was put forward. This is nearly five percentage points higher than the simple average shown in table 4-1 for 1998, which suggests that more investment is indeed needed.[16] The investment analyses for this project come to similar conclusions, based on studies of individual countries and sectors.[17] Comparisons with other regions also indicate that Latin America needs higher investment, even if there is disagreement on the precise numbers.[18]

Trends in labor productivity levels are similar to those for investment. A large increase in productivity occurred between 1950 and 1980 (an annual average increase of 2.8 percent), a decline in the 1980s (1.2 percent, on average), and a recovery to previous peak levels by 1998 (2.0 percent annual growth in the 1990s). Nonetheless, only Argentina, Chile, and Colombia had productivity levels in 1998 above those of 1980; Bolivia and Peru fell particularly far behind in this period (see table 4-2).

The general view in the literature, which is reinforced by our case studies, is that productivity trends are closely linked to investment. Greater

16. ECLAC (1996, pp. 51-59).
17. See Moguillansky and Bielschowsky (2000).
18. See Stallings (1995) for a comparison of investment rates and other aspects of the development process in Latin America, East Asia, Southeast Asia, and Sub-Saharan Africa.

Figure 4-2. *Investment and Labor Productivity Trends, 1950–98*[a]

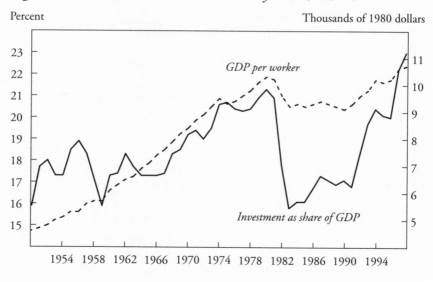

Percent   Thousands of 1980 dollars

Source: Project database.
a. Based on simple averages for eight project countries (excluding Jamaica).

amounts of capital per worker should therefore result in increased output per worker. Figure 4-2 illustrates the link for the simple averages of investment and labor productivity among the project countries. As expected, the two have similar trajectories, although productivity falls much less than investment during the 1980s.

Of course, investment is not the only factor that affects productivity. Higher rates of education are among the most important determinants of productivity, as will be seen later in the chapter. Other factors that have been found to be important determinants of labor productivity include the age and health of the labor force, management and organizational arrangements in the firm, technological advances, and public sector activities such as training and support for research and development.[19]

In one of the project volumes, Katz argues that it is necessary to take into account macroeconomic conditions (especially interest and exchange

19. Recent theory on endogenous growth stresses that human capital is a complement to physical capital, as is organizational improvement or disembodied technical progress. For a summary of this literature, see Aghion and Howitt (1998).

rates), sectoral factors (namely, the market structure, the regulatory framework, and institutions), and firm level variables (particularly the accumulation of technological capabilities, organizational models, and entrepreneurial strategies) to understand trends in labor productivity. The incorporation of technological change depends on the interaction of firms, governments, research centers, and financial institutions, which together constitute the so-called national innovation systems. Katz argues that innovation systems in Latin America underwent two important changes after the reforms. The reduction of state involvement in technological efforts resulted in an increased privatization of the determinants of technological progress. In addition, foreign presence increased dramatically through the substitution of domestic by foreign inputs and a larger presence of transnational corporations (TNCs) in the production structure.[20]

Overall, in the 1990–98 period, when the effects of the reform process began to be felt in Latin America and the Caribbean, investment and productivity improved somewhat, but this mainly represented a recovery from the losses suffered during the debt crisis. Chile was an important exception, doing well on both indicators. Most other countries improved on one or the other. The two largest countries in the region, Brazil and Mexico, face serious challenges on both; their ability to raise investment and productivity rates will have a significant impact throughout the region.

Post-Reform Phases of Investment and Technological Change

Analyzing the reforms' impact on investment and productivity is a complex task because many things were happening simultaneously. In addition, the reforms themselves had different effects over time. The project studies of individual country experiences suggest the need to distinguish a transitional period from a consolidated one in order to understand the potential impact of the reforms. Given the timing of the initiation of the reforms, almost all of the project countries are still in the transition period. Extrapolating on the basis of what has occurred up till now could result in quite misleading conclusions. Recognizing the various phases enables us at least to speculate on the more permanent aspects in light of what we are able to measure of past trends.[21]

---

20. Katz (2000, chapter 6).

21. The idea of investment phases is developed in Moguillansky and Bielschowsky (2000, chapter 1); see this source for further detail.

At a high level of abstraction, the new environment created by the reforms and macroeconomic variables can be conceptualized as consisting of three phases based on the type of factors influencing investment.[22] During the years after the reform process began, positive and negative transitory factors dominated the decisionmaking environment. Only later would these transitory factors dissipate, leaving actors to make decisions based on the permanent signals that determine investment in any capitalist society, such as macroeconomic stability, anticipated demand, relative prices, and technological upgrading. Such factors are relevant for industrialized countries as well as Latin America and for any point in time. During the transition period between the destruction of the old economic model and the consolidation of the new one, the transitory factors operate alongside the permanent ones, such that the three phases are not mutually exclusive. Even so, we can identify a first phase that is dominated by negative transitory factors. These are replaced by positive transitory factors in the second phase and by permanent factors in the third phase, when the transition is complete and the new model is consolidated.

The negative transitory factors that dominated the initial post-reform phase tended to depress investment. Economic actors were very cautious because the immediate post-reform period was characterized by singular uncertainty. Most of the rules of the game had changed, and the governments that had made those changes still lacked credibility in the eyes of potential investors; it was unclear whether the reforms would be continued. Relative prices were also changing rapidly, while domestic and especially international competition was becoming much more relevant than before. The uncertainty caused by the initiation of the reform process itself was greatly magnified when macroeconomic conditions or international economic trends were unstable or negative. As described above, this was the case with most of the project countries. Conditions ranged from hyperinflation at the macroeconomic level to an almost total lack of liquidity on the international side.

Investment in fixed capital was highly unusual under such uncertainty; firms tended to defer irreversible decisions until the situation became clearer. They reacted defensively, rationalizing production processes and introducing disembodied technical change to increase productivity. This typically involved adopting new management techniques, reducing product mix,

---

22. On a less abstract level, firms and productive sectors in a given country tend not to be simultaneously at the same phase. The level of abstraction of stylized facts permits us to concentrate on traits that are key to the analysis in this chapter.

increasing the use of imported inputs, dismissing workers, and downsizing. In the extreme, the new rules and prices sent such strong negative signals that firms decided to shut down plants that were no longer competitive.

The second phase featured a quite different set of transitory factors that raised investment above "normal" levels, but these processes set in only when the initial uncertainty and lack of credibility had been at least partially overcome. These investments tended to be one-time occurrences, because as soon as the desired target was reached, less investment related to that target was needed.

The first factor stimulating this type of investment involved the modernization of equipment to reduce costs. Following the rationalization process, but still defensive in orientation, modernizing investment aimed to raise quality and productivity by replacing old equipment that was substantially behind international standards. Such investments had a very high marginal return since they could rehabilitate capital stock that would otherwise have become obsolete. A second factor pertained to the new export orientation. At least some economies required large new investments to support a sharp increase in the export coefficient, which derived from new market opportunities including those from participation in regional integration schemes. These investments were sometimes earmarked for new product development, but more typical was the expansion of existing facilities and upgrading to meet the quality demands of foreign customers.

Strategic repositioning of transnational corporations also led to temporary increases in investment. The reforms opened new possibilities for TNCs, which had frequently been banned from certain sectors of Latin American economies. New investment was necessary to take advantage of new opportunities. In addition, TNCs were less deterred by uncertainty than were domestic firms, since their new investments represented a much lower share of their total capital.[23] A final factor involved investment related to privatizations. While privatizations per se do not provide new investments, new investments often accompany privatizations, either through legal obligations (such as those in Bolivia or Peru) or through attempts to raise productivity in newly acquired firms.

The first post-reform phase thus features abnormally depressed investment because of the predominance of negative transitory factors, whereas positive transitory factors are the most significant in the second phase,

---

23. We are talking here only of new (greenfield) investment or expansion. Purchase of existing firms would not involve new investment from a national accounts perspective, as opposed to that of an individual firm.

causing investment to rise beyond what it would be under normal conditions. The third phase emerges when the transitory factors disappear or have relatively little weight in comparison to permanent investment incentives. At this point, the transition is complete, and the new model determines economic performance. Whether the new model will feature higher investment-to-GDP ratios than the previous one is an empirical question that cannot be determined before the fact.

The case studies of the project countries find evidence to support the existence of the three phases.[24] The reforms were not a homogeneous process in the region, in terms of either the moment in which they were initiated or the form in which they were implemented. Chile and Argentina began the process in the 1970s; the latter reversed course after a few years, only to return to the reforms with renewed vigor in the 1990s. Bolivia, Costa Rica, and Mexico began transforming their economies in the second half of the 1980s, while Peru, Colombia, and Brazil (together with Argentina) did so at the beginning of the 1990s. This timing sequence meant that the reforms were initiated in the various countries under markedly different macroeconomic circumstances and in varying international contexts. In Colombia and Costa Rica, the reforms were launched in an environment of macroeconomic stability, while the remaining countries initiated reforms in the context of powerful internal and external disequilibria.

The resulting uncertainty strongly influenced investor response to the reforms. In those countries that initiated the reforms under conditions of recession, gross fixed investment fell as a percentage of GDP during the years immediately following the reforms (see table 4-3). Not only were the coefficients well below the peaks reached during the 1970s and 1980s, they also tended to be below or at most comparable to the minimum levels achieved during the earlier decades. Exceptions to this pattern included Costa Rica, which began its reforms under positive macroeconomic conditions, and Bolivia and Peru, where the previous minimums occurred during years of extreme political instability (1983 and 1985, respectively).

Following the period during which investment coefficients declined, all countries went through a period of more stable macroeconomic conditions (namely, lower inflation and higher growth) and a generally more favorable international context.[25] These conditions led to rising investment,

24. See Moguillansky and Bielschowsky (2000, chapter 1).

25. The recovery of the investment coefficients occurred within the particular international context of the 1990s, except in Chile, where the recovery took place during the 1980s (see table 4-4). Three elements establish the favorable context of the 1990s: greater access to foreign financing, buoyant external demand, and high export prices.

Table 4-3. *Investment Coefficients for the Initial Post-Reform Period Compared to Previous Levels*
Percent

Country	Initial post-reform phase		Minimums and maximums for the pre-reform period (1970–90)[a]			
	Years	Coefficient	Year	Minimum	Year	Maximum
Argentina	1990	12.7	1989	14.7	1977	26.7
Bolivia	1985–89	13.2	1983	9.1	1978	19.9
Brazil	1990–93	14.5	1984	16.3	1975	25.8
Chile	1974–76	14.6	1975	14.9	1970	21.6
Colombia	1990–91	13.5	1989	15.2	1982	17.8
Costa Rica	1986–91	20.5	1982	14.3	1979	26.6
Mexico	1985–90	17.1	1983	16.6	1981	26.5
Peru	1990–92	17.7	1985	16.0	1975	27.6

Source: Adapted from Moguillansky and Bielschowsky (2000), on the basis of project data.

a. Except in the case of Chile, where a lack of information makes it necessary to use the period 1970–75.

at least in part because of the positive transitory factors mentioned earlier: modernization, exports, privatizations, and TNC strategies. As a result, investment coefficients rose above their minimums for the 1970s and 1980s, albeit still below the maximum levels achieved during those decades (see table 4-4). Only in the second half of the 1990s did the coefficients tend to reach levels similar to those observed for the pre-reform period.

Our analysis indicates that of the eight countries with investment data available, only Chile has reached the third phase when the reforms are consolidated and investment is determined by normal factors. Arguably such a point was reached in 1990, when the new democratic government assumed power and proceeded to follow macroeconomic policies that did not differ significantly from those of its military predecessor, which had initiated the reform process. The investment coefficient in Chile in the third phase has been far higher than in its own past as well as higher than in other countries in the region in the present. The same will not necessarily characterize a third phase in all of the other countries, nor will such performance necessarily continue in Chile.[26]

---

26. For an important discussion of the reasons for Chile's success, see Moguillansky (1999).

Table 4-4. *Investment Coefficients for the Post-Reform Period*
Percent

Country	Phase 1		Phase 2		Phase 3	
	Years	Coefficient	Years	Coefficient	Years	Coefficient
Argentina	1990	12.7	1991–98	20.5	...	...
Bolivia	1985–89	13.2	1990–98	17.9	...	...
Brazil	1990–94	14.7	1995–98	16.8	...	...
Chile I[a]	1974–76	14.6	1977–81	16.7	...	...
Chile II[a]	1982–85	14.2	1986–89	18.3	1990–98	25.1
Colombia	1990–91	13.5	1992–98	17.8	...	...
Costa Rica	1986–91	20.5	1992–98	23.2	...	...
Mexico	1985–90	17.1	1991–98[b]	19.7	...	...
Peru	1990–92	17.7	1993–98	23.3	...	...

Source: Moguillansky and Bielschowsky (2000), on the basis of project data.
a. Chile is listed twice to distinguish two reform periods.
b. Does not include 1995.

Chile now has twenty-five years of experience with reformed policies, far longer than any other country. Bolivia, Costa Rica, and Mexico have been carrying out reforms for about fifteen years, but none has yet entered the third phase. In Bolivia, the privatizations were begun late in the reform process, and the resulting investment boom generated by foreign investment is still being sustained by legal obligations that accompanied the sale of state firms. Costa Rica has enjoyed a recent surge of investment associated with the repositioning of transnational firms in the region; this is driving the investment rate above what would probably be normal levels. In Mexico, the inconsistency between the reforms and macroeconomic policies eventually led to a major financial crisis in 1994–95. The resulting devaluation and accompanying export boom are still providing transitory incentives for investment. In addition, an inflow of foreign investment has resulted from the North American Free Trade Agreement (NAFTA). Thus all three cases need a few more years before investment coefficients stabilize at their new normal levels.

The remaining four cases—Argentina, Brazil, Colombia, and Peru—have less than a decade of experience with the reforms, so it is not surprising that they are still in a transition period. Brazil, in particular, did not escape hyperinflation until 1994, and other types of macroeconomic instability, especially a large fiscal deficit, are still creating a situation of substantial uncertainty. This was compounded, of course, when the international financial crisis spilled over into the Brazilian economy and eventually resulted in the January 1999 devaluation.

Beyond the relatively short time period involved, Argentina, Colombia, and Peru have encountered additional problems that conflict with the consolidation process. Argentina and Peru have been subject to particularly volatile growth patterns. Argentina, with a fixed exchange rate regime, was highly exposed to changes in international financial flows. Peru suffered from stop-go growth caused by macroeconomic imbalances and exacerbated by climatic phenomena. Reform implementation in Colombia conflicted with other policy goals, especially decentralization and a large increase in social spending. The result has been a deviation from Colombia's traditional stable economic performance, which has caused great uncertainty in recent years and a reduction in investment.

The Impact of the Reforms on Investment

Investment and productivity trends result from the behavior of relevant actors, who respond to the macroeconomic context, the international environment, and the enactment of reforms under different degrees of uncertainty. To better ascertain the significance of these determinants of investment behavior, we employed an econometric model in which the dependent variables are gross fixed investment as a percentage of GDP and investment in machinery and equipment as a percentage of GDP. The independent variables are the change in output lagged one period (the accelerator effect), indicators of macroeconomic instability (in particular, the change in consumer prices, the variation of the real exchange rate, and the burden of external debt), the international environment (that is, foreign direct investment inflows), and the economic reforms.

The results of the econometric analysis are generally consistent with the expectations arising from the literature on investment as well as the previous discussion (see table 4-5).[27] The coefficient on lagged output was positive and significant; its value was notably greater for the regressions referring to machinery and equipment than for those measuring total investment. This is consistent with the points made earlier about the negative

---

27. These results are similar to those achieved by Lora and Barrera (1997). They are also compatible with those of Fernández Arias and Montiel (1997) and Servén and Solimano (1993). The authors thank Claudio Pini for carrying out the econometric analysis.

Table 4-5. *Determinants of Investment Rates*[a]

Independent variable	(1)	(2)	(3)	(4)	(5)	(6)	(7)	(8)
GDP (–1)	1.168	1.831	1.905	1.259	2.993	2.833	2.33	2.859
	(4.794)	(7.577)	(6.976)	(5.356)	(9.641)	(11.826)	(9.308)	(12.300)
External debt	–0.209			–0.196			–0.194	
	(–8.293)			(–7.105)			(–4.390)	
Foreign direct investment				0.038				0.017
				(3.319)				(0.686)
Inflation	–0.040	–0.051	–0.059	–0.035	–0.070	–0.071	–0.050	–0.070
	(–3.745)	(–3.529)	(–3.712)	(–3.308)	(–4.414)	(–4.912)	(–2.955)	(–4.922)
Real exchange rate							–0.04	
							(–2.501)	
Average reform index			0.018		0.265			
			(0.228)		(2.468)			
Privatization index		0.327				0.533	0.372	0.557
		(4.542)				(7.924)	(3.941)	(7.589)
Trade reform index		0.025				0.408	0.219	0.369
		(0.360)				(4.166)	(2.296)	(3.862)
Summary statistic								
R^2	0.716	0.612	0.595	0.745	0.488	0.520	0.599	0.523
Adjusted R^2	0.687	0.575	0.561	0.716	0.445	0.474	0.545	0.472
Number of observations	112	128	128	109	128	128	112	125

Source: Authors' regressions based on Moguillansky and Bielschowsky (2000); t statistics are shown in parentheses.

a. The dependent variable for equations 1–4 is gross fixed investment as a share of GDP, while for equations 5–8 it is investment in machinery and equipment as a share of GDP. The model is a panel, using fixed effects and ordinary least squares estimation, for data on eight countries (Argentina, Bolivia, Brazil, Chile, Colombia, Costa Rica, Mexico, and Peru) for the period 1979–95. Independent variables are first differences of the logs of GDP with a one-period lag (the accelerator relation), the logs of external debt as a share of GDP with a one-period lag, foreign direct investment as a share of GDP, the coefficient of variation for the consumer price index, the coefficient of variation for the real exchange rate, and the three-year average of the reform indexes described in chapter 3.

impact of a recessionary macroeconomic context on investment performance immediately after the reforms, as well as with the strong recovery in investment in machinery and equipment that takes place with advances toward stabilization.

The variation of the real exchange rate, the consumer price index, and the external debt burden had the anticipated negative effects on investment, highlighting the importance of uncertainty during the first phase for encouraging wait-and-see behavior. Foreign direct investment (FDI) had a positive and significant impact on total investment, although its magnitude is small. This makes sense given that even at its high point in 1997–98, FDI represented on average less than 20 percent of total investment in the principal recipient countries in the region. Moreover, an important part of this flow was directed toward the purchase of existing assets, both through participation in the privatization of public enterprises beginning in the early 1990s and through private sector mergers and acquisitions. This was especially true after the crisis of 1995, and it extended even to Chile following the recession of 1998–99.

The average reform index had a positive impact on both dependent variables, although it is significant only for equations explaining investment in machinery and equipment. Among the indices of specific reforms, that corresponding to privatization was positive and highly significant in all cases. Trade reform was significant only for investment in machinery and equipment, as was to be expected given the elevated presence of imports in that sector.

Reforms and Growth

At this time a major problem for any study of the reforms is the relatively short period they have been in effect. As already indicated, Chile is the single exception, since the reforms there began in the mid-1970s. A second group of countries implemented reforms in the mid-1980s, while in the majority of the project countries the reforms date only from around 1990. Since it is unreasonable to expect that the full benefits of the reforms would appear in the short run, this factor must be taken into account in interpreting the results. We use two approaches to deal with this problem of timing. First, we put special emphasis on the 1991–98 period when examining growth outcomes; this gives the maximum possible time frame for the impact of the reforms to be manifested. Second, we report on some econometric results that cover a longer period, 1970–95, since a few countries undertook some reforms in the 1970s.

Table 4-6. *Periodization of Economic Growth, 1950–98*

Country	Base period	Crisis period	Post-crisis period Recovery	Post-crisis period Growth
Argentina	1950–1980	1980–1990	1990–1992	1992–1998
Bolivia	1950–1978	1978–1986	1986–1990	1990–1998
Brazil	1950–1980	1980–1992	. . .	1992–1998
Chile	1950–1970	1970–1984	1984–1987	1987–1998
Colombia	1950–1980	1980–1986	. . .	1986–1998
Costa Rica	1950–1980	1980–1985	. . .	1985–1998
Jamaica	1950–1974	1974–1986	. . .	1986–1998
Mexico	1950–1980	1980–1986	1986–1989	1989–1998
Peru	1950–1980	1980–1990	1990–1994	1994–1998

Source: Hofman (2000), on the basis of project data.

An additional problem of timing emerges from the particular growth pattern in Latin America in the last two decades, which exhibited minimal growth in the 1980s followed by a reactivation in the 1990s. This pattern lends itself to the possible confusion of a period representing recovery from recession with that of growth per se. We therefore examine the growth trajectory of each of the project countries and define a post-crisis "growth period" as beginning when aggregate GDP returned to the peak before the recession of the 1980s. Table 4-6 shows these periods for each country, including a base period, a crisis period, a post-crisis recovery period (if relevant), and a growth period.[28]

Table 4-7 uses this periodization to organize the data on behavior of GDP between 1950 and 1998. The simple average for the nine countries shows that annual growth in the base period was 5.2 percent, falling to 0.2 percent in the crisis period. The post-crisis period, which is divided into recovery and growth subperiods, had average annual rates of 5.3 and 4.0 percent, respectively. In other words, GDP expanded somewhat more slowly on average in the recent growth period than it did in the base period. A final point of importance concerns the comparison between the growth period and the 1990s, which was identified earlier as being of particular interest for our analysis since it represents the most recent results. The average growth rate for the 1990s at 3.9 percent was slightly

28. For further details, see Hofman (2000).

Table 4-7. *GDP Growth in Selected Periods, 1950–98*[a]
Percent

| Country | Base period | Crisis period | Post-crisis period | | 1990s (1991–98) |
			Recovery	Growth	
High growth					
Argentina	3.8	−1.1	10.1	4.5	5.8
Bolivia	3.5	−1.7	3.5	4.3	4.3
Chile	3.9	1.4	5.2	7.6	7.7
Peru	4.9	−1.2	5.1	4.2	4.6
Simple average	4.0	−0.7	6.0	5.2	5.6
Low growth					
Brazil	7.0	1.3	...	2.4	1.8
Colombia	5.1	2.8	...	3.8	3.6
Costa Rica	6.5	0.2	...	4.0	4.0
Jamaica	5.5	−1.2	...	2.1	0.2
Mexico	6.5	1.0	2.4	3.3	3.1
Simple average	6.1	0.8	...	3.1	2.5
Simple average, total	5.2	0.2	5.3	4.0	3.9
Weighted average, total	6.0	0.8	4.9	3.4	3.2

Source: Hofman (2000), on the basis of project data.
a. Average annual compound growth rate.

lower than the 4.0 percent found during the growth period. Four of the nine countries saw their growth rates decline slightly in the 1990s with respect to the growth period as a whole, and Jamaica saw almost no growth at all in that decade.

These calculations all use simple averages, which give equal weight to the nine countries. Growth outcomes, however, demonstrate a substantial difference between the simple and weighted averages. As indicated in table 4-7, the weighted averages show a sharper decline from the base period with respect to the 1990s, from 6.0 percent to 3.2 percent. The reason becomes clear on analyzing individual country performance.

The four countries that grew most slowly in the base period (Argentina, Bolivia, Chile, and Peru) were the fastest growing in the 1990s. This group also grew substantially faster in the 1990s than in its own past (with the exception of Peru, which grew at about the same rate). On average among the four, growth in the base period was 4.0 percent, rising to 5.6

Table 4-8. *Per Capita GDP Growth in Selected Periods, 1950–98*[a]
Percent

Country	Base period	Crisis period	Post-crisis period		1990s (1991–98)
			Recovery	Growth	
High growth					
Argentina	2.1	−2.6	8.7	3.2	4.6
Bolivia	1.2	−2.9	1.3	2.1	1.8
Chile	1.6	−0.2	3.5	5.4	6.1
Peru	2.1	−2.7	3.3	2.4	2.8
Simple average	1.8	−2.1	4.2	3.3	3.8
Low growth					
Brazil	4.1	−0.7	. . .	0.8	0.1
Colombia	2.3	1.3	. . .	2.0	1.9
Costa Rica	3.1	−2.6	. . .	1.4	1.4
Jamaica	2.4	−1.5	. . .	1.4	−1.0
Mexico	3.5	−2.0	0.4	1.7	1.2
Simple average	3.1	−1.1	. . .	1.5	0.7
Simple average, total	2.5	−1.5	3.4	2.3	2.1
Weighted average, total	3.2	−1.3	3.1	1.7	1.5

Source: Hofman (2000), on the basis of project data.
a. Average annual compound growth rate.

percent in the 1990s. The largest increase was found in Chile, where growth rates nearly doubled.

The remaining five countries (Brazil, Colombia, Costa Rica, Jamaica, and Mexico) grew more slowly in the 1990s than in the base period and more slowly in the 1990s than did the other four countries. This group did especially poorly in the 1990s per se. The simple average growth rate of the five in the base period was 6.1 percent, compared to 3.1 percent in the growth period and 2.5 percent in the 1990s. The most dramatic declines in growth occurred in Brazil, Mexico, and Jamaica; since the first two are the largest countries in the region, this explains the difference between the simple and weighted averages shown in table 4-7.

A similar pattern emerges if we use per capita rather than aggregate growth rates (see table 4-8). Among the nine countries as a group, the gap between growth in the base period and in the 1990s is smaller in per capita terms than in aggregate terms, since population growth rates fell during the postwar decades. At the country level, the main difference is with respect to Peru. While Peru was a high-growth country in comparison with others in the 1990s, it nevertheless grew a bit slower in the 1990s in aggregate terms than it did in the base period; in per capita terms, in contrast, growth increased in the 1990s over the base period. Note also that while the high- and low-growth countries do not overlap in the 1990s with respect to aggregate growth rates, in per capita growth Colombia (in the slow-growth group at the aggregate level) slightly exceeded Bolivia (in the high-growth group).

Accounting for Differences in Growth

Growth among the nine countries as a whole thus fell between the base period and the 1990s, although two subgroups demonstrated contrasting behavior. The reasons for these trends can first be approximated through a growth-accounting framework, which divides overall growth into three components: labor accumulation, capital accumulation, and total factor productivity.[29]

Table 4-9 shows the trends with respect to factor accumulation for all countries except Jamaica. The group of eight countries as a whole increased labor input between the base period and the 1990s. Since hours worked fell in most countries, this increase implies a larger number of persons working. Capital accumulation, in contrast, fell sharply between the base period and the later years.

The two subgroups displayed diverging tendencies. For the group of faster-growing countries, the growth rate of labor input more than doubled, rising from 1.2 percent in the base period to 2.7 percent in the 1990s. Argentina's contribution to this result, however, was minimal. In the slower-growing countries, the rate actually fell from 2.7 percent to 2.4 percent, as a result of decreases in Colombia and especially Brazil. The next chapter on employment uncovers a similar pattern: employment problems in the region were especially severe in Argentina, Brazil, and Colombia, where employment creation was slow throughout the 1990s.

Capital accumulation experienced a relatively small decline in the fast-

29. The growth-accounting framework is controversial and not completely consistent with other types of analysis used in the volume. Among the problems that should be kept in mind are the following: (1) the framework assumes a steady-state economy; (2) the residual (total factor productivity) captures much more than productivity; and (3) there are serious measurement problems involved. On measurement problems, see Griliches (1998).

Table 4-9. *Factor Inputs to Growth, 1950–98*[a]
Percent

Country	Labor input (hours worked)			Capital accumulation		
	Base period	Post-crisis growth period	1991–98	Base period	Post-crisis growth period	1991–98
High growth						
Argentina	1.2	1.5	1.5	4.9	2.9	2.5
Bolivia	1.0	3.5	3.5	2.8	3.3	3.3
Chile	0.4	2.9	2.8	4.2	6.2	6.8
Peru	2.0	2.9	3.0	5.0	3.7	2.9
Simple average	1.2	2.7	2.7	4.2	4.0	3.9
Low growth						
Brazil	2.9	1.4	1.4	9.8	2.7	2.6
Colombia	2.3	2.0	2.0	4.1	3.8	3.8
Costa Rica	2.9	3.4	3.1	7.2	4.4	4.6
Mexico	2.6	3.0	3.1	7.7	2.4	2.4
Simple average	2.7	2.5	2.4	7.2	3.3	3.4
Simple average, total	1.9	2.6	2.6	5.7	3.7	3.6

Source: Hofman (2000), on the basis of project data.
a. Average annual compound growth rate.

growing countries, from 4.2 percent to 3.9 percent; the large declines in Argentina and Peru were partially offset by increases in Bolivia and especially Chile. In the slow-growth group, the fall was much more dramatic, from 7.2 to 3.4 percent, with three of the four countries suffering substantial declines.[30] Despite these different tendencies with respect to the past, the two groups had similar growth rates for both labor input and capital accumulation in the 1990s. The variation within groups was much higher than the variation between groups. This suggests that other variables must explain much of the difference in GDP growth rates in the 1990s.

Labor input in table 4-9 is measured simply by the number of hours worked. It would be useful, however, to be able to adjust these figures to reflect changes in the quality of labor input. Fortunately, researchers have

30. These results may appear to be inconsistent with the previous discussion of the investment coefficient; it has to do with the way capital stock is calculated, as explained below.

devoted considerable attention to this topic. The most important component of quality, considered to have a direct effect on productivity, is the level of education and its rate of change. An individual's level of education affects the type of work he or she can do and the efficiency with which the work is performed. The number of years of formal education of the population between 15 and 64 years of age is the main indicator available for measuring quality change. Differences between this and better measures are probably small at the primary and secondary level, if not the tertiary level.[31]

In most Latin American countries, the education systems have undergone noteworthy expansion in recent decades. They still display shortcomings, however, in the quality of their results, their degree of adaptation to the requirements of the economic and social environment, and the extent to which they are accessible to different strata of society.[32] In the case of the project countries, average years of education rose from six and a half to ten years between the base period and the 1990s. Despite all the differences between the fast- and slow-growing countries, the average education level for the two groups was virtually identical throughout the 1950–98 period although there are significant differences between individual countries.[33]

To measure capital stock, we use the generally accepted perpetual inventory model.[34] This methodology disaggregates capital stock into several types with different service lives: machinery and equipment (15 years), nonresidential construction (40 years), and dwellings (50 years). In any given year, investment adds to capital stock, while some stock is withdrawn in the accounting sense due to the end of its useful life as defined above, even though it may continue to be used in practice.[35]

31. The preferred measure would be level of education of the labor force rather than the population as a whole. In addition, neither the educational level of the population as a whole nor that of the labor force takes into account the important element of on-the-job training.

32. ECLAC/UNESCO (1992).

33. Data in equivalent years of education. For more detail, see Hofman (2000).

34. On the methodology, see Goldsmith (1951). Among the problems with this measure are that it takes no account of whether these assets are actually in use at any particular moment. The reform process presents an additional problem: much of the existing stock of capital may become obsolete as trade liberalization brings access to the latest international technology. These quality issues cannot be captured in this methodology.

35. This implies that two countries with the same amount of new investment in a given year may have quite different accumulation rates. The one with the more rapid accumulation in the past will have a lower rate of accumulation in the present, since more stock will be withdrawn from use.

An important aspect of physical investment is that it embodies technical progress in the form of quality improvements in successive vintages of
capital. The quality effect of physical investment comes from three sources:
embodied technical progress, change in the average age of capital stock,
and change in its composition. With respect to composition, the most
important aspect is the relative weight of machinery and equipment compared to residential and nonresidential construction. Among the eight countries, this component increased in Argentina, Chile, Colombia, Costa Rica,
and Mexico, while it fell in Brazil and Peru and remained about constant in
Bolivia. In absolute terms, Brazil and Peru had the lowest share of machinery and equipment, with 33 and 21 percent, respectively, in comparison
with an average for the eight countries of 42 percent.[36]

The average age of capital stock showed mixed trends. For nonresidential construction, age declined in all cases between 1950 and 1980, but it
increased or stayed constant during the 1980s and continued to increase in
all cases except Chile and Bolivia in the 1990s. Machinery and equipment
followed similar trends until 1990, when average age began to fall in all
eight countries.

Technical progress and the resulting productivity were very unevenly
distributed. Indeed, it is with respect to productivity that we can begin to
distinguish between the high- and low-growth countries in the 1990s
rather than only with respect to their own past performance. Factor inputs grew at fairly similar rates when compared across the two groups;
education levels were also nearly identical. As table 4-10 shows, however,
productivity trends for labor and capital increased at very different rates.
Labor productivity among the faster-growing group rose by four times
the rate found among the slower-growing set (2.9 percent in comparison
to 0.7 percent). With respect to productivity of capital stock, the fast-
growing countries had an average rate of increase of 1.6 percent, while
the others fell slightly.

These results are summarized in the data for total factor productivity, which report a figure for productivity of all factors combined as well

---

Likewise, capital stock growth trends could be quite different from, and perhaps even have a different
sign than, those for investment. (The differences in project countries with respect to investment and
capital stock over the 1950–98 period can be observed by comparing tables 4-1 and 4-9.)

36. Hofman (2000).

Table 4-10. *Growth of Labor and Capital Productivity, 1950–98*[a]
Percent

Country	Labor productivity (hours worked)			Capital productivity		
	Base period	Post-crisis growth period	1991–98	Base period	Post-crisis growth period	1991–98
High growth						
Argentina	2.5	2.9	4.3	−0.8	1.8	2.7
Bolivia	2.5	0.8	0.8	0.7	1.0	1.0
Chile	3.5	4.6	4.8	−0.3	1.3	0.9
Peru	2.9	1.3	1.6	−0.1	0.5	1.7
Simple average	2.9	2.4	2.9	−0.1	1.2	1.6
Low growth						
Brazil	3.9	1.0	0.4	−2.6	−0.3	−0.7
Colombia	2.8	1.8	1.6	0.9	0.0	−0.2
Costa Rica	3.5	0.8	0.9	−0.7	−0.3	−0.6
Mexico	3.8	0.3	0.0	−1.1	0.9	0.7
Simple average	3.5	1.0	0.7	−0.9	0.1	−0.2
Simple average, total	3.2	1.7	1.8	−0.5	0.7	0.7

Source: Hofman (2000), on the basis of project data.
a. Average annual compound growth rate.

as other residual elements not captured in the analysis. Table 4-11 shows data for two measures: total factor productivity and doubly-augmented total factor productivity. The latter takes into account quality improvements in both labor and capital as well as their quantitative changes. We find the same pattern as for labor and capital productivity. The fast-growing countries increased their productivity between the base period and the 1990s, going from 1.9 percent to 2.8 percent on the basic measure and from 0.9 to 1.9 percent with respect to augmented productivity. (Bolivia was an exception to the trend, as the productivity growth rate fell.) The slower-growing countries, in contrast, saw the basic measure decline from 2.3 to 0.7 percent and the augmented measure fell from 1.1 percent to −0.4 percent. These tendencies were repeated in each of the individual countries.

Table 4-11. *Growth of Total Factor Productivity, 1950–98*[a]
Percent

Country	Total factor productivity			Doubly augmented total factor productivity		
	Base period	Post-crisis growth period	1991–98	Base period	Post-crisis growth period	1991–98
High growth						
Argentina	1.5	2.4	4.0	0.6	1.6	3.2
Bolivia	2.0	1.2	1.2	0.9	0.0	0.0
Chile	2.0	3.9	3.9	1.2	2.8	2.8
Peru	1.9	1.3	2.0	0.9	0.8	1.5
Simple average	1.9	2.2	2.8	0.9	1.3	1.9
Low growth						
Brazil	2.6	0.7	0.1	1.4	−0.3	−0.7
Colombia	2.4	1.2	1.1	1.4	−0.1	−0.3
Costa Rica	2.2	0.6	0.7	1.2	−0.4	−0.3
Mexico	1.8	0.9	0.7	0.5	0.0	−0.3
Simple average	2.3	0.9	0.6	1.1	−0.2	−0.4
Simple average, total	2.1	1.6	1.7	1.0	0.6	0.8

Source: Hofman (2000), on the basis of project data.
a. Average annual compound growth rate.

To summarize the relative contributions to growth rates of labor accumulation, capital accumulation, and productivity, three of the four fast-growing countries (Argentina, Chile, and Peru) saw the main contribution from increased productivity, while all of the other countries relied more heavily on factor accumulation (see table 4-12). Insofar as productivity is a crucial determinant of a country's ability to compete in the world economy, this would suggest that the group of countries that grew fastest in the 1990s—largely on the basis of higher productivity—will enjoy additional advantages in the future.[37]

37. An important debate on the relative merits of growth through factor accumulation or productivity began shortly before the Asian crisis broke out. See Krugman (1994) and responses (Gibney and others, 1995; Rostow, 1995).

Table 4-12. *Contributions to GDP Growth, 1950–98*
Percent

Country	Base period			Post-crisis growth period			1991–98		
	Labor	*Capital*	*TFP*[a]	*Labor*	*Capital*	*TFP*[a]	*Labor*	*Capital*	*TFP*[a]
High growth									
Argentina	18	43	39	24	30	45	9	23	68
Bolivia	19	24	57	49	23	28	49	23	28
Chile	7	41	52	21	27	51	21	29	51
Peru	23	38	39	40	28	32	37	20	42
Simple average	17	37	46	34	27	39	29	24	47
Low growth									
Brazil	31	32	37	35	36	29	47	45	8
Colombia	24	29	47	26	41	32	27	43	29
Costa Rica	25	41	34	56	31	13	44	38	18
Mexico	19	53	28	32	39	29	35	42	22
Simple average	25	39	36	37	37	26	38	42	20
Simple average, total	21	38	41	36	32	32	34	33	33

Source: Hofman (2000), on the basis of project data.
a. Total factor productivity.

The Impact of the Reforms on Growth

The four countries identified as aggressive reformers in chapter 3 were the same ones that grew most rapidly in the 1990s; the cautious reformers, in contrast, grew more slowly. On the surface, this relation appears to provide evidence that more reforms lead to higher growth, but the situation is actually much more complicated. The reforms worked together with macroeconomic and international trends. The elimination of hyperinflation, in particular, had a very positive impact on growth. In addition, the aggressive reformers chose to undertake many reforms in a very short time period because they were in such dire straits with respect to hyperinflation and negative growth in the preceding years; their economies were much more distorted than others and this was often accompanied by problems of governability. Not surprisingly, the change in policy orientation led to new investment and an acceleration of growth rates, after a period in which economic actors waited to see if the new policies would be continued.

Initially, of course, this expansion was only recovery from the previous recession, but it eventually became growth per se. This can be thought of as a type of regression to the mean trajectory, though with respect to rates rather than levels. One of the mechanisms bringing about the increase in growth has to do with potential investments (and therefore productivity increases) that were not undertaken in those countries with poor initial conditions. Once the changes were carried out, and assuming the other factors were also favorable, the potential for especially high growth rates was present for some period of time.[38]

The group of countries that had been doing reasonably well in the pre-reform period had less reason to undertake major structural changes in their economies. Although they did implement gradual and selective reforms, they got a smaller boost from them because of the lack of a reservoir of unexploited opportunities. These countries also encountered serious macroeconomic problems that had a negative effect on growth rates. Mexico and Brazil already had high inflation rates at the beginning of the reform period. The type of stabilization policies they followed, which relied on an overvalued exchange rate, eventually resulted in foreign exchange crises. Colombia, Costa Rica, and Jamaica also began to suffer macroeconomic disequilibria during the 1990s. The causes were *sui generis*: a desire to ex-

---

38. Note the parallel situation with respect to the phases of investment; of course, the two are related insofar as investment is an important determinant of growth rates.

Table 4-13. *Determinants of Per Capita GDP Growth*[a]

Independent variable	(1)	(2)	(3)	(4)
Investment coefficient	0.179	0.181	0.178	0.186
	(11.103)	(11.102)	(11.114)	(11.508)
International activity level	0.040	0.050	0.040	0.038
	(3.528)	(3.604)	(3.600)	(3.420)
Exchange rate variation	−0.049	−0.050	−0.043	−0.049
	(−5.841)	(−5.981)	(−5.280)	(−5.993)
Crisis dummy	−0.018	−0.018	−0.020	−0.018
	(−4.209)	(−4.093)	(−4.636)	(−4.046)
Average reform index	0.034			
	(2.121)			
Trade reform index		0.027		
		(1.667)		
Capital account index			0.056	
			(3.486)	
Privatization index				0.052
				(2.437)
Summary statistic				
R^2	0.60	0.60	0.61	0.59
Adjusted R^2	0.57	0.57	0.58	0.56
Number of observations	198	198	198	198

Source: Authors' regressions; t statistics are shown in parentheses.

a. The dependent variable is the first difference of the logs of per capita GDP. The model is a panel, using fixed effects and ordinary least squares estimation, with data on nine countries (Argentina, Bolivia, Brazil, Chile, Colombia, Costa Rica, Jamaica, Mexico, and Peru) for the period 1970–95. Independent variables are the first difference of the logs of investment as a share of GDP, first difference of the logs of exports to developed countries, the coefficient of variation of monthly movements of the exchange rate, a dummy whose value is 1 during crisis periods (varying by country), and the average level for the previous five years of the reform indexes described in chapter 3.

pand social spending in Colombia at the same time that a substantial share of central government revenues had been decentralized to the regions; the failure of an important bank in Costa Rica; and a one-time hike in the inflation rate in Jamaica, caused by the delayed effects of a monetary and credit expansion in the late 1980s. In the cases of Colombia and Jamaica, overvaluation of the exchange rate was also a significant factor.

In addition to these qualitative links between reforms and growth, several econometric exercises provide further insights into the relation between the two variables (see table 4-13). The results are closely related to those discussed earlier with respect to the model to explain investment perfor-mance. Both sets of equations are based on short-run models that test the impact of the reform indexes (plus other variables) on the annual change in investment or GDP. In the case of the growth equations, the dependent variable was change in GDP per capita between 1970 and 1995. Indepen-dent variables included investment, a variable representing the international environment, a volatility measure, a dummy for crisis years during the period, and the reform indexes.[39]

Investment always has a positive and significant effect on growth. This is clearly consistent with the growth-accounting analysis, in which invest-ment is one of the key determinants of growth. Nonetheless, investment becomes less important with the addition of other variables into the analy-sis, since the latter may work through their impact on investment. Invest-ment also has a different impact on growth in different sectors, as will be seen in chapter 6.

To measure the impact of the international environment, the growth rate of exports from developing countries to member countries of the Or-ganization for Economic Cooperation and Development (OECD) is used as a proxy of the international activity level. This is meant to reflect the expansionary or contractionary stance of the world economy, which our analysis suggests would play an important part in determining growth pat-terns. As expected, the coefficient is positive and significant.

To test for the expected negative effect on growth of macroeconomic instability, two variables were tried: the annual inflation rate and the coef-ficient of variation of the monthly levels of the real exchange rate. Coeffi-cients on both were negative and significant, but the latter led to a better fit of the model so only this variable is reported in table 4-13. These results are consistent not only with the extensive literature on the determinants of growth, but also with the discussion earlier in the chapter on the negative impact of macroeconomic instability on investors.

A dummy was used to capture the effect of the worst crisis years in the period, where the years vary by country. Its coefficient was negative and significant, suggesting that these particular years had relevance beyond that captured in the other variables.

The reform indexes, including both the aggregate index and several of the individual ones, had a positive and significant effect on growth. The coefficients suggest that an increase of 10 percent in the average reform

39. The authors want to thank Lucas Navarro for his role in carrying out the econometric analysis.

index would produce an increase of about 0.2 percent in GDP growth rates. This result is based on the long-run impact of the reforms. That is, the reform variable in table 4-13 is the five-year average of the reform index. Regressions using the current-year value, the three-year average, and the five-year average found an increasingly positive impact with larger coefficients and higher significance levels. Only the five-year average was significant at the 5 percent level. While the impact appears to be small, this depends on the pre-existing growth rate; the lower the rate, the more important the reform-generated increment. This point relates back to the aggressive versus cautious reform categories presented in chapter 3. Specifically, for the aggressive reformers with their low or negative growth rates in the period leading up to the reforms, the increment is more significant than for the cautious reformers with higher base rates.

The individual indexes that proved to be significant included import liberalization, privatization, and the opening of the capital account. Neither the tax nor financial reform indexes were significant. These results with respect to the reforms are similar to those found in the regressions with investment, except that the capital account index was not significant for explaining the latter.[40]

Growth and the External Sector

A final topic of importance to the reform-growth process has to do with changes in the relation between growth and the international economy as a result of the reforms. The expectation was that post-reform growth would be more export oriented, even if not necessarily export led. A greater emphasis on exports, together with more efficient import substitution, would produce a trade surplus or a lower trade deficit. This section investigates the role played by exports in the new economic model and examines changes in imports as well. The data provide the basis for evaluating the impact on the trade balance, which is a key aspect of the sustainability of the new economic model. A trade deficit, in turn, must be financed by external savings.

40. Since the model employed concentrated on the short-term links between growth and the various explanatory variables, variables normally found in long-run growth equations were not always relevant. One example is the insignificance of education, which is a stalwart of long-term models. The results of the model discussed here are usefully compared with those in Escaith and Morley (forthcoming), which uses the project data to construct a long-term growth model. In this model, for example, education is highly significant, as are structural characteristics of the economies.

The export coefficient has indeed increased in all eight of the project countries.[41] From 1980 to 1990, using the 1990-based data, the average export coefficient rose from 14.3 to 19.6 percent. Between 1990 and 1998, using the 1995-based series, the coefficient increased from 16.7 to 23.5 percent. The 1980s, then, experienced an average increase of 37 percent, with another 41 percent added in the 1990s. As usual, the averages mask big differences across countries. Mexico's coefficient nearly tripled between 1980 and 1998, and Costa Rica's coefficient nearly doubled, while Chile's had already increased significantly in the 1970s. Argentina and Brazil also saw large increases, although they started from very low initial levels. Even after the increases, Argentina and Brazil only export about 10 percent of their GDP, compared with over half in Costa Rica and nearly one-third in Chile and Mexico (see table 4-14). The trend in the import coefficients was quite different from that of exports over the same period. The import coefficient declined slightly in 1980–90 and then rose by 68 percent between 1990 and 1998. Import behavior was somewhat more homogeneous among countries than was the case for exports. Most countries underwent a decline or only a small increase in the 1980s and a large rise in the 1990s.

Whether the export boom in the 1980s and 1990s constituted export-led growth is a tricky question, since disagreement exists in the literature on what the term means.[42] In the 1980s, exports in the project countries grew rapidly, but GDP was practically stagnant. Two factors produced this results. Export coefficients in all project countries except Chile and Costa Rica were very low at the beginning of the 1980s. The increase in exports thus could not have an important impact on growth. In addition, to increase exports countries had to become more competitive, which implied the substitution of imported inputs for domestic supply, as shown in chapter 6. Moreover, value added in the fast growing *maquila* exports was usually below one-fourth of their value. As a result, the value added of exports did not grow as fast as the export value. Consequently, the net effect on growth was much smaller than would be expected if domestic content had not decreased. Exports continued to grow rapidly in the 1990s, becoming more diversified in both composition and destination, but the question remains about their contribution to the rest of the economies. One study on Chile argues that growth was export-led because of positive spillover effects on

---

41. These data are consistent with those in table 2-1, which show exports growing much faster than GDP in the last two decades.

42. See discussion of the different definitions in García, Meller, and Repetto (1996).

Table 4-14. *Export and Import Coefficients, 1980–98*[a]

Percent

Country	1980[b]		1990[b]		1990[c]		1998[c]	
	Export	Import	Export	Import	Export	Import	Export	Import
Argentina	5.7	9.7	10.5	4.8	8.8	3.8	11.0	13.9
Bolivia	14.5	15.7	18.7	20.8	19.2	25.0	20.4	32.2
Brazil	5.0	7.9	8.2	6.6	7.1	4.0	8.7	11.5
Chile	24.3	35.5	33.6	30.1	26.6	20.8	33.5	30.1
Colombia	17.4	21.4	21.6	17.5	13.3	8.9	17.5	21.6
Costa Rica[d]	23.5	34.1	34.4	41.1	33.6	35.9	51.0	51.9
Mexico[d]	10.3	17.3	18.6	19.8	14.8	18.0	32.2	33.7
Peru	13.6	13.5	11.5	11.4	10.4	9.7	13.4	17.1
Simple average	14.3	19.4	19.6	19.0	16.7	15.8	23.5	26.5

Source: Project database, on the basis of ECLAC statistics.

a. Exports and imports as a share of GDP.

b. Based on 1990 dollars.

c. Based on 1995 dollars.

d. *Maquila* exports and imports are included for Mexico and for Costa Rica in 1998.

Table 4-15. *Trade Balance as a Share of GDP, 1950–98*
Percent[a]

Country	1950–73	1974–82	1983–91	1992–98
Argentina	0.2	1.0	2.5	–2.3
Bolivia	4.9	5.3	–4.5	–7.7
Brazil	–1.8	–4.4	2.3	–0.3
Chile	3.1	–3.9	4.6	3.0
Colombia	–0.8	–0.1	0.4	–3.1
Costa Rica	–3.6	–7.0	–2.3	–1.0
Mexico	–0.9	–1.0	3.3	–2.4
Peru	2.0	–1.7	1.7	–3.2
Simple average	0.4	–1.5	1.0	–2.1

Source: Project database, on the basis of ECLAC statistics.
a. Calculated in constant dollars.

nontradables sectors.[43] Similar studies are needed for other countries before any firm conclusions can be reached on the role of export in growth.

Table 4-15 puts the trade situation into a longer-term perspective. A small positive trade balance characterized the 1950–73 period.[44] This was followed by a swing toward deficits in the latter half of the 1970s, as imports exceeded exports when foreign capital flooded into the region in the form of private bank loans. Once the debt crisis broke and Latin American countries no longer had access to international capital markets, they had to generate trade surpluses to service their debt. On average, this period of surpluses lasted from around 1982–83 until the early 1990s, when access to capital markets was again a possibility and trade deficits matched capital account surpluses. Such an externally based account is incomplete, however, because it overlooks the internal factors that contributed to the deficits. The reforms themselves played an important role, especially trade liberalization, privatization, and the opening of the capital account, as did pent-up demand for consumer goods and new demand for investment goods.

Current account deficits may play a positive role in economic growth because their financing implies that the country receives external savings.

43. See García, Meller, and Repetto (1996).
44. This result is based on simple averages. Weighted averages demonstrate a small deficit in the 1950–73 period, mainly because of the deficit in Brazil.

Problems arise, however, when deficits reach levels that cannot be sustained. Increasing current account deficits in the economies of the region raise new concerns about their vulnerability. By the late 1990s, trade deficits alone reached nearly 3 percent of GDP on average among the project countries. To this must be added an additional 2 percent for factor payments in a typical country, which means that the current account deficits approached 5 percent.[45] Recent history indicates that this level is about the limit of what the capital markets are willing to finance, even in a period of abundant liquidity.

Thus, the vulnerability issue is a very important one with two separate but related components. One centers on the behavior of the current account, both the trade balance and factor payments (dividends and interest). Although the current account is usually in deficit in developing countries, we have seen that the size of the deficit varied substantially. In the face of the expectation that the reforms would shrink deficits, the opposite occurred through the end of the 1990s. To evaluate the significance of this trend, we need to know whether investments are underway that might narrow the gap.

The other component of external vulnerability concerns the type of foreign capital that finances the current account deficit. Chapter 2 presented evidence of two diverging trends in capital inflows in the 1990s compared to the period before the debt crisis. On the one hand, the volatility of inflows rose because of the increased role of short-term capital. On the other hand, foreign direct investment constituted an increased share of total inflows. Since FDI is the most stable kind of capital, and it is often linked to exports, governments implemented policies to attract this type of flow.

Overall, the issue of external vulnerability remains high on the agenda in Latin America and the Caribbean, as was shown during the economic downturn in South America in 1998–99. In some ways, the reforms exacerbated the problem through the unrestricted opening of the capital account in many countries. At the same time, the new investment resulting from the reforms may be producing exports that are less sensitive to wide price fluctuations. One measure of the success of the reforms and associated policies in the future will be their capacity to reinforce the latter while minimizing the former.

45. This figure of 5 percent is the counterpart of the figure for external finance of investment, as discussed earlier in the chapter.

Conclusions

In most project countries in the 1990s, investment and labor productivity recovered their previous levels after significant declines in the 1980s. As measured by simple averages, both variables are now back to or a little above their levels at the end of the import-substitution period. A similar pattern occurred for growth among project countries, but the recovery process in this instance was less complete; growth in the 1990s remained below that in the 1950–80 base period. Predicting the future growth path requires evidence on investment and productivity at the sectoral level.

On the aggregate level, the reforms—especially privatization and trade liberalization, but also the capital account opening—had a positive impact on both investment and growth. According to the econometric evidence, this impact was fairly small, although qualitative evidence at the sectoral and firm levels presented in chapter 6 suggests that the reforms may have been more important than the econometric evidence indicates. We have no econometric evidence with respect to productivity, but the growth accounting exercises suggest that this was the crucial factor in explaining the behavior of high-growth versus low-growth countries. The reforms led to a more efficient allocation of resources, but macroeconomic stabilization also played a significant role.

The performance of investment, productivity, and growth was heterogeneous across countries. Three cases exhibit a consistent pattern with respect to the three variables. In Chile, all three variables increased substantially in comparison with earlier periods, while in Mexico and Brazil all three declined (or remained constant in the case of investment in Mexico). These consistent patterns are the expected ones since investment, productivity, and growth are known to reinforce each other, but most of the countries had a more mixed performance.

Chile achieved a virtuous circle among the three variables only from the mid-1980s, more than a decade after its reforms began; earlier post-reform economic performance had been extremely volatile. Positive outcomes, including increases in factor inputs and productivity of all factors, were stimulated by macroeconomic policies that became consistent with the reforms, thanks to the policy shift after the crisis of the early 1980s. These policies reduced uncertainty through close collaboration between public and private sectors. In addition, although Chile was the recipient of substantial amounts of foreign capital, it kept its external accounts under control through rapid export growth and a high domestic savings rate, including a fiscal surplus.

Brazil and Mexico, in contrast, have yet to stimulate a sustained, positive relation among investment, productivity, and growth, although Mexico may be heading in this direction with policy adjustments following the 1994–95 crisis. The key factor in both cases was inconsistency between the reforms and macroeconomic policy, centering on the use of the exchange rate to tame inflation. In Mexico, this led to a large current account deficit that made investors hesitant to undertake major projects, which might have stimulated higher growth. The situation in Brazil was more serious. The reforms had to co-exist with hyperinflation until 1994, and then the high interest rates to protect the overvalued exchange rate both enlarged the fiscal deficit and hindered investment. While the situation changed partially after the January 1999 devaluation, the outcome is not yet clear.

The other cases demonstrate a mixed pattern, with either investment or productivity exceeding their previous levels, but not both. Among the mixed cases, Argentina, Bolivia, and Peru saw an increase in growth compared with the base period, while it fell in Colombia and Costa Rica. On the surface, the difference was explained by productivity trends, but the factors underlying productivity probably related back to the initial conditions when the reforms began. That is, the former group of countries faced especially negative circumstances and had thus lost past opportunities for investment and productivity gains in comparison with their more successful neighbors. Once the reforms were implemented and macroeconomic conditions became more stable, they quickly began to catch up, in large part through increased access to foreign capital flows. Whether these gains will persist remains to be seen. Countries that had been doing well previously did not have this opportunity for an easy catch-up; they may even have lost out in terms of investment to the other group.

The reforms did not eliminate, and may have exacerbated, external vulnerability. Trade deficits returned to levels not seen since the 1970s. The increased role of volatile short-term capital flows in financing the deficits led to new problems for macroeconomic management. Moreover, given the trade and current account deficits, a sharp drop in financial flows could cause serious recession if governments have to slow their economies to prevent foreign exchange crises. This process was evident in the aftermath of the international crisis in 1998 and especially 1999. Again, we need more evidence at the sectoral and microeconomic levels to evaluate future prospects.

Aggregate-level analysis can provide useful insights into patterns of investment, productivity, and growth, and it can also provide evidence for linking the reforms to these processes. It can depict the heterogeneity among countries with respect to investment and growth and give clues to the sustainability of the process. At the same time, an aggregate level of analysis, which is typical of the vast majority of studies on the reforms, leaves many questions pending, most notably with regard to the types of structural change that have taken place in the various economies and the characteristics of the investment and productivity trends that are underway. These are essential pieces of information for making policy recommendations to improve existing policies.

5 | Employment and Equity: Continuing Challenges

The impact of the structural reforms on employment and equity has attracted less attention than the relation between reforms and growth.[1] The empirical analyses that have been carried out have generally found that the reforms had a negative impact on both employment generation and equity. This result is opposite to that predicted by the literature of the late 1970s and early 1980s, which provided the theoretical underpinnings for the reforms.

That literature argued that removing the distortions caused by the import substitution industrialization (ISI) model would generate more employment, especially for unskilled workers.[2] Several mechanisms were specified to link the reforms to increased employment. The most basic was that a more efficient allocation of resources would facilitate faster growth, and faster growth would result in more job creation. This would occur even if the elasticities remained the same, but the elasticities were

1. This chapter draws extensively on data and analysis in Weller (2000) and Morley (2000). These authors are not responsible for the conclusions that are drawn here.

2. Perhaps the most important of the early works that argued for structural reforms and linked them to the "employment problem," were those of Krueger (1978, 1981–83). The fact that Krueger served as chief economist of the World Bank in the early 1980s gave her opinions a weight well beyond academic circles.

also expected to be more favorable, owing to a shift in investment and the production structure. Investment and technical change were projected to be more labor intensive once the alleged biases in favor of capital and against labor were eliminated. An increased emphasis on exports would also create jobs, because exports were thought to be more labor intensive than import-competing products. This last point was consistent with the sectoral analysis, which asserted that agriculture and light industry would be especially favored under a new trade strategy. Finally, it was increasingly argued that if the high costs of hiring workers were lowered, more jobs would be created.

The mechanisms for increasing equity were closely related to those for expanding employment.[3] The most obvious link was through the creation of new low-skill jobs, which would presumably be filled by those who were unemployed or underemployed and thus had very low incomes. Insofar as many of these new jobs were created in rural areas, they would help alleviate the greatest pockets of poverty, which were located there. It was also expected that the greater demand for unskilled labor would have a positive impact on the relative wages of those who were already employed. That is, the wage differential between skilled and unskilled workers would decrease, thus improving the distribution of income. The gap between profits and wages was also expected to decrease, given some evidence that protection had increased the former at the expense of the latter. Finally, reducing the productive role of the state would free up funds that could be devoted to social expenditure in benefit of poorer groups.

The empirical literature on the impact of the reforms is paying increasing attention to employment; an important example is a recent set of studies by the Inter-American Development Bank (IDB).[4] The International Labour Organization (ILO) has also studied the topic extensively.[5] Both the IDB and ILO argue that the growth rate of employment was lower in

3. While there is no doubt that the proponents believed the reforms would benefit employment, there is more disagreement about whether better income distribution was an explicit goal of the reformers. Balassa and others clearly said that it was (1986, pp. 93–94), as did Krueger (1983, pp.186–87). Williamson specifically excluded it from the Washington Consensus measures, saying that the Washington of the Reagan-Bush years had no interest in the subject (1990, pp. 413–14; 1993, p. 1329). Perhaps Bulmer-Thomas's conclusion that the new economic model was "not primarily adopted" to reduce poverty and improve distribution is the best summary (1996, p. 310).

4. IDB (1998b); see also World Bank (1995b and 1995c); ECLAC (1997); Edwards and Lustig (1997).

5. See especially the annual *Panorama Laboral de América Latina y el Caribe.*

the 1990s than in the last half of the 1980s, unemployment rose, informality increased, and improvement in real wages mainly benefited skilled workers. The explanation and remedy for these problems differ, however, with the IDB stressing the need for more flexible labor markets and the ILO more protection for workers.

Academic analysts, as well as ECLAC and the IDB, have done more work on equity. These studies express a difference of opinion on the impact of the reforms per se. While all authors agree that the distribution of income in Latin America is the most unequal in the world, the IDB analysis stresses that inequality increased primarily during the lost decade of the 1980s and that it did not get any worse during the 1990s. IDB authors go so far as to argue that the reforms actually improved distribution in comparison with what it would otherwise have been.[6] The studies included in the Bulmer-Thomas and Berry volumes, in contrast, argue that the reforms have led to further deterioration of an already deplorable situation.[7]

This chapter analyzes employment, equity, and the linkages between the two, always at the aggregate level. We argue that both employment and equity deteriorated as a result of the reforms, but that the changes were less dramatic than is often believed. While job creation slowed somewhat in the 1990s with respect to the 1950–80 base period, mainly because of slower GDP growth, the more serious problems arose because of the low quality of many new jobs. Primary distribution of income—the measure most closely related to the functioning of the economy—deteriorated somewhat in most of the project countries. This trend would probably be more pronounced if we had the proper data. Nonetheless, significant offsetting factors were also at work, especially the end of hyperinflation and the long-run impact of education trends; the household distribution patterns therefore changed less than was predicted, by either proponents or critics of the reforms.[8]

The chapter begins with demographic and educational shifts and their role in determining long-term trends in both employment and equity. It then moves to the impact of the reforms on employment, unemployment, and wages. Next it focuses on the wage differential and its role in linking labor markets and income distribution. The following sections examine

6. Londoño and Székely (1997); IDB (1997). For annual data and analysis of distribution trends, see ECLAC's *Social Panorama of Latin America*.

7. Bulmer-Thomas (1996); Berry (1998).

8. In his volume for the project, Morley (2000) stresses the lack of change in distribution. Our emphasis is slightly different, mainly because we give greater weight to the lack of data on the wealthy.

primary and household income distribution, analyzing their respective determinants in addition to the wage differential, with emphasis on the reforms. The final empirical section discusses the impact of social expenditure on employment and equity. We again conclude by identifying the questions that can and cannot be answered by aggregate-level analysis.

The Supply Side: Demography and Education

Experts clearly agree that long-term trends in employment are determined by changes in the labor supply. Specifically, changes in the economically active population (EAP) over the long run are explained by changes in the size of the working-age population (WAP) and the extent to which that population decides to participate in the labor market (the total participation rate, or TPR). The latter two variables have followed different trends in Latin America in the postwar period. On the one hand, as the demographic transition proceeds, the annual growth rate of the WAP is falling, reducing pressure on the labor market. On the other hand, the degree of labor force participation, which is the outcome of both long-term processes and temporary fluctuations, is still increasing, mainly because of greater female participation.

Among the nine project countries, Argentina, Chile, and Jamaica had the lowest rates of WAP growth in the 1990s with less than 2 percent per year, while Bolivia, Costa Rica, Mexico, and Peru had rates over 2.5 percent; Brazil and Colombia were in between. WAP trends are affected by migratory flows as well as by birth and death rates. In Argentina and Costa Rica, immigration contributed to a quickening of the WAP growth rate, while in Bolivia, Jamaica, Mexico, and Peru, emigration reduced this variable.

The participation rate reflected offsetting trends. As mentioned above, the most important factor raising the TPR was the increasing role of women in the labor force. Other processes, however, worked to reduce participation rates, including urbanization, growth in the education system, and increased coverage of the pension system. This second group of factors meant that people entered the labor force later and retired earlier. As a consequence, the TPR in the region as a whole grew by 0.2 percentage points per year between 1990 and 1997–98, thus maintaining the trend of the previous decade. Figure 5-1 combines the effects of demographic and participation changes to show their impact on the growth of the economically active population, which fell from 2.9 percent in the 1980s to 2.5 percent in the 1990s.

Figure 5-1. *Changes in Labor Supply, 1950–2000*[a]

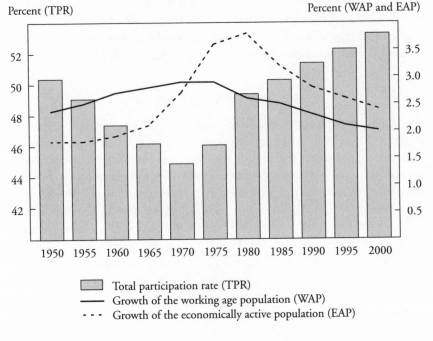

Percent (TPR)   Percent (WAP and EAP)

☐ Total participation rate (TPR)
— Growth of the working age population (WAP)
- - - Growth of the economically active population (EAP)

Source: Weller (2000).
a. Based on weighted averages for twenty Latin American countries.

These long-term trends are always subject to short-term variations caused by temporary economic circumstances. The TPR is particularly prone to fluctuate around its long-term trend rate, owing to the impact of supply and demand factors that change over the course of the business cycle. These variations consist mainly of people entering and leaving the labor market. Most of these people pertain to the secondary labor force, that is, household members who do not usually generate most of the family income.

The TPR fluctuates around its average in both the expansion and contraction stages of the cycle, and not always in the same direction. When the economy is expanding beyond its long-term trend rate, the TPR may increase because extra employment opportunities encourage people who were formerly inactive to seek work. If the expansionary phase of the cycle is a prolonged one, however, the TPR may fall as participants from the secondary labor force withdraw from the market to continue their studies or to take advantage of other opportunities. During downturns in the cycle (below the long-term trend), equivalent situations arise. The TPR may increase as the secondary labor force returns to the market; if the adverse economic conditions persist, participation may decline as people lose confidence in their prospects of finding work.[9]

The other important change in the labor force had to do with levels of education and experience. In terms of educational attainment, the general education indexes of the region at the beginning of the 1990s were quite good by international standards, especially for primary and tertiary education, although they lagged somewhat in the case of secondary schooling.[10] By the middle of the decade, almost all countries had achieved gross enrollment rates of close to 100 percent at the primary level, and enrollment at the higher levels had also increased.[11] Although young people spent more time in the education system, a high proportion of the labor force still had a very low level of education in most of the project countries. The situation was particularly serious in Brazil, where almost 60 percent of the work force had six years of schooling or less in the mid-1990s.[12] At the same time, the demographic transition and especially the fall-off in WAP growth led to an increase in the average age of the region's economically active population, meaning that the work force was more experienced and that pressure from the supply of inexperienced people had eased.

Changes in the education profile of the population have important implications for equity. Improving the education level at the bottom of the income distribution is one of the most important ways of making the distribution less regressive. The effect of increasing education at the other end of the distribution is more ambiguous: increasing the supply of skilled labor should drive down the wage premium of these individuals, but as long as demand is increasing faster than supply, the opposite will occur. Population trends interact with shifts in education stock. As the older generation

9. In the 1990s, for example, the TPR in Latin America went through the following fluctuations: (1) rising in the context of growth, due to a perception of opportunities from the demand side (1991–93); (2) falling, still in a growth situation, due to a lessening of pressure from the supply side (1994); (3) rising at a time of recession, due to greater supply pressure (1995); (4) falling in a recession, due to a perception that the demand situation was poor (1996); (5) a return to the first stage as growth recovered (1997); and (6) increasing participation during recession as in 1995 (1998).

10. IDB (1993).

11. ECLAC (1999d).

12. Weller (2000), on the basis of consultant reports. For a discussion of education problems in Brazil, see Birdsall and Sabot (1996).

Table 5-1. *Employment Growth and Elasticities, 1950s to 1990s*[a]
Annual weighted average

Period	GDP growth	Growth of employment	Employment elasticity re: output	Growth of wage employment	Wage employment elasticity re: output
1950s	5.1	1.9	0.4	2.5	0.5
1960s	5.7	2.3	0.4	2.7	0.5
1970s	5.6	3.8	0.7	4.7	0.8
1980s	1.2	2.9	2.6	2.4	2.0
1990–97	3.7	2.2	0.6	2.2	0.6
Average	4.3	2.6	0.9	2.9	0.9

Source: Weller (2000), on the basis of official statistics.

a. For the 1950s to 1970s, employment growth corresponds to growth of the labor force. From the 1950s through the 1980s, 20 countries are included; for 1990–97, the number is 17.

with poorer education levels disappears from the scene and the younger generation obtains more education than their parents and grandparents, this will eventually lead to greater equality.[13]

The Impact of the Reforms on Employment

The strong correlation between the labor supply and the generation of total employment causes difficulties for the analysis of labor demand and its possible relation to changes brought about by the reforms. To minimize this problem, we concentrate on trends among wage earners, a category more closely related to labor demand. Table 5-1 illustrates the differences between total employment and wage earners, as well as changes over time; it shows economic growth by decade in the postwar period, creation of total and wage employment, and the respective elasticities. Leaving aside the 1980s, which were clearly atypical,[14] elasticities did not differ significantly in the 1990s from the 1950–80 period. Insofar as the 1990s reflected the impact of the reforms, it can be inferred that the reforms did

13. For an analysis of the impact of demography on equity, see Duryea and Székely (1998).

14. Especially high elasticities in the 1980s resulted from an increasing labor supply in the face of very slow growth; nonetheless, the EAP was growing more slowly than in the 1970s.

Table 5-2. *Employment Growth and Elasticities, 1990–97*

Country	Growth of employment	Employment elasticity re: output	Growth of wage employment	Wage employment elasticity re: output
Argentina	1.7	0.4	2.3	0.5
Bolivia	6.6	1.6	4.7	1.1
Brazil	1.2	0.3	1.1	0.3
Chile	2.5	0.3	3.3	0.4
Colombia	1.4	0.3	1.1	0.2
Costa Rica	2.7	0.8	2.7	0.8
Jamaica	1.2	0.9	2.2	1.6
Mexico	2.9	1.1	4.0	1.5
Peru	3.8	0.6	1.7	0.3
Simple average	2.7	0.7	2.6	0.7

Source: Weller (2000), on the basis of official statistics.

not affect—either positively or negatively—the quantitative relationship between GDP growth and employment creation. Rather, what stands out in the table for the last decade are lower growth rates, which led to more sluggish employment creation, especially for wage earners.

The data in table 5-1, however, are weighted averages for the Latin American region, and as we have seen in previous chapters, comparisons over time based on weighted averages can be misleading because of the changing behavior of the largest economies. Table 5-2 focuses on the simple averages for the nine project countries during the 1990s. These were somewhat more positive than the weighted regional averages with respect to employment creation (mainly because of the relatively poor employment performance in Brazil) although not for elasticities. The nine countries displayed important differences, however: a relatively low elasticity for wage employment in five cases (Argentina, Brazil, Chile, Colombia, and Peru), a high elasticity in three (Bolivia, Jamaica, and Mexico), and an average elasticity in Costa Rica.

Moving from aggregate employment statistics to the types of jobs that were created in the 1990s, table 5-3 contrasts wage and nonwage work in the nine countries. The number of wage earners increased more slowly than the self-employed: 2.5 percent versus 2.7 percent on average for the

Table 5-3. *Employment Growth by Type of Job, 1990s*
Percent

Country (period)	Wage earners			Self-employed	Domestic service	Family members	Others	Total
	Private	*Public*	*Total*					
Change in employment								
Argentina (1991–97)	1.7	3.2	1.8	-1.0	2.3	n.a.	0.9	1.1
Bolivia (1990–97)	5.5	-1.4	4.7	5.5	-2.9	11.6	16.1	5.5
Brazil (1992–97)	1.1	1.0	1.1	1.5	3.8	-1.9	3.1	1.2
Chile (1990–97)	n.a.	n.a.	3.3	2.4	-0.6	-4.2	0.2	2.5
Colombia (1991–97)	1.4	-0.6	1.1	4.0	0.1	-7.5	-1.4	1.4
Costa Rica (1990–97)	3.5	0.1	2.7	2.8	2.8	-4.4	7.8	2.7
Jamaica (1989–96)	3.1	-1.8	2.2	-0.5	n.a.	-4.2	14.7	1.2
Mexico (1991–97)	4.1	3.4	4.0	4.1	8.4	3.0	-5.1	3.4
Peru (1991–97)	4.3	-4.7	1.7	5.3	1.7	n.a.	n.a.	3.8
Simple average	3.1	-0.1	2.5	2.7	2.0	-1.1	4.5	2.5
Contribution to total change								
Argentina (1991–97)	86.9	13.8	100.7	-20.0	14.7	0	4.5	100.0
Bolivia (1990–97)	42.8	-1.4	41.4	34.7	-2.8	12.3	14.4	100.0
Brazil (1992–97)	45.0	4.0	49.0	34.2	22.5	-15.7	10.0	100.0
Chile (1990–97)	n.a.	n.a.	84.1	22.4	-1.4	-5.5	0.3	100.0
Colombia (1991–97)	47.4	-3.7	43.8	92.0	0.2	-31.3	-5.0	100.0
Costa Rica (1990–97)	63.9	0.7	64.6	20.0	4.4	-6.7	17.7	100.0
Jamaica (1989–96)	122.0	-16.5	105.5	-11.8	0	-16.0	22.2	100.0
Mexico (1991–97)	57.9	4.3	62.2	28.7	9.0	11.2	-11.0	100.0
Peru (1991–97)	32.3	-13.9	18.4	81.0	0.6	0	0	100.0
Simple average	n.a.	n.a.	63.3	31.2	5.2	-5.7	5.9	100.0

Source: Weller (2000), on the basis of national household surveys.

nine. Given the employment structure, however, new wage jobs accounted for 63 percent of all new employment, while self-employment contributed 31 percent. Within the wage-earner category, private sector jobs increased at a 3 percent annual rate, while public sector jobs shrank.

In three of the nine countries (Bolivia, Colombia, and Peru) wage jobs grew more slowly than total employment, in part because private firms could not compensate for the significant contraction of employment in the public sector. In Argentina, Chile, Jamaica, and Mexico, wage-earner categories grew faster in relative terms, increasing their weight in the total employment structure. In Brazil and Costa Rica, wage earners as a group grew at about the same rate as total employment.

According to ILO data, the increase in the number of wage earners in the private sector in the 1990s was concentrated in microenterprises (that is, with fewer than six workers) and small firms (between six and twenty workers). Jobs in these two groups grew at 3.7 percent between 1990 and 1998 in comparison to only 2.3 percent in medium-size and large firms.[15] The ILO's concept of the informal sector, which has permeated the literature on employment, combines jobs in the microfirm and the nonwage categories. Although the definition of the concept centers on the productivity level of firms, in practice it has been measured by a proxy that groups microenterprises, the self-employed, domestic service, and nonremunerated family members. On this basis, nearly 60 percent of new jobs in the seven project countries with data available were in the informal sector. They were especially prevalent in Brazil, where formal sector jobs fell in absolute terms, and in Colombia. Informal jobs were least important in Argentina and Chile.[16] The idea behind the concept of the informal sector is that this type of job is of low quality, with poor working conditions, low salaries and productivity, and a lack of legal and social protection. Clearly this is not completely true, since both the self-employed and some microenterprises include good jobs. The concept continues to be used because of lack of information on the characteristics of such occupations and the assumption that the majority are indeed precarious.

More precarious yet is the situation of the unemployed, whose presence in Latin America increased. Unemployment fell only slightly in the 1990s in comparison to the 1980s, despite higher growth of GDP. Average

15. ILO (1999). The figures are based on weighted averages for twelve countries.

16. Estimated from data in ILO (1999). No information is available for Bolivia and Jamaica. Note that these estimations of increased informality are substantially lower than those shown in previous ILO publications, due to changes in definitions and sampling methods.

Table 5-4. *Unemployment Rates, 1990–98*

Percent

Country	1990	1991	1992	1993	1994	1995	1996	1997	1998
Argentina	7.4	6.5	7.0	9.6	11.5	17.5	17.2	14.9	12.9
Bolivia	7.3	5.8	5.4	5.8	3.1	3.6	3.8	4.4	4.1
Brazil	4.3	4.8	5.8	5.4	5.1	4.6	5.4	5.7	7.6
Chile	7.8	8.2	6.7	6.5	7.8	7.4	6.4	6.1	6.4
Colombia	10.5	10.2	10.2	8.6	8.9	8.8	11.2	12.4	15.3
Costa Rica	5.4	6.0	4.3	4.0	4.3	5.7	6.6	5.9	5.4
Jamaica	15.3	15.4	15.7	16.3	15.4	16.2	16.0	16.5	15.5
Mexico	2.7	2.7	2.8	3.4	3.7	6.2	5.5	3.7	3.2
Peru	8.3	5.9	9.4	9.9	8.8	8.2	8.0	9.2	8.4
Simple average	7.7	7.3	7.5	7.7	7.6	8.7	8.9	8.8	8.8

Source: Project database, on the basis of ECLAC statistics.

unemployment in the project countries in 1980–89 was 9.2 percent, falling to 8.2 percent in 1990–98.[17] Not surprisingly, unemployment jumped in Mexico and Argentina in 1995, although jobs recovered fairly quickly in Mexico. Later in the decade, unemployment rose in Colombia, in particular, and in Brazil, as GDP growth rates fell in those two countries, and unemployment rates remained high in Argentina. Table 5-4 shows that the simple average for unemployment in project countries rose from 7.6 percent in 1994 to nearly 9.0 percent in 1995 and remained at that level through 1998. With the generalized fall in growth rates in South America in 1999, unemployment reached historic highs in that subregion.

The other side of the labor market equation involves remunerations. Average real wages in the formal sector in Latin America as a whole, as well as in the project countries, improved during the 1990s or at least held their own. In Argentina, Mexico, and Peru, however, wages in 1998 were lower than in 1980 (see table 5-5). Because of the especially large drop in Peru between 1980 and 1990, the simple average for the nine countries also remained lower in 1998 than in 1980. In five countries, real wages fell at

17. The sharp drop in Jamaica's traditionally high rates of unemployment skews the simple averages. Excluding Jamaica, unemployment among project countries actually rose from 6.9 to 7.2 percent between the 1980s and 1990s.

Table 5-5. *Average Real Wages in the Formal Sector, 1980–98*
1990 = 100

Country	1980	1991	1992	1993	1994	1995	1996	1997	1998
Argentina[a]	130.0	101.4	102.7	101.3	102.0	100.9	100.7	100.2	99.1
Bolivia[b]	64.9	93.4	97.1	103.6	111.8	112.6	113.9	123.1	127.5
Brazil[c]	91.3	85.2	83.3	91.5	92.2	95.7	103.3	106.0	106.1
Chile[d]	95.4	104.9	109.6	113.5	118.8	123.6	128.7	131.8	135.3
Colombia[e]	85.0	97.4	98.6	103.2	104.1	105.4	107.0	109.8	108.4
Costa Rica[f]	115.8	95.4	99.3	109.5	113.6	111.4	109.1	110.0	117.6
Jamaica[g]	103.4	71.4	75.4	91.6	108.4	105.0	106.7	117.5	120.9
Mexico[a]	128.3	106.5	114.3	124.5	130.4	113.5	102.3	101.1	103.9
Peru[h]	309.3	115.2	111.1	110.2	127.4	116.7	111.2	110.4	108.2
Simple average	124.8	96.8	99.0	105.4	112.1	109.4	109.2	112.2	114.1

Source: Weller (2000), on the basis of official statistics.
a. Manufacturing industry.
b. Private sector in La Paz; figure for 1980 is actually for 1985.
c. Workers covered by social and labor legislation.
d. Average wages of nonagricultural workers until April 1993; then general index of hourly wages.
e. Blue-collar workers in manufacturing.
f. Workers affiliated with social security system.
g. Nonagricultural workers in the private sector; figure for 1980 is actually for 1986.
h. Private sector workers in Lima.

the beginning of the 1990s but then recovered (Bolivia, Brazil, Colombia, Costa Rica, and Jamaica). Mexico and Peru experienced the opposite trend, with an early increase followed by declines; in the Mexican case, this trend was clearly the result of the 1995 financial crisis. In Argentina, the elimination of inflation was accompanied by nearly constant real wages. Only Chile had continuous increases throughout the decade.

Theory tells us that there should be a trade-off between wages and volume of employment created. On the surface, this does not appear to have occurred among project countries during the 1990s. That is, wages rose everywhere (except Argentina), but both employment and unemployment behavior varied widely across countries (with increased unemployment in Argentina).[18] One hypothesis is that regional labor markets are far

18. Econometric analysis in Weller (2000) shows a negative relationship between employment creation and wages, but the coefficient is not significant. See table 5-7 in this chapter.

Table 5-6. *Changes in Labor Market Indicators, 1990s*[a]

Country	Occupation level[b]	Unemploy-ment[c]	Wage employment[d]	Real wage[e]	Labor productivity[f]
Argentina	−	−	+	=	+
Bolivia	+	+	−	+	−
Brazil	−	−	=	+	+
Chile	+	+	+	+	+
Colombia	=	−	−	+	+
Costa Rica	+	=	=	+	+
Jamaica	−	=	+	+	−
Mexico	+	−	+	+	=
Peru	+	−	−	+	+

Source: Weller (2000), based on consultant reports.

a. The evaluation refers to changes between the beginning of the 1990s and 1998 (Bolivia and Peru: 1997). + means a favorable change; - means an unfavorable change; = means very little or no change.

b. Change in the rate of employment (employed as share of WAP).

c. Change in unemployment rate (unemployed as share of EAP).

d. Growth of wage employment with respect to total employment.

e. Change in real average wages in the formal sector.

f. Change in average labor productivity.

from equilibrium, but a proper analysis of this topic would require better data than are currently available. Sectoral-level data are particularly important, since labor markets in Latin America tend to be heavily segmented by sectors as well as by other characteristics.

Table 5-6 provides a simple qualitative summary of various changes: the employment rate, unemployment, wage employment compared to total employment, real wages, and labor productivity. The table assigns a plus where conditions improved, a minus where they deteriorated, and an equal sign where they remained relatively constant, which enables us to compare across issue areas and across countries. The most positive trends occurred with respect to real wages, which were often linked to productivity rises. Rising unemployment appears to be the biggest problem; it was also frequently related to productivity but in an inverse direction. Changes in the level and type of employment (wage earners as a share of total new jobs) occupy intermediate positions in the nine countries.

Table 5-6 also provides the basis for comparing labor market results across the nine countries. If we convert the pluses and minuses into +1 and

−1, Chile clearly emerges at the top with positive marks in all five categories (a score of 5). Costa Rica follows with a score of 3, reflecting a weaker performance in unemployment and the creation of wage jobs. Mexico also displays a relatively positive pattern, with a score of 2, despite the increased unemployment and drop in wages resulting from the 1994–95 crisis. Bolivia and Peru scored 1 in this exercise. Both faced increasing informalization in the 1990s; Bolivia also suffered from low productivity and Peru from unemployment and underemployment. Argentina, Brazil, Colombia, and Jamaica had the most difficult labor conditions. They shared a general set of characteristics featuring weak generation of employment (and thus high unemployment), accompanied by increases in productivity (except Jamaica), but only moderate growth of salaries.

How do the overall trends among labor variables and the specific differences among countries relate to the reforms? Up till now, we have been examining trends in the 1990s as a proxy for the post-reform period, but Weller's book for the project provides elements to link reforms and employment more directly. Table 5-7 reports the results of an econometric exercise to test the relevance of several variables, including the reforms.[19] The table first shows a basic equation in which growth of employment is the dependent variable, and GDP growth, salaries, a trend term to represent technological progress, the real exchange rate, and economic openness are independent variables. Only the growth rate, together with the real exchange rate and the openness variable, are statistically significant at the 5 percent level. Equations (2) through (4) add three measures of the reform index. These include the average reform index, trade reform, and capital account opening, expressed in five-year averages. All coefficients are negative and significant.

Two main conclusions emerge from the table. First, expansion of output is closely related to the generation of employment. Our hypothesis, which is embodied in figure 1-1 (chapter 1), is that GDP growth is the main transmission mechanism between the reforms and the quantitative dimension of employment. The implication is that the weak growth rates of the 1990s—in comparison to the earlier years of the postwar period, not to the 1980s—caused a good part of the employment problem. The stop-go pattern that characterized growth in the 1990s further hindered job

---

19. Weller (2000, chapter 4). The econometric analysis was carried out by Lucas Navarro.

Table 5-7. *Determinants of Employment Creation*[a]

Independent variable	(1)	(2)	(3)	(4)
GDP	0.402	0.389	0.299	0.331
	(6.168)	(6.022)	(5.046)	(5.469)
Real wages	−0.050	−0.031	−0.033	−0.040
	(−1.014)	(−0.655)	(−0.707)	(−0.837)
Trend	−0.077			
	(−1.494)			
Real exchange rate	0.046	0.043	0.041	0.049
	(2.136)	(2.082)	(2.088)	(2.288)
Trade openness	−0.148	−0.079	−0.082	−0.113
	(−2.317)	(−1.138)	(−1.230)	(−1.802)
Average reform index		−0.063		
		(−2.776)		
Trade reform index			−0.066	
			(−2.866)	
Capital account index				−0.030
				(−2.586)
Summary statistic				
R^2	0.377	0.392	0.395	0.387
Adjusted R^2	0.284	0.301	0.305	0.296
N	78	78	78	78

Source: Weller (2000); t statistics are shown in parentheses.

a. The dependent variable for all equations is the first difference of the logs of the number of occupied persons. The model is a panel, using fixed effects and ordinary least squares estimation, for data on six countries (Argentina, Brazil, Chile, Colombia, Costa Rica, and Mexico) for the period 1985–98. Independent variables are the first difference of the logs of GDP, the real wage in the formal sector, an index of the real exchange rate, the ratio of exports plus imports to GDP, and the reform indexes described in chapter 3. All variables except GDP and wages are five-year averages.

creation. High and stable growth of output would appear to be a crucial prerequisite for increasing job growth.

A second conclusion drawn from the econometric analysis is that the reforms hindered the growth of employment.[20] The coefficient indicates that a 10 percent increase in the average reform index led to a decline in employment creation of about 0.4 points. As was the case with the analysis

20. These results are consistent with such studies as IDB (1997) and Márquez and Pagés (1998).

of growth, the importance of the impact varies with the base rate of employment growth. The higher this rate, the smaller the negative impact. Of course, in so far as the reforms increase growth, this partially offsets the negative impact of the reforms per se. Nonetheless, the direct effect is clearly negative. This conclusion holds for both the average reform index and for trade and capital account reforms. It also holds in both the short and medium run.

Although not shown in the table, other exercises indicate that the negative impact was especially strong for the manufacturing sector.[21] There are at least two reasons that the sectoral analyses provide stronger conclusions. On the one hand, the data are of better quality than for the labor force as a whole. Also only wage earners are included, such that labor supply factors are weaker as a determinant of employment creation. On the other hand, manufacturing is the sector most likely to have been hurt by increased imports deriving from trade reform.

The impact of the reforms on employment occurred in distinct phases. As discussed in the previous chapter, investors hesitated to put new money into big projects in the immediate aftermath of the reforms, especially since these were frequently accompanied by macroeconomic instability. The resulting uncertainty led them to concentrate on defensive activities, which included disembodied technological change, cost cutting, downsizing, and layoffs; this pattern was especially prevalent in the tradables sectors. Only after the reforms gained more credibility did firms begin to invest and hire more workers.

Using annual data to examine the pattern of employment in the pre-reform, reform, and post-reform periods for each of the nine project countries, Weller confirms that phases existed in employment as well as in investment.[22] Not surprisingly, the employment patterns were not simple. While employment generally fell in the immediate aftermath of the reforms, particular country characteristics and the international context caused significant differences. For example, the sequencing of stabilization and reforms appears to have been important, as were sociopolitical aspects of domestic conditions at the time the reforms were initiated. The evolution of the international economy, especially with respect to the availability of international finance, was also relevant.

---

21. Weller (2000, chapter 4). For the manufacturing sector, the adjusted R^2 rises from the range of .22 to .28 shown in table 5-7 to a range of .52 to .60. The size of the coefficients also increases.

22. Weller (2000, chapter 4).

Another factor that has to be taken into account is the previous situation with respect to employment itself. Three of the four aggressive reformers (Argentina, Bolivia, and Peru) had experienced significant declines in employment rates prior to the reforms, because of especially difficult internal conditions that led people to withdraw from the labor market.[23] For this reason, participation rates surged after the reforms and stabilization, which stimulated increased employment from the supply side and offset the expected downturn. The tendency toward lower elasticities and employment rates could also be counteracted by especially dynamic GDP growth rates.

Inconsistency between the reforms and the macroeconomic policies accompanying them further weakened the ability of many economies to create jobs. An overvalued exchange rate, in conjunction with the trade opening, stimulated imports, and undermined exports. Firms that produced import-competing goods were under special pressure, and part of their initial response was to dismiss workers. In addition, the combination of reforms and an overvalued exchange rate affected the relative prices of capital and labor, lowering the former with respect to the latter. The outcome was an incentive to substitute capital for labor, especially unskilled labor. This set of issues is better studied at the sectoral level, since not all sectors were affected in the same way; the analysis will thus be taken up in the next chapter.

Wages and the Wage Differential

As discussed above, real wages increased in the 1990s in all nine project countries, with the exception of Argentina where they remained stationary throughout the decade. This conclusion, however, is based on the behavior of average wages in the formal sector, and in some cases data are only available for the capital city or are limited to the manufacturing sector. A great deal of work is clearly needed to improve the data on remunerations in general, but our particular concern in this section is to decompose average wages to see what happened to the remunerations of different categories of workers. The literature suggests the wage differential is a key link between labor markets and income distribution.[24]

---

23. The fourth aggressive reformer, Chile, also had a decline in the employment rate, but in this case it was due to a long-term decline in the participation rate.

24. Bulmer-Thomas (1996); ECLAC (1997); IDB (1998b).

Table 5-8. *Wage Differentials by Education Level, 1990s*[a]
Percent

Country (period)	University graduates vs. average wage		University graduates vs. 7–9 years of education	
	Initial year[b]	Final year[c]	Initial year[b]	Final year[c]
Argentina (1991–97)	164.3	169.6	218.3	227.9
Bolivia (1989– 96)	235.0	292.9	251.8	506.4
Brazil (1992–97)	380.2	383.5	553.2	553.3
Chile (1990–96)	231.6	247.9	366.1	448.6
Colombia (1988–95)	222.2	261.6	276.7	327.2
Costa Rica (1990–96)	285.0	273.2	323.1	316.7
Mexico (1991–97)	182.1	232.1	160.1	302.2
Peru (1991–97)	220.7	275.0	321.0	403.1
Simple average	240.1	267.0	308.8	385.7

Source: Weller (2000), on the basis of consultant reports.
a. Ratio of average wages of specified groups.
b. Initial year of period indicated for each country.
c. Final year of period indicated for each country.

The aim is to study the divergence (if any) in trends between the wages of high- and low-skill workers. This can be operationalized in several ways; the most common is by educational level. Weller compares two versions of an education-based wage gap during the 1990s: (1) the difference between wages for workers with university education and those with the average remuneration level of the sample and (2) university graduates versus those with 7-9 years of schooling (the equivalent of complete primary education, or perhaps a bit more depending on the educational structure of each country) (see table 5-8). The second method generally resulted in a larger differential.[25] An increase in the differential is found in all cases except Costa Rica, although it is small in Argentina and negligible in Brazil.

Morley uses slightly different periods and compares university graduates to those having only primary education. His data indicate a similar pattern with some exceptions.[26] For example, the differentials in Argentina and Brazil were substantially larger than those shown in table 5-8, and Chile, like Costa Rica, suffered no increase in the wage gap. These differ-

25. Weller (2000, chapter 6).
26. Morley (2000, chapter 5).

ences are accounted for partly by the difference in base years for the comparisons. Morley's analysis of Chile is based on the period 1987–96, while Weller uses 1990–96. The difference was crucial since the wage gap shrank in the 1987–90 period, only to open up again in the 1990s. Furthermore, the group used for comparison with university graduates in the Morley analysis was broader than that used by Weller; it included workers with less than complete secondary education, rather than primary. Morley also included Jamaica, which was excluded by Weller for lack of information. Finally, Weller used wage earners as the population for analysis, whereas Morley used the population as a whole. These kinds of differences clearly affect the results, so care must be taken in interpreting them. Nonetheless, the majority of trends are similar in the two sources.

Another way to operationalize the wage differential is to compare results for white-collar and blue-collar workers. Data are available for a number of countries including Chile, Colombia, Costa Rica, Mexico, and Peru. Almost all cases show the same pattern as that embodied in the educational comparisons: white-collar workers received larger wage increases than did blue-collar workers, again with the exception of Costa Rica.[27]

Both of these measures point to a widening gap in wages based on skill level, which is the opposite of what proponents of the reforms expected. Theoretical analysis would point to relative prices favoring cheaper capital over more expensive labor as the main cause of the phenomenon. This change in relative prices would lead to a substitution of labor by capital and thus a higher capital-labor ratio. According to data gathered by Morley, however, relative price trends did not manifest themselves in any consistent pattern with respect to the capital-labor ratio in project countries. The ratio rose in Brazil, Chile, Costa Rica, and Mexico in the 1990s, fell in Argentina, Bolivia, and Peru, and remained about the same in Colombia and Jamaica.[28]

If relative prices do not explain the widening wage gap, one alternative is firm restructuring that was not associated with skilled labor as a complement to capital. For example, restructuring that involved increased use of

27. García-Huidobro (1999); Ramírez and Núñez (1999); Montiel (1999); López (1999); Saavedra and Díaz (1999). There is also some indication of an increased wage gap between small and large firms, but the differences are not large and information is not available for many countries (Weller, 2000).

28. Morley (2000, chapter 5). Morley's calculations are based on the Penn Tables. Other project data shows a somewhat closer relationship, but there still is no strong correlation between the wage gap and the capital-labor ratio.

outsourcing for services could lead to the employment of more skilled workers in the tertiary sector and fewer unskilled workers within the firm itself. The operation of the labor market provides another explanation: the declining strength of unions probably played a role in some countries, since less-skilled workers were less likely to be represented by labor unions, as did policy with respect to the minimum wage, which has frequently been allowed to lag with respect to the average wage.

Trends in Primary Income Distribution

The income distribution that is most closely linked to outcomes from the labor market is the primary distribution, which measures income accruing to the factors of production. The available data mainly consider labor and to a limited extent capital; we have no data on other factors, notably land. This distribution, in which the unit of analysis is the individual, differs from the household-based measures that are most commonly cited, and the trends may be different. The primary distribution is the most relevant, however, insofar as we are trying to understand the impact of the reforms on distribution, and the operation of the labor market is a key intervening factor. Note that it does not incorporate the role of unemployment since it includes only those individuals with "earned" income.[29]

Table 5-9 shows both primary and household distributions for project countries, as calculated by Morley from consultant reports.[30] All of the data come from the household surveys that are now routinely administered throughout the region. These instruments provide a great deal of information on household characteristics and on certain types of income. Nonetheless, they have two major flaws in terms of studying the impact of the reforms on distribution. First, they do not necessarily include all types of income; for example, profits would not normally be included. Second, they do not sample the wealthiest groups in society, which we have reason to believe were primary beneficiaries of the reforms.[31] The analysis below

29. It is extremely complicated to go from primary to household distribution on an empirical basis. A simulation method for doing so is being used in a joint UNDP/ECLAC/IDB project; see Vos and others (forthcoming).

30. Morley (2000, chapter 5).

31. Examples of the processes through which this may have occurred include the sale at subsidized prices of many state firms, one-time gains on the newly reinvigorated regional stock markets, privileged access to newly liberalized financial markets to leverage existing capital, tax reforms that lowered marginal rates on the highest incomes, high interest rates that benefited holders of financial wealth, and the use of public money to rescue private sector banks.

Table 5-9. *Primary and Household Distribution of Income*

Country	Pre-reform	Post-reform	Latest
Primary distribution[a]			
Argentina[b]	.293 (1986)	.268 (1991)	.283 (1996)
Bolivia[b]	.668 (1985)	.486 (1989)	.595 (1996)
Brazil	.680 (1985)	.700 (1990)	.710 (1997)
Chile	n.a.	.658 (1987)	.636 (1996)
Colombia[b]	.582 (1988)	.596 (1993)	.625 (1996)
Costa Rica	n.a.	.490 (1988)	.478 (1995)
Jamaica	n.a.	n.a.	n.a.
Mexico	.200 (1984)	.270 (1989)	.290 (1996)
Peru	.579 (1985)	.502 (1991)	.485 (1996)
Household distribution[c]			
Argentina[a]	.407 (1986)	.461 (1991)	.486 (1996)
Bolivia[a]	.590 (1985)	.430 (1989)	.480 (1996)
Brazil	.590 (1985)	.610 (1990)	.590 (1997)
Chile	n.a.	.560 (1987)	.553 (1996)
Colombia	.516 (1978)	.531 (1991)	.533 (1995)
Costa Rica	.500 (1986)	.466 (1988)	.456 (1995)
Jamaica[d]	.436 (1989)	.382 (1993)	.369 (1996)
Mexico	.474 (1984)	.537 (1989)	.540 (1994)
Peru	.519 (1985)	.467 (1991)	.435 (1996)

Source: Morley (2000), on the basis of consultant reports.

a. Theil index. Wide differences in the size of the index for primary distribution are because of the particular subgroups of the population that were analyzed.

b. Urban only.

c. Gini coefficient.

d. Expenditure rather than income data.

thus probably underestimates the impact of the reforms in increasing inequality.

We were able to study the primary distribution in only eight of the nine project countries; data are not available for Jamaica. The Theil index is used for measuring the primary distribution. (For information on this index and a comparison with the better known Gini coefficient, see box 5-1.) Three patterns can be distinguished among the cases. A first involves declining inequality in Chile (in the 1990s), Costa Rica, and Peru. Prereform measures were not available for Chile or Costa Rica, but comparing the early post-reform years with the latest available observation shows that inequality decreased slightly. A second pattern is found in Brazil, Colombia, and Mexico, where inequality increased from the pre-reform period to the latest year. Again, none of the changes was very large. Finally, Argentina and Bolivia followed a mixed pattern with a decline in inequality between the pre-reform and early post-reform period, after which inequality began to rise again. It is important to stress that these results pertain only to reforms in the 1980s and 1990s. Both Chile and Argentina suffered significant increases in inequality during their reform experiences in the 1970s, although it is hard to determine whether this arose because of the reforms per se or the repressive policies of the military governments.[32]

Data on trends in household distribution for all nine project countries are also shown in table 5-9, this time using the Gini coefficient. In the majority of the cases, the patterns are similar to those for primary distribution. The most important exception is the continuing increase in inequality in Argentina in the household data. This difference is likely due to the fact that the household data capture the impact of unemployment, which was rising rapidly in Argentina. In addition, Brazil does not demonstrate a clear trend in household distribution. There is also an earlier observation for Costa Rica, which indicates that inequality fell throughout the period as in the primary distribution. Finally household distribution data (of expenditure) are available for Jamaica; they show greater equality over the period.

The trends in primary distribution are related to trends in the wage gap. For the first two groups of countries above, the wage gap generally behaved in the same way as the distribution measures. That is, the wage gap shrank in Chile and Costa Rica and income distribution improved.[33] Likewise, the gap widened in Brazil, Colombia, and Mexico, and income distribution became more unequal. The situation is more complicated for Argentina, Bolivia, and Peru. These countries experienced very high inflation around the time the reforms were implemented. Theory and empirical evidence tell us that lowering high inflation will have a positive impact on distribution because inflation levies a heavy tax on the poorest groups in society.[34] This factor was at least partially responsible for the one-time improvement of distribution in Argentina and Bolivia, after which inequality

32. On distribution in the 1970s, see Berry (1998). On Argentina in the 1970s, see Altimir and Becarria (1999); on Chile, see Larrañaga (1999).

33. This is according to the Morley data, which differ for Chile in comparison with Weller's data; see earlier discussion in the text.

34. Morley (1995, especially chapter 7).

Box 5-1. *Two Measures of Inequality*

There are various measures of inequality, all of which are highly correlated. This chapter uses two measures: the Gini coefficient and the Theil index.

Definitions

The **Gini coefficient** is a summary statistic derived from the Lorenz curve. This curve plots cumulative percentages of total income received against cumulative percentages of income recipients, starting with the smallest income recipient. The Gini coefficient gives the area between the observed Lorenz curve and the line of absolute equality as a proportion of the total area under the line of absolute equality. The formal representation is:

$$G = (N + 1)/N - (2/N) \sum_i q_i$$

N is the number of equal-sized groups (for example, income deciles) into which the population is divided
q_i is the cumulative share of income received by each group

In principle, the Gini can vary between 0 (perfect equality) and 1 (perfect inequality). In practice, it normally varies between around 0.25 and 0.60.

The **Theil index** is a measure of income inequality within a specific population. If a population is partitioned in a definite number of groups such that each individual in the population belongs to one and only one group, the index can be decomposed into two elements. One component (B) measures the contribution of inequality *between* groups' average incomes to total income inequality. The other component (W) measures the contribution on inequality *within* each group to total inequality. Likely groups would involve education, sector, region, and so on. The formal representation is:

began to increase again, in line with the skill gap. Peru presents a special case in that the wage gap increased substantially, but the index suggests that inequality fell slightly. This seemingly greater equality was really less dispersion around a declining average income in the 1985–90 period; that is, everyone was getting poorer.[35] In the 1990s, per capita income growth was positive although poverty continued to rise.

35. A similar phenomenon, but in a more extreme form, holds for Jamaica. Although no data are available for primary distribution, household income distribution was improving during a period in which per capita income was falling.

$$T = B + W = \sum_i y_i \ln(y_i/p_i) + \sum_i y_i T_i$$

T is the Theil index for the total population
y_i is the income share of the ith group
p_i is the population share of the ith group
T_i is the Theil index for the ith group

The Theil index varies between 0 (perfect equality) and log N (perfect inequality), where N is the size of the population. The index can be normalized to fall into a 0 to 1 range.

Advantages

The main advantage of the **Gini coefficient** is that its values are easily interpretable. A disadvantage is that different Lorenz curves can have the same Gini coefficient.

The main advantage of the **Theil index** is that it is decomposable. Its two components indicate the sources of inequality.

Differences

For any given distribution of income, the relative level of the Gini and the Theil would be similar although the Theil has a slightly wider range. The two indexes give different weights to different parts of the distribution under consideration. The Gini coefficient gives more weight to the middle part of the distribution, while the Theil gives more weight to the lowest deciles.

Further evidence on the process behind the inequality trends can be obtained by decomposing the Theil index to cast light on sources of inequality. Decompositions were carried out for a number of variables: education, occupation, age, gender, and rural-urban location. Table 5-10 shows the education decomposition, which is the most important. The total indexes (which are generally the same as those shown for primary distribution in table 5-9) are divided into two components: variation in inequality explained by differences between groups with different levels of education and variation explained by differences within those same groups; together

Table 5-10. *Decomposition for Theil Index of Education*

Country	Total Theil			Percent contribution to total variation — Variation within groups			Variation between groups		
Argentina	1986 0.293	1991 0.268	1997 0.283	1986 73.0	1991 70.9	1997 66.1	1986 27.0	1991 29.1	1997 33.9
Bolivia	1985 0.668	1989 0.486	1996 0.595	1985 88.2	1989 80.0	1996 70.3	1985 11.8	1989 20.0	1996 29.7
Brazil	1985 0.772	1990 0.854	1997 0.809	1985 61.1	1990 61.8	1997 65.0	1985 38.9	1990 38.2	1997 35.0
Chile	n.a.	1987 0.653	1996 0.636	n.a.	1987 100	1996 77.9	n.a.	1987 0	1996 22.1
Colombia	1988 0.432	1993 0.522	1996 0.457	1988 73.3	1993 76.5	1996 63.5	1988 26.7	1993 23.5	1996 36.5
Costa Rica	n.a.	1988 0.355	1995 0.328	n.a.	1988 68.9	1995 62.6	n.a.	1988 31.1	1995 37.4
Jamaica	1989 0.341	1993 0.26	1996 0.251	1989 96.0	1993 83.2	1996 83.6	1989 4.0	1993 16.8	1996 16.4
Mexico	1984 0.20	1989 0.27	1996 0.29	1984 80.0	1989 77.8	1996 89.7	1984 20.0	1989 22.2	1996 10.3
Peru	1985 0.537	1991 0.435	1996 0.386	1985 87.9	1991 90.6	1996 79.0	1985 12.1	1991 9.4	1996 21.0

Source: Morley (2000), on the basis of consultant reports.

the two must sum to 100 percent. Groups, in this case, were usually defined as those with less than primary education, completed primary schooling, completed secondary schooling, and some university education or more.

Differences between average incomes of groups with different education levels (for example, average income of university graduates versus that for people with only primary education) were a significant and rising source of inequality in this analysis. According to table 5-10, the differences between groups generally explain anywhere between one-fifth and one-third of inequality in the primary distribution of income.[36] The share increased in every country except Brazil and Chile. This evidence is broadly consistent with trends in the skill differential, suggesting that differences in education, which have always been an important factor in distribution, have become even more important in recent years.

According to Morley, the relatively small change in income distribution in many of the countries seems to result from two offsetting features of the changing education structure of the labor force and its effect on labor market outcomes. On the one hand, inequality increased as a greater share of income went to the most-educated segment of society. The skill-intensive growth of the 1990s further increased the variance of income among the educated: post-reform growth created opportunities that were primarily open to the best educated, not just the well educated. On the other hand, progressive trends were also at work. Improvements in education moved people up the distribution. This is progressive because a smaller fraction of the labor force was in the lower end of the distribution. It is especially important because the variance of income among the less educated was in many cases bigger than it was for the better educated (for example, greater differences in income among workers in microenterprises than among those working for large firms). On balance, even in most countries with rising wage inequality, these various effects just about cancelled each other out, and the distribution changed less than would have been expected on the basis of the wage differentials alone.[37]

As important as wage differentials and intergroup inequality were, Morley indicates that they only explained about one-third of total income variance. That means that two-thirds must have come from other sources. Some of these sources are captured in the other decompositions that were

36. Jamaica has a lower level of between-group variation, probably due to the use of expenditure rather than income data. Expenditure data are known to be more equally distributed than those for income.

37. For more details on this argument, see Morley (2000, chapter 5).

carried out. Differences in average income across occupational groups proved to be the second largest source of inequality after education, accounting for anywhere from 20 to 38 percent of the total. Although each of the country studies had a different breakdown of occupations, the typical one included owners or employers, employees, self-employed or the informal sector, and in some cases also government and agriculture. Thus, for example, if the average income of employers increased in comparison to employees, this would increase between-group variance. Of the seven countries with data available with respect to occupation, all saw an increase in between-group variance in the 1990s, although the change was small in Brazil and Colombia; data are unavailable for Chile and Jamaica.[38]

Gender and urban-rural location do not appear to have been important sources of inequality; each accounted for less than 10 percent of the total despite big differences in income between groups. Although this result contradicts some studies that focus on the importance of urban-rural differentials, it is due to the way that the Theil index is calculated. The small share of women in the work force and of the rural population in the total population holds down the between-group variance.

The case study on Argentina combined the various factors just discussed into a single analysis, to arrive at the cumulative impact of between-group variance in education, occupation, age, and sector. Each was added after taking account of the impact of those already in the analysis. Together, they explained 48 percent of the variance in inequality among the entire work force of Greater Buenos Aires in 1986 before the reforms and 58 percent in 1997. When the population was limited to wage earners, the percentages were five to seven points higher.[39]

The most important result of the decomposition analysis was to reinforce the importance of educational differences in creating inequality, as already suggested in the behavior of the education-based skill gap. Additional evidence on this effect comes from special studies carried out by project consultants on the top income groups in the household surveys. According to Morley's analysis of these studies, decomposition of the Theil index between university graduates and all others showed that the contribution of the university group to overall inequality was so great that it completely offset favorable trends in the rest of the population. Put another way, earnings inequality would have declined in every country, with

38. Morley (2000, chapter 5).
39. Altimir and Beccaria (1999).

the possible exception of Argentina, had it not been for increased inequality within the university group and between it and everyone else.[40]

The Impact of the Reforms on Household Income Distribution

The more extensive data that exist on household distribution, in comparison with primary distribution, enable us to move beyond before-and-after analysis and to estimate directly the impact of the reforms on equity. To do so, Morley constructed a regression model for the nine project countries (plus seven others) for the period 1970–95.[41] The strategy was to build a model based on variables identified in the literature as affecting distribution and then to add the reform indexes (see table 5-11).

In contrast to almost all other studies, Morley finds evidence of the existence of a so-called Kuznets curve.[42] This is the inverted U-shaped curve discovered by Simon Kuznets in the 1950s to fit the relation between income and its distribution in the United States and Britain. Kuznets argues that on the way up the income curve, distribution becomes more unequal, while beyond an inflection point, inequality falls. A representation of the basic Kuznets curve is shown in figure 5-2.

Two trend terms in the model describe changes in the shape of the Kuznets curve. The first, which is in the intercept of the equations, is negative and significant, suggesting a downward shift of the curve over time; this is progressive since inequality does not rise as much in the period of increasing inequality. This process is illustrated by the shift between curves (1) and (2) in figure 5-2. The second trend term, which interacts with the income term itself, is positive and significant. The interpretation here is that the left-hand slope of the Kuznets curve becomes steeper over time, while the right-hand side becomes flatter and the inflection point shifts to the right. Growth becomes less progressive, since countries encounter greater inequality in the early years and it takes them longer to reach the positive part of the curve. This change is illustrated in curve (3).

The regression model reinforces the previous discussion about the importance of education and its unequal impact on remunerations, de-

40. Morley (2000, chapter 7).

41. The other seven were the Dominican Republic, Ecuador, El Salvador, Honduras, Paraguay, Uruguay, and Venezuela (Morley, 2000, chapter 4).

42. (Kuznets, 1955). The reason that this study differs from others with respect to the Kuznets curve is that it has a much larger number of observations and covers a longer period of time.

Table 5-11. *Determinants of Gini Coefficient of Income Inequality*[a]

Independent variable	(1)	(2)
Income	−0.0001	−0.0001
	(−7.971)	(−7.246)
1/income	−336.4263	−251.9830
	(−4.002)	(−3.394)
Inflation	0.0138	0.0165
	(1.703)	(1.979)
University education	−0.0039	−0.0093
	(−1.381)	(−3.564)
Primary education	0.2311	0.1441
	(3.258)	(2.032)
Trend	−0.0030	
	(−3.176)	
Trend * income	0.0000	0.0000
	(7.146)	(5.780)
Average reform index	0.0633	
	(2.900)	
Privatization index		0.0604
		(3.011)
Tax reform index		0.0514
		(2.717)
Financial reform index		−0.0228
		(−2.337)
Capital account index		−0.0156
		(−0.918)
Trade reform index		0.0282
		(1.620)
Urban sample dummy	−0.0320	−0.0305
	(−6.704)	(−6.325)
Expenditure survey dummy	−0.0838	−0.0813
	(−2.862)	(−2.726)
ECLAC survey dummy	−0.0530	−0.0523
	(−9.448)	(−9.565)
Household survey dummy	−0.0154	−0.0132
	(−3.018)	(−2.729)
Summary statistic		
R^2	0.976	0.979
Adjusted R^2	0.973	0.976
Number of observations	262	262

Source: Morley (2000); t statistics are shown in parenthesis.

a. The dependent variable is the Gini coefficient. The model is a panel, using fixed effects and ordinary least squares estimation for data on seventeen countries, for the period 1970–95. Independent variables are GDP per capita; the inverse of GDP per capita; a dummy for inflation (1 if over 1000 percent per year, otherwise 0); percent of population with university education; percent of population with less than primary education; a trend term; a trend term multiplied by GDP per capita; the current level of the reform indexes (described in chapter 3); and dummies for urban only sample, expenditure rather than income data, samples where ECLAC was the source, and household rather than individual data.

Figure 5-2. *Examples of Kuznets Curves*

Inequality

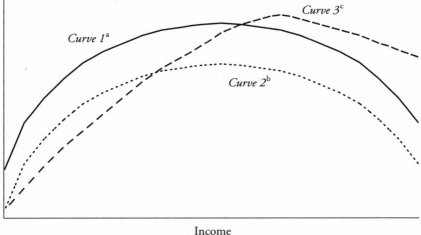

Income

a. Basic Kuznets curve.
b. Kuznets curve modified by trend term in intercept.
c. Kuznets curve modified by trend term interacting with income.

pending on the amount of education an individual has. A low level of education (no more than primary schooling) has a large negative effect on income distribution. The higher the share of such people in a society, the more unequal the distribution will be. Conversely, university education is progressive, but the effect is much less important than the low-schooling variable.

The model suggests that inflation is regressive, at least at very high levels. Inflation episodes of over 1000 percent have a negative impact on distribution. This is consistent with the point made earlier that ending hyperinflation in several countries may have helped lower inequality, at least in the short run. Lower levels of inflation do not seem to have much impact on inequality.

The distribution of land is the model's only measure of asset distribution. This variable is significant only with the use of a random effects model (which has a single intercept for all countries). In that case, the unequal distribution of land in Latin America has a negative impact on the distribution of income, as would be expected. If a fixed effects model is used, the individual country intercepts appear to absorb the effect of land distribution, and the variable loses its significance.[43]

With respect to the impact of the reforms on the level of the Gini coefficient, the equations indicate that the overall reform variable had a small, but negative, effect on distribution. This confirms the qualitative, case-study evidence from sources such as Bulmer-Thomas and Berry.[44] The size of the coefficient on the overall reform index means that increasing the index by 10 percent would increase the Gini coefficient by two thirds of a percentage point.

Two notes of caution need to be added about the impact of the reforms. First, when we discuss the effects of the reforms, other variables are being held constant. If the reforms increased the growth rate or lowered inflation, as they seem to have done in some countries, the positive effect of those two factors may have outweighed the direct negative effect of the reforms themselves. Second, some of the individual reforms may have had different, offsetting impacts, such that particular reform packages may have produced different effects depending on which components were implemented. This finding draws into question the frequent assumption in the literature that the reforms were a mutually reinforcing package. Clearly this was not the case with respect to income distribution.[45]

To further study this last point, Morley disaggregates the overall reform index into the five components presented in chapter 3: trade liberalization, domestic financial liberalization, capital account opening, tax reform, and privatization. Interpreting the impact of the individual reforms is complicated. To enlarge the sample, surveys with different characteristics were used, including some surveys that cover only urban areas, together with others that are based on a national sample. A dummy was included in the equations in the case of an urban-only sample to capture the difference. The dummy was always significant and negative, meaning that inequality was lower in urban areas than in a country as a whole. This then provides three possible sets of observations: urban only, national, and a combination of the two (including the urban dummy). The model presented in table 5-11 is the combined sample.

While the three samples give relatively similar results for the aggregate reform index, they provide quite different results for the individual re-

43. Other variables, including inflation and higher education, also have a larger impact if individual country coefficients are not incorporated into the model.

44. Bulmer-Thomas (1996); Berry (1998).

45. See the correlation matrix of the individual reforms in chapter 3 (note 7).

Table 5-12. *Impact of Individual Reform Indexes on
Household Income Distribution*

Type of reform	Combined sample	Urban sample	National sample
Import liberalization	Regressive	Regressive	Regressive*
Capital account opening	Progressive	Progressive *	Progressive*
Tax reform	Regressive*	Regressive	Regressive*
Domestic financial liberalization	Progressive*	Regressive*	Regressive
Privatization	Regressive*	Progressive	Regressive

Source: Morley (2000).
* Significant at 1 percent level.

forms. That is, at least some of the individual reforms appear to have be-haved differently in urban and rural settings. Table 5-12 summarizes the outcomes. Three of the reforms provide consistent results across the three samples: trade liberalization and tax reform were always regressive, and capital account opening was always progressive. In some cases, the coefficients are statistically significant, while in other cases they are not. Domestic financial reform and privatization appear regressive in two of the three samples, but each is progressive in one sample, suggesting that we really do not know enough about these two reforms to make a judgment.

The regressive impact of tax reform is not at all surprising. Tax reform was defined to involve lowering the maximum rates on personal and corporate taxes and shifting from direct to indirect (value added) levies. Even though evidence suggests that tax evasion is prevalent in Latin America, some taxes were paid at the high rates, so that the shift in types and rates of taxes would be expected to increase inequality.[46] If this led to more invest-ment and jobs, as argued by supply-side economists in the United States, such an effect would be captured in other variables.

The effect of trade reform on income distribution is more controver-sial. While Londoño and Székely, for example, find a positive relation be-tween trade reform and equality, Morley's results are consistent with other studies in finding a negative relation.[47] In particular, trade reform appears

46. ECLAC (1998b).
47. Londoño and Székely (1997). There are several differences between the Londoño and Székely analysis and the one reported here: they use only urban samples, they cover a much shorter time period, and they do not include other variables in their equations. Hence, the different results are not surprising. Other studies that find a negative relation include Robbins (1996) and, to some extent, Spilimbergo, Londoño, and Székely (1997).

to be more regressive in the national than in the urban regressions, suggesting that the negative effect on agriculture of the loss of protection and subsidies was more significant than the loss of protection in manufacturing. As was discussed earlier in this chapter, it was expected that trade opening would favor unskilled labor in general and agriculture in particular, which would have improved distribution; we have already seen that this did not happen.

Finally, opening the capital account appears to have been progressive. This particular reform has received little attention to date, so we do not have any results to compare. One way in which increased foreign capital would affect distribution would be through lowering interest rates in the domestic market as larger firms go abroad to seek funds. Another mechanism involves reducing the profit rates (consistent with other results on factor distribution) of local entrepreneurs and financial institutions. Whether it would also have the additional progressive impact of increasing the demand for labor depends on the type of foreign capital and the response of local firms.

The Impact of Social Expenditure on Equity

Given the extraordinarily high degree of inequality in Latin America and the Caribbean, many proponents of the reforms have looked to government social expenditure, particularly on education and health, as a way to mitigate inequality. Such expenditure would have the added advantage of simultaneously promoting growth by improving the quality of the labor force. To close this chapter then, we examine the evolution and impact of social expenditure. The analysis is not easy: appropriate data are scarce, and they are generally not comparable across countries. Nonetheless, we can obtain some initial insights into the question at hand; a more detailed analysis must await better information.

In chapter 3, we found that social spending increased in all nine project countries in the 1990s in comparison with the previous decade. Nonetheless, as seen in table 5-13, priorities varied across countries in terms of human capital expenditure (that is, education and health) versus other types of expenditure (in particular, social security). The distinction is important since education (especially primary education) and health are the most progressive types of expenditure in that a large share goes to low-income families. Social security benefits, in contrast, go mostly to middle-income

Table 5-13. *Social Expenditure on Human Capital, 1990–97*

Country	Education[a] 1990–91	Education[a] 1996–97	Health[a] 1990–91	Health[a] 1996–97	Human capital[b] 1990–91	Human capital[b] 1996–97	Share of social expenditure[c] 1990–91	Share of social expenditure[c] 1996–97
High spending[d]								
Argentina	228	334	274	362	502	696	41.1	44.3
Brazil[e]	55	43	115	89	170	132	35.7	23.2
Chile	89	167	72	128	161	295	35.5	40.8
Costa Rica	113	153[f]	174	193[f]	287	346[f]	64.6	62.8[f]
Medium spending[d]								
Colombia	70	113	26	95	96	208	52.7	53.3
Jamaica	114	132[f]	61	64[f]	175	196[f]	74.5	80.2[f]
Mexico	113	153	141[g]	164[g]	254	317	89.9	90.1
Low spending[d]								
Bolivia	28	59	11	14	39	73	71.4	61.2
Peru	31	37	10	8	41	45	n.a.	55.3
Simple average	93	132	98	124	192	257	58.2	56.8

Source: Mostajo (2000), on the basis of ECLAC's Social Development Division database.
a. Expenditure in 1997 dollars.
b. Sum of education and health.
c. Human capital as a share of social expenditure.
d. Ranked according to total social expenditure (see table 3-8).
e. Only includes central (federal) government.
f. Only 1996.
g. Includes social security.

groups.[48] Consequently, an initial, very broad indicator to analyze the distributive impact of social spending is the allocation among different uses.

Table 5-13 indicates that per capita spending on education and health rose in almost all countries in the 1990s. The largest increase was in Colombia, with a 117 percent rise; Chile and Bolivia also had large increases of 84 and 87 percent, respectively. Human capital as a share of social expenditure followed a different pattern: countries with a tradition of high social expenditure had large social security programs and thus high expenditures in this area; they had a correspondingly smaller share devoted to human capital. This pattern held for all project countries except Costa Rica. In Argentina, Brazil, and Chile, less than half of social spending was on human capital, while in the medium- and low-expenditure countries (plus Costa Rica) the majority was devoted to this purpose. Since Mexican statistics combine health and social security expenditures, it is impossible to make such a comparison. If we assume that education and health expenditures were approximately equal, then Mexico would fit in the second group with a high share of human capital in social expenditure. Comparing the early and late 1990s, human capital as a share of social spending rose in five of the eight countries with information available, although the simple average fell slightly from 58 to 57 percent.

Going beyond the share allocated to human capital, figure 5-3 provides a more specific measure of the redistributive impact of primary education and health spending for eight of the nine project countries. (No data are available for Mexico.) Based on an index of concentration, which shows the ratio of social spending directed to the poorest 20 percent of the population compared to the richest 20 percent, the figure demonstrates that primary education is more focused on the poor than is health. In addition, it shows the very wide range of behavior with respect to spending in the two areas; this diversity is found both across countries and between the two types of expenditure. In the case of Colombia, for example, spending on health is regressive (the concentration index is around 1) while primary education spending is very progressive (an index of nearly 9). Argentina is equally redistributive in both areas since both indexes are around 8.

Table 5-14 provides more detailed evidence on the behavior of total social spending in the four project countries with data available (Argentina, Brazil, Chile, and Colombia). The first indicator is a targeting index, which compares the amount of social expenditure received by poor groups

48. See discussion in ECLAC (1999c).

Figure 5-3. *Index of Concentration: Primary Education and Health*[a]

Primary education

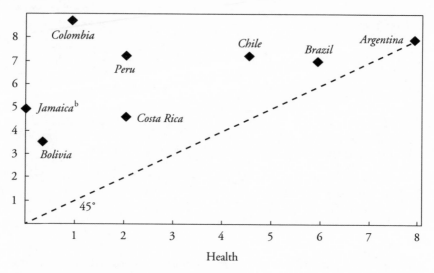

Health

Source: Mostajo (2000), based on country studies.
a. Ratio of benefits of bottom 20 percent to top 20 percent.
b. No information available on health.

of the population (according to individual country standards) compared to their share in the population as a whole. Although the data indicate that some redistribution occurred, the country with the highest share still did not reach a level of 2, which would mean that the poor received twice the expenditure as the average citizen. In general, all countries were somewhat redistributive, but there is still space for greater targeting if countries desire to follow such a policy.

The second measure in the table is the concentration index discussed earlier. On this measure, Chile stands out with spending directed to the bottom quintile representing more than seventeen times the share to the top quintile, whereas the others range between two and three times. High concentration of social expenditure among low-income groups in Chile did not result from a much higher share of social expenditure going to the lowest quintile. The main determinant was the small share going to the top quintile in comparison with other countries (2 percent and 12 percent respectively). Argentina and Brazil present fairly similar distribu-

Table 5-14. *Redistributive Impact of Social Expenditure, 1990s*

Country (year)	Targeting index[a]	Concentration index[b]	Share of social expenditure received by the poor (percent)[c]
Argentina (1998)	1.8	3.4	23.6
Brazil (1994)[d]	1.5	3.0	48.1
Chile (1996)	1.9	17.3	37.6
Colombia (1992)	1.3	1.9	56.3
Simple average	1.6	6.4	41.4

Source: Mostajo (2000), based on country studies.

a. Ratio of the percent of social expenditure received by the poor to the percent of the poor in the population.

b. Ratio of the percent of social expenditure received by the poorest 20 percent of the population to the percent of the social expenditure received by the richest 20 percent.

c. The definition of the poor varies by country.

d. Data include only the state of São Paulo.

tions of social expenditure, although the former is relatively more progressive since a smaller share goes to the top two quintiles. Colombia shows the least progressive situation among the four countries; the lowest quintile receives the smallest share in the sample, while the top quintile receives the largest.[49]

The third indicator shows the percentage of total social expenditure received by groups defined as poor in each country. The share varies between about one-fourth and one-half of the total. While this indicator needs to be considered in conjunction with the share of the population that is poor in each country (the ratio shown in the targeting index), it nonetheless is useful in demonstrating the potential for additional targeting of social expenditure.

In terms of the distributive impact, table 5-15 shows that social expenditure significantly increased household incomes of the lowest quintile. The effect on incomes ranged from 41 percent in Colombia to 142 percent in Argentina, with an average of 87 percent. In other words, calculating the monetary equivalent of the benefits provided through the social programs and adding them to the autonomous income of the households, social spending has significant impact on the welfare of the poorest 20 percent of the

49. Mostajo (2000), based on country studies (Government of Argentina, 1999; Government of Chile, 1998; IPEA, 1999; and Vélez, 1996).

Table 5-15. *Impact of Social Expenditure on Income Distribution, 1990s*

| Country (year) | Top quintile income/lowest quintile income | | Increase in the income of the lowest quintile (percent) |
	Excluding social expenditure	Including social expenditure	
Argentina (1998)	14.2	6.1	142.2
Brazil (1994)[a]	24.6	12.6	97.6
Chile (1996)	14.8	8.9	68.0
Colombia (1992)	11.0	7.9	41.2
Simple average	16.2	8.9	87.3

Source: Mostajo (2000), based on country studies.
a. Data include only the state of São Paulo.

population. For example, social benefits accounted for 31 percent of total consumption of this quintile in Colombia and 54 percent in Argentina.

Social expenditure also had a positive impact on income distribution, reducing the gap between the income of the highest and lowest income quintiles. Without social expenditure, the income of highest quintile on average among the four countries would have been sixteen times higher than that of the lowest quintile; with social expenditure the ratio fell to nine. Concentration of social expenditure on the lowest quintile explains most of the reduction of the gap, independently of the characteristics of the income distribution in the country. The largest reductions in the gap occurred in Argentina and Brazil. This positive impact of social spending resulted mainly from expenditure on education and health, which accounted for about 75 percent of total expenditure received by low-income groups.[50]

Based on the meager data we have, then, the picture is heterogeneous across countries: some countries appear to have done better than others in distributing social expenditure in a progressive way. This depends partly

50. Mostajo (2000), based on country studies. These results do not appear as positive when Latin American countries are compared with other regions of the world. Even including social expenditure, the average gap in the four countries in table 5-15 is larger than the gap excluding social expenditure in middle-income countries such as Ireland, Israel, and Spain or low-income countries such as India and Indonesia. The average income gap excluding social expenditure was 5 in the former and 6 in the latter. In Malaysia and Thailand, the relative shares were 12 and 9 before social expenditure, still well below the Latin American level (calculated from World Bank, 2000). For a more extensive comparison of inequality across regions, see Stallings, Birdsall, and Clugage (2000).

on the historical evolution of social spending programs in each case. Those with a longer trajectory tended to have large social security systems that drained money from other, more progressive functions. Even given these historical constraints, however, some countries have done more than others in targeting spending on lower-income groups.

We have no systematic quantitative data about how the distributional impact of social spending was affected by the reforms, but qualitative information provides some insights. Targeting of social policies in the 1970s and 1980s was weak. In most countries, social expenditure was either purely compensatory or closely linked to social benefits to employees in the formal sector. In both cases, institutional fragmentation, poor management, and the action of interest groups led to inefficiency in the allocation of expenditure.[51] In the 1990s, many governments became more concerned with the issue of poverty alleviation and tried to increase the targeting of social spending.[52]

At the same time, it would appear that the share of primary education and basic health expenditures have declined in importance over the course of the decade. Of the five countries for which calculations can be made (Bolivia, Chile, Colombia, Costa Rica, and Jamaica), all except Costa Rica experienced a fall in the share of these indicators as a share of total social expenditure per capita between 1980-81 and the latter part of the 1990s.[53] This falling share, in the face of higher per capita spending, may represent backsliding in terms of poverty alleviation, although it may also indicate that governments are trying to respond to multiple demands with limited resources. Governments tend to perceive a tradeoff within social expenditure between poverty alleviation (which would imply increased spending on basic services, which are far from universally available) and greater competitiveness for the economies (which would point to greater spending at the secondary and university levels of education). While some experts have

51. Mostajo (2000), based on country studies.

52. Many official government statements point in this direction. For example, the Chilean Ministry of Planning and Cooperation says: "Social expenditure was more selective [in 1990–96] with a stronger concentration on the poorest sectors in the country. In addition to a general increase in resources allocated to social expenditure, targeting has increased" (Government of Chile, 1996, p. 232). Similarly, the Argentinean government says: "Public social expenditure is concentrated on the sectors with the lowest income and it is progressive, a characteristic that was strengthened between 1996 and 1998" (Government of Argentina, 1999, p. 14). Authors' translation.

53. These figures are calculated on the basis of table 3-8 from chapter 3 and table 10 in Ganuza, León, and Sauma (1999). The latter reports on a recent study of social expenditure sponsored by the United Nations Development Program (UNDP), ECLAC, and UNESCO.

argued that no such trade-off exists, the perception remains an impediment to greater targeting of expenditure.[54]

In summary, our evidence on the distributive impact of social expenditure points to three conclusions. First, based on data for four of the nine project countries, it would appear that social expenditure had a strong redistributive impact. The poor generally received a large amount of social expenditure on basic services, which substantially reduced the income gap between rich and poor. Nonetheless, there is still substantial scope for increased targeting. Second, we have no direct evidence on whether the trend toward a large share for the poor was strengthened as a result of the reforms. Since qualitative evidence suggests that targeting increased in the 1990s, and special attention was paid to reducing poverty, it seems likely that the redistributive impact of expenditure also increased. At the same time, the need for greater competitiveness as a result of the reforms stimulated the concern to improve human capital in Latin American and Caribbean countries. Third, much remains to be done in terms of improving the stock of human capital. In addition, given the very high levels of income concentration in the region, improving distribution via social spending and other means has become an end in itself in a number of countries.

Conclusions

This chapter has shown that both employment and equity trends in the 1990s are a source of concern. While the elasticities of employment creation with respect to GDP growth were about the same as the average for the postwar period as a whole, GDP growth was slower, and therefore employment growth also declined, especially with respect to wage earners. This was partly due to supply factors, since the increase in the economically active population slowed from its peak in the 1970s, but demand was also slack and volatile in many countries. The quality of new jobs suffered as well. The substantial majority (six of ten) were in microenterprises or self-employment. While good jobs can certainly be found in both of these categories, the bulk are characterized by low productivity and low wages, and they frequently lack access to benefits. The reforms were not able to change secular trends; perhaps it was naïve to expect that they would. In-

---

54. On this argument, see Birdsall, Graham, and Sabot (1998). Their book is indeed titled *Beyond Tradeoffs*.

deed, they may have exacerbated problems by increasing the heterogeneity in the labor market.

With respect to equity, the trends are less clear. Our evidence suggests that little change occurred as a result of the reforms, but that evidence is based on incomplete data. In particular, the data leave out the very group that is likely to have benefited most: namely, the wealthiest in society. What our data do enable us to say is that educational differences became more significant as a result of the reforms (and of technological progress more generally). This translated into special opportunities for the best educated, and it was reflected in a growing skill premium between the best educated and others. Other factors were also at work, including demographic trends, the end of hyperinflation, and some progressive aspects of education. These frequently offset the regressive impact of wage differentials. While governments' social expenditure ameliorated inequality in the region to some extent, it still remains the highest in the world.

Within this overall picture, countries displayed important differences with respect to employment and equity, just as they did in the areas of investment, productivity, and growth. The good performers were not always the same as in the previous analysis, however, and the pattern was far more complex. The attempt to characterize the heterogeneity across the nine project countries on labor and equity measures during the 1990s led to the definition of four groups. Chile and Costa Rica showed a relatively positive performance on both variables, while Argentina, Brazil, and Colombia suffered setbacks on both. In Bolivia and Mexico, strong employment growth was unable to prevent increased inequality, but in Jamaica and Peru mediocre labor market performance was accompanied by lower inequality.

These patterns were related to the reforms, but also to many other factors, economic and social, historical and contemporary, which are beyond the scope of this book. The econometric evidence discussed earlier suggested that the reforms had a negative (if small) impact on both employment and equity. Argentina, Brazil, and Colombia were examples of this prediction. All three began their reforms in the 1990s, so they had little time to put a new economic model into operation during the decade. More important, macroeconomic policies in the three countries were frequently inconsistent with the reforms, leading to substantial uncertainty among potential investors. This resulted in volatile growth, which had negative implications for employment and thus for equity.

Chile and Costa Rica, by contrast, were able to offset any negative impulses coming from the reforms through stable macroeconomic policies that helped promote investment and growth. (Clearly we are referring to Chile in the 1990s; during the first fifteen years of Chilean reforms, both employment and equity showed highly negative trends.) Steady growth led to relatively satisfactory employment growth with an emphasis on wage jobs, constant or declining rates of unemployment, and moderate or high growth of productivity and salaries. The shrinking wage differential helped produce greater equality on the primary distribution measures (and household distribution in Costa Rica). High levels of social spending also accompanied the reforms in the context of a relatively even distribution of education.

The remaining four cases, where employment and equity variables moved in opposite directions, have more complicated roots. Bolivia and Mexico began their reforms in the mid-1980s, and by the early 1990s both had begun to enjoy quite dynamic rates of job creation. In Mexico, the financial crisis interrupted the positive dynamic, doubling rates of unemployment and depressing real wages. Although increased growth was beginning to make a dent in these problems by the end of the decade, our latest distributional measures (to 1996) do not reflect the incipient recovery in the labor market. Bolivia's case is different, since it was the country with the most stable growth pattern during the 1990s. The failure of Bolivia's strong job creation to produce more progressive distributional trends is probably linked more closely to the quality of jobs created than to quantitative trends, as in Mexico. Since most of Bolivia's new jobs were in the informal sector, heterogeneity increased between these new jobs of a relatively precarious nature and the small number of high-skill jobs. This is reflected in the especially large increase in the skill premium in Bolivia.

Finally, Jamaica and Peru displayed the anomalous pattern of mediocre labor market performance together with increased equality. Labor market problems in the two countries had different characteristics. Unemployment was typically high in Jamaica, although it did not increase in the 1990s. While job creation was sluggish, it centered on wage jobs with rising remunerations but stagnant productivity. Peru, by contrast, created a relatively large number of jobs, but most were in the informal sector; wages increased until mid-decade but then began to fall. Wages in 1998 were far below those for 1980. These labor market patterns were combined with more progressive distribution in both countries, but less dispersion of income did not necessarily mean greater welfare for the population. The case of Jamaica is clear, since per capita income fell during the 1990s. A similar situation was found in Peru between 1985 and 1991. Some improvement took place in the 1990s, when the poorer groups in the country improved their relative position, but poverty continued to increase even though distribution improved. As the authors of the Jamaica study on income distribution said, "The decline in inequality in Jamaica . . . hardly provides a lesson for other reforming economies to emulate."[55]

These characterizations are based on aggregate-level data. As a consequence, they can not address many of the factors that would cast light on both employment and distributional trends, especially differential behavior by size of firm and different characteristics by sector. Sectoral and microeconomic analyses are necessary to find out what kinds of firms are creating jobs, how fast they are doing so, and how productivity and wages vary across types of firms. After examining such data in the next chapter, we will be in a better position to explain the complex relations between the reforms, employment, and equity and to make policy recommendations for improvements.

55. King and Handa (2000).

6 | Heterogeneity in Responses of Sectors and Firms

A basic tenet of the analytical framework presented in chapter 1 is that the impact of the economic reforms on growth, employment, and equity depends on the way in which they modify firm behavior regarding investment and the incorporation of technological progress. After studying the impact of the reforms at the aggregate level in the previous two chapters, we now turn to the behavior of economic actors in response to the reforms, identifying the most important determinants of their actions and their main effects.[1]

Although the reforms did not aim at promoting specific sectors or firms, neither were they meant to be neutral. At the sectoral level, expectations focused on increasing the share of exports in total output and reducing that of formerly protected sectors. This would be a straightforward result of moving from import substitution to an export-led growth model. A central objective of the reforms was to overcome the strong anti-export bias that had developed under protection policies, because the resulting trade deficits represented a serious constraint on growth. The long-run

---

1. This chapter draws heavily on information and analysis developed in Moguillansky and Bielschowsky (2000), Katz (2000), and Weller (2000), although our conclusions do not necessarily coincide with those reached in the three works.

sustainability of an export orientation would depend to a large degree on whether the reforms could overcome, or at least reduce, external constraints on growth.

Not all kinds of potential exports were expected to benefit equally from the reforms. Trade liberalization and the phasing out of industrial and agricultural policy, which was believed to have artificially increased labor costs and reduced the cost of capital, would lead a country to specialize in areas in which it had comparative advantages. The proponents of the reforms generally assumed that Latin America's comparative advantage lay in unskilled labor; they therefore predicted two additional outcomes. First, labor-intensive sectors would produce the most dynamic export performance and, consequently, the most rapid growth and employment creation. Second, small firms, which presumably specialize in labor-intensive sectors, would grow faster than larger ones, which were concentrated in capital-intensive, protected sectors.[2]

The growth of labor-intensive export sectors and the share of small firms in such sectors are therefore outcomes against which we should assess the impact of the reforms at the microeconomic level. But that is not the whole story. The reforms—especially privatization and capital account liberalization—also aimed at reducing the share of government, eliminating state-owned enterprises, and promoting foreign direct investment (FDI) flows into the region. As a consequence, subsidiaries of transnational corporations (TNCs) were expected to be increasingly important players under the new rules of the game, providing technological and managerial skills to improve efficiency in sectors in which countries had comparative advantages.

The reforms aimed at changing firm behavior, but they were not the only cause of the changes analyzed in this chapter. As was the case in earlier sections of the book, firms were also influenced by macroeconomic policy decisions, the dynamics of the international context, particularly regarding finance, technology, and demand, and longer-term lagged effects (inertia) of economic changes that had taken place much earlier. We do not attempt to isolate the effects of the reforms. Instead, we analyze how growth and employment at the sectoral and microeconomic levels were influenced by a

---

2. For example, Balassa and others state: "The proposed measures will be of special benefit to small and medium-sized businesses, which have particularly suffered the consequences of high protection, the lack of imported inputs, and price controls. At the same time, such businesses provide a large potential source of employment creation in Latin America" (1986, p. 94).

combination of the reforms and other, sometimes contradictory, economic signals.

The analysis begins with an overview of the impact of the reforms on the sectoral structure of the economy as a whole. We then disaggregate further, focusing on producers of exportables in the most important tradables sectors, namely agriculture, mining, and manufacturing.[3] We also discuss the services sectors that strongly influence the international competitiveness of exports, including electricity and telecommunications. These services are among the most important areas in terms of the impact of the privatization reforms. At the microeconomic level, we consider the behavior of specific firms, particularly in highly concentrated sectors with very few players. The focus of the analysis, however, is on the dynamics of different types of firms defined according to size and ownership, including subsidiaries of transnational corporations, large domestic firms (usually part of diversified conglomerates), small and medium-size enterprises, and state-owned enterprises.[4]

The Sectoral Dynamics of the Economy as a Whole

At the most general level, structural change in Latin American production was moderate after the reforms. Table 6-1 shows that the tradables sectors continued their long-term trend of reducing their share in the region's economies. They were less important as a share of output in 1998 than they were before the reforms began. Despite the similar downward trend, countries demonstrate substantial differences in the share of tradables.[5]

Analyzing data for output structure at the single-digit level of the International Standard Industrial Classification for the nine countries in 1970,

3. Definitions of tradables versus nontradables sectors vary considerably. In this chapter, we use the most straightforward definition: all sectors that produce goods are considered tradables, and services are considered nontradables. This definition presents shortcomings, for example when applied to tourism, a services sector that is an important source of foreign exchange in several project countries (Costa Rica, Jamaica, and Mexico). Other services are also becoming increasingly tradable (for example, banking and insurance).

4. We do not discuss technological and structural changes within firms. For a detailed analysis of firm behavior at the plant level in the manufacturing, mining, and telecommunication sectors, see Katz (2000, chapters 3 and 4). For an analysis of changes within large domestic conglomerates operating in the manufacturing sector, see Peres (1998).

5. Of the nine project countries, Bolivia, Colombia, and Peru had the highest share of tradables in 1997 (an average of 43 percent of total output among the three); Brazil, Mexico, and Jamaica were at the opposite extreme (only 28 percent on average), while Argentina, Chile, and Costa Rica were in between the others (an average of 37 percent).

Table 6-1. *Sectoral Value Added as Share of Total Output, 1970–98*[a]
Simple average in percent

Year	Agriculture	Mining	Manufacturing	Services[b]
1970	14.3	5.5	22.5	57.7
1980	12.2	6.0	22.6	59.2
1985	12.6	5.3	21.8	60.3
1990	12.6	5.3	21.3	60.8
1998	11.2	5.1	19.7	63.9

Source: Project database, on the basis of ECLAC statistics.
a. Includes Argentina, Bolivia, Brazil, Chile, Colombia, Costa Rica, Jamaica, Mexico, and Peru.
b. Includes construction.

1980, 1990, and 1997 uncovers only four types of significant, repeated changes during the period after the reforms: a decline in manufacturing in Brazil, Chile, Colombia, and Jamaica; an increase in financial services in Argentina, Chile, Costa Rica, Jamaica, Mexico, and Peru; an increase in transportation and communications in Bolivia, Chile, Costa Rica, and Jamaica; and a decline in government in Bolivia, Brazil, Chile, and Costa Rica. No comparable data are available for the last category in Argentina and Mexico.[6]

These four changes are linked to the reform process in fairly direct ways. The decline in manufacturing in the four countries was related to the trade opening that increased the competition faced by local producers; a similar phenomenon occurred in Argentina during the first reform phase in the 1970s. For Mexico, with its large *maquila* (in-bond) industry, manufacturing as a share of total output increased between 1985 and 1997. Likewise, the decline in the role of government was compatible with the new emphasis on the leading role of the private sector. Only in Colombia did government participation increase after the reform period began. The increased importance of finance, transportation, and communications is a logical complement to the reform process, since all are necessary for raising a country's competitiveness.

Previous chapters highlighted the fast pace at which exports grew, both in value and in volume, after the early 1980s and particularly in the 1990s.

6. The criterion used to define a significant change was a shift of two or more points of GDP. The category "other services" was not included, since its content varies substantially across countries.

Unlike the trends observed for output, the sectoral structure of exports changed significantly in those decades, and different sectoral patterns of growth clearly emerged within the project countries.

Primary products and semi-manufactures accounted for 89 percent of the value of Latin American exports in 1970 but less than 40 percent 1998 (including *maquila*); the other 60 percent was accounted for by manufactured goods, whose share was just 11 percent of the total in 1970 (see table 6-2). These averages hide sharp national differences. They are skewed by the weight of the largest exporter (Mexico), whose foreign sales are highly diversified. When Mexico is excluded from the statistics, for example, primary products and semi-manufactures still accounted for 61 percent of Latin American exports in 1998, and manufactured exports drop from 60 percent of the region's total to 36 percent. *Maquila* exports have played an important role in Mexico's boom in manufacturing exports, but that is not the whole story. When we exclude the *maquila* from Mexico's total exports, the share of manufacturing is still 73 percent, that is, twice the average for the other eight project countries.

Within manufacturing, traditional industries and natural resource–based sectors moderately increased their share in total Latin American exports in 1970–98, while foreign sales from labor-intensive and capital-intensive industries increased strongly in the 1990s (see table 6-3). Manufactured goods with higher technological content also represented an increasing share of manufactured exports. Once more, the dynamics change dramatically when Mexico is excluded from the statistics. When Mexico is included, labor-intensive industries grew from less than 4 percent of total Latin American exports in 1970 to 27 percent in 1998. When Mexico is excluded, they accounted for only 10 percent in 1997 (see table 6-4). *Maquila* exports again played an important role, but do not fully explain the difference. Capital-intensive industries had more than twice as large a share in Mexico's exports in 1998 than in the other eight project countries. The only other project country that had an export dynamic similar to Mexico's was Costa Rica, where labor-intensive manufactures rose from 5 percent of total exports in 1980 to about 28 percent in 1998. The other seven project countries diversified their manufacturing exports more in the 1970s and 1980s than in the 1990s.

Mexico's integration into the North American market (mainly but not exclusively through *maquila* exports) gave it a very different export structure and performance from other large and medium-size countries in the region. As a consequence, Mexico is the only project country that made a

Table 6-2. *Structure of Mexican versus Regional Exports, 1970–98*[a]

Percent of total exports

Year	Primary products			Semi-manufactures			Manufactures		
	Mexico	Other 8	Total	Mexico	Other 8	Total	Mexico	Other 8	Total
1970	45.3	53.7	52.6	26.7	37.3	36.0	27.7	8.5	11.0
1980	80.7	38.7	49.8	9.7	37.2	29.9	9.5	23.4	19.7
1985	67.7	36.4	46.7	14.3	35.2	28.3	17.9	27.2	24.1
1990	46.8	30.2	35.0	13.7	37.1	30.4	38.7	30.9	33.1
1998 (including *maquila*)[b]	9.9	30.0	19.8	6.5	31.0	18.6	83.2	36.3	60.0
1998 (excluding *maquila*)[b]	17.6	30.0	25.4	8.7	31.0	22.9	73.1	36.3	49.7

Source: Project database, on the basis of ECLAC statistics.

a. Weighted averages; includes Argentina, Bolivia, Brazil, Chile, Colombia, Costa Rica, Jamaica, Mexico, and Peru. Totals do not add to 100 percent because other exports are not included.

b. Does not include Jamaica.

Table 6-3. *Structure of Manufacturing Exports, 1970–98*[a]

Percent of total exports

Year	Traditional industries	Natural resource–based industries	Labor-intensive industries	Capital-intensive industries	High-tech industries[b]
1970	2.7	2.5	3.8	2.1	2.2
1980	5.7	3.0	6.4	4.7	2.6
1985	5.2	5.8	8.2	4.9	2.9
1990	7.1	8.1	9.5	8.4	4.3
1998[c]	9.7	5.5	26.9	17.9	21.6

Source: Project database, on the basis of ECLAC statistics.

a. Weighted averages; includes Argentina, Bolivia, Brazil, Chile, Colombia, Costa Rica, Jamaica, Mexico, and Peru.

b. Includes high-tech labor- and capital-intensive industries already included in the previous two columns.

c. Does not include Jamaica.

significant gain in market share in world exports to the industrialized countries (see table 6-5). Costa Rica and Chile also increased their market shares, but at a slower pace than Mexico.

Investment and technical progress are the main long-term forces behind the dynamics of GDP, employment, and export growth. The response of investment to the reforms at the sectoral level is particularly useful for identifying specialization and growth trends, which may still be too weak to be detected at the aggregate level. The extent to which investment trends point to a strengthening of sectors that produce tradable goods in general and exports in particular is a key element in our final assessment of the impact of the reforms.

Analyzing particular sectors and the types of firms operating within them also enables us to understand the effects of the two reforms that were most important for aggregate investment trends (namely, trade liberalization and privatization). It also makes it possible to determine the degree to which the dynamism of investment extended to different kinds of firms (for example, small and large, national and foreign).

The determinants of sectoral investment are found in the interaction among the economic reforms, macroeconomic policy, and the international context. Together, these lead to the emergence of new firms, market structures, and business strategies. The reforms had an especially powerful impact on the emergence of new economic actors and market structures. These

Table 6-4. *Structure of Mexican versus Regional Manufacturing Exports, 1970–98*[a]

Percent of total exports

	Labor-intensive industries		Capital-intensive industries		High-tech industries[b]	
Year	Mexico	Other 8	Mexico	Other 8	Mexico	Other 8
1970	11.7	2.6	6.7	1.4	7.6	1.4
1975	9.1	6.2	7.7	4.0	5.1	2.7
1980	3.1	7.5	3.6	5.1	1.4	3.0
1985	10.6	7.1	3.3	5.7	2.4	3.2
1990	14.3	7.6	15.2	5.7	5.6	3.7
1998 (including *maquila*)[c]	43.6	9.7	23.4	12.2	36.8	6.1
1998 (excluding *maquila*)[c]	23.9	9.7	31.6	12.2	19.9	6.1

Source: ECLAC, on the basis of official statistics.

a. Weighted averages. Includes Argentina, Bolivia, Brazil, Chile, Colombia, Costa Rica, Jamaica, Mexico, and Peru. Does not include exports from traditional and natural resource–based industries.

b. Includes high-tech labor- and capital-intensive industries already included in the previous two columns.

c. Does not include Jamaica.

processes reduced barriers to entry, changed the operation of specific markets through privatization and deregulation, and determined the evolution of investment.

Investment data at the sectoral level are particularly poor in Latin America.[7] National statistics are available for only six of the nine project countries (Bolivia, Brazil, Chile, Colombia, Costa Rica, and Peru), and the information is not comparable across countries. The coefficient of sectoral investment as a share of GDP before and after the reforms demonstrate heterogeneous dynamics (see table 6-6). Investment in tradables sectors grew significantly in Bolivia, Chile, Colombia, and Costa Rica, while it decreased in Brazil and Peru. In manufacturing, the coefficients doubled in Chile and improved significantly in Costa Rica.

The sectoral structure of investment also showed very heterogeneous behavior.[8] Overall, tradables accounted for only one-fifth to one-third of

7. Improving these data was a major contribution of the work presented in Moguillansky and Bielschowsky (2000).

8. Shares were calculated by dividing sectoral investment coefficients from table 6-6 by total investment coefficients from Moguillansky and Bielschowky (2000, appendix A-1).

Table 6-5. *Latin America's Share in World Exports to the Industrialized Countries, 1980 and 1996*
Percent

Country	1980	1996
Argentina	0.35	0.24
Bolivia	0.04	0.02
Brazil	1.01	0.83
Chile	0.23	0.28
Colombia	0.25	0.25
Costa Rica	0.07	0.10
Jamaica	0.06	0.05
Mexico	1.26	2.27
Peru	0.21	0.09

Source: Authors' calculations, on the basis of ECLAC's CAN software.

total investment. They strongly increased their share in Chile and Colombia, rose moderately in Costa Rica, fell slightly in Brazil, and fell strongly in Bolivia and Peru. Patterns within tradables were also different across countries. Higher shares in total investment sometimes resulted from a country's comparative advantage (for example, mining in Chile and Colombia), and other times reflected long-term development policies (for example, manufacturing in Brazil).

Table 6-7 uses these data, together with qualitative evidence collected by project consultants for two of the three countries not included in table 6-6, to rate the dynamism of sectoral investment in eight of the project countries. Two general trends emerge. First, at this broad level of analysis just one sector (telecommunications) increased its share in total investment and showed a higher investment-to-GDP ratio after the reforms in all eight countries. Second, only one country (Chile) showed high investment performance for almost all sectors in the 1990s than in the 1980s.[9]

GDP and employment growth were a joint result of the dynamics of investment and the incorporation of technical progress; the ratio between them gives us one measure of productivity. While total factor productivity would be a preferable measure, we use average labor productivity as a proxy

9. We should keep in mind that a pre-reform period in Chile would mean the 1960s and early 1970s, for which sectoral investment data and qualitative evidence are unavailable.

Table 6-6. *Investment Coefficients by Sector, 1970–97*
Percent of GDP

Country and sector	Pre-reform	Post-reform Phase 1	Phase 2	Phase 3
Bolivia	*1970–84*	*1987–89*	*1990–97*	. . .
Tradables	n.a.	5.11	6.16	
Oil and natural gas		3.40	3.94	
Manufacturing		1.40	1.47	
Mining		0.31	0.75	
Infrastructure	n.a.	1.56	2.72	
Electricity		0.83	1.69	
Water and sewage		0.32	0.17	
Telecommunications		0.41	0.86	
Brazil	*1970–89*	*1990–94*	*1995–97*	. . .
Tradables	5.05	2.60	3.80	
Oil and natural gas	0.95	0.50	0.40	
Manufacturing	3.90	2.00	3.30	
Mining	0.20	0.10	0.10	
Infrastructure	4.58	2.34	2.18	
Electricity	1.83	0.91	0.55	
Water and sewage	0.35	0.19	0.13	
Telecommunications	0.62	0.49	0.70	
Transportation	1.78	0.75	0.80	
Chile	*1970–73*	*1980–85*	*1986–89*	*1990–97*
Tradables	n.a.	5.18	6.32	8.98
Oil and natural gas		0.93	0.80	0.81
Manufacturing		1.87	2.31	3.81
Mining		2.38	3.21	4.36
Infrastructure	n.a.	4.68	4.14	5.59
Electricity		1.82	1.56	1.52
Water, sewage, roads, and harbors		1.47	1.15	1.71
Telecommunications		0.47	0.68	1.50
Other infrastructure		0.92	0.75	0.86

Table 6-6. *Investment Coefficients by Sector, 1970–97 (continued)*
Percent of GDP

Country and sector	Pre-reform	Post-reform		
		Phase 1	Phase 2	Phase 3
Colombia	1975–89	1990–91	1992–95	. . .
Tradables	3.33	3.30	4.69	
Oil and natural gas	0.96	1.05	2.22	
Manufacturing	2.37	2.25	2.47	
Infrastructure	4.04	3.52	5.84	
Water	0.30	0.35	0.60	
Telecommunications	0.37	0.40	0.71	
Electricity	1.95	1.68	2.45	
Transportation	1.42	1.09	2.08	
Costa Rica	1970–85	1986–91	1992–94	. . .
Tradables	5.89	7.36	8.26	
Agriculture	1.75	2.45	2.82	
Manufacturing	4.14	4.91	5.44	
Infrastructure	5.71	5.87	7.79	
Electricity and tele-				
communications	1.90	1.83	2.60	
Transportation	3.81	4.04	5.19	
Peru	1970–89	1992–93	1994–97	. . .
Tradables	7.99	4.18	4.79	
Agriculture	0.38	0.75	0.79	
Oil and natural gas	0.74	0.21	0.22	
Manufacturing	4.84	2.23	2.84	
Mining	2.03	0.99	0.94	
Infrastructure	3.94	3.48	3.84	
Electricity and water	0.81	1.14	1.24	
Transportation and tele-				
communications	3.13	2.34	2.60	

Source: Moguillansky and Bielschowsky (2000).

Table 6-7. *Dynamism of Sectoral Investment after the Reforms*[a]

Country	Mining	Oil and gas	Manufacturing	Telecommunications	Electricity	Transportation
Argentina	Medium	High	Medium	High	Medium	Medium
Bolivia	Medium	Medium	Low	High	High	n.a.
Brazil	Low	Low	Medium	High	Low	Low
Chile	High	Medium	High	High	High	High
Colombia	n.a.	High	Medium	High	Medium	Low
Costa Rica	n.a.	n.a.	High	High	High	High
Mexico	n.a.	Medium	Medium	High	Medium	High
Peru	Medium	Low	Low	High	Medium	High

Source: Moguillansky and Bielschowsky (2000), on the basis of the project sectoral studies.

a. High (low) dynamism implies that the investment-to-GDP coefficients were bigger (smaller) after the reforms than in the pre-reform period, except for Argentina and Chile, for which the base period is the early 1990s and early 1980s respectively. When coefficients are not significantly different between periods, dynamism is qualified as medium.

Figure 6-1. *Average Labor Productivity by Sector, 1970–98*[a]

Thousands of 1980 dollars (purchasing power parity)

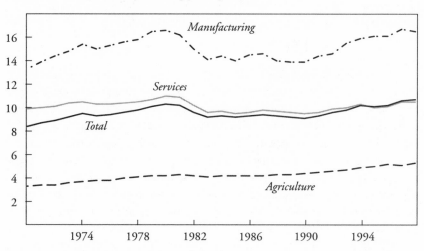

Source: Hofman (1999), on the basis of project data.
a. Based on simple averages for the nine project countries.

because of lack of data on capital utilization at the sectoral level. Figure 6-1 shows trends in labor productivity for the nine countries, disaggregated into three broad sectors of activity. Average labor productivity declined in the 1980s and then rose in the 1990s. By 1997–98, however, it barely exceeded the level of 1980. At the sectoral level, productivity increases accelerated in agriculture as the result of significant processes of modernization and declining employment. In manufacturing, productivity suffered a sharp decline in the 1980s and then grew again. Finally, the services sector excluding utilities overcame the stagnation of the 1980s as average productivity began to rise, albeit at slow rates.

This review of sectoral dynamics raises four important issues. First, the share of tradables in GDP fell moderately, while their share in employment dropped, as will be seen later in the chapter. We need to identify the forces that led to the corresponding increase of employment in services and ask whether they were related to the reforms. Second, project countries exhibited two distinct export patterns. Mexico's different performance regarding manufacturing exports was a result of its integration in the North American economic area in general and of the *maquila* operations in particular. With the exception of Costa Rica, the other countries maintained and sometimes increased their specialization in primary products and natural resource–based semi-manufactures. We now need to determine the impact of these different patterns of specialization on production and employment.

Third, investment did not flow mainly to tradables and potential exports, and some nontradables, such as telecommunications, experienced very fast growth. Within the investment that went to the tradables sectors, a disaggregated analysis must now examine whether it was concentrated in export-oriented subsectors. It is also necessary to find out why other infrastructure sectors did not perform as well as telecommunications. Finally, a deeper analysis of the heterogeneous dynamics of productivity needs to explore whether the overall picture of relatively slow productivity growth in services is hiding more dynamic sectors that are crucial for the competitiveness of the tradables sectors.

These questions require a more detailed analysis of specific sectors. The following sections present such an analysis of manufacturing, agriculture, mining, electricity, and telecommunications, focusing on the dynamics of investment and the incorporation of technological progress in each sector. Employment is considered separately because of the different breakdown of available information.

Specialization and Heterogeneity in Manufacturing

The most important change in the structure of manufacturing production in the 1970s and 1980s was the increase in the relative weight of subsectors that process natural resources, particularly in Argentina, Brazil, Chile, and Colombia.[10] In the 1990s, in contrast, metal products and the automobile industry were the most dynamic (see table 6-8). The weight of activities such as textiles, garments, leather products, and footwear in the production structure diminished throughout the three decades. These trends, together with the evolution of investment in the sector, reflect the significant specialization process that occurred in manufacturing after the reforms.

10. These subsectors present important economies of scale, are highly capital-intensive, and produce homogeneous goods, such as paper and cellulose, basic chemicals, iron and steel, and nonferrous metal products. See Katz (2000, chapter 2).

Table 6-8. *Growth Rate of Value Added and Employment in Manufacturing Subsectors, 1990–96*[a]

Percent

Subsector	Value added	Employment
Metal products, excluding transportation equipment	4.5	–1.1
Transportation equipment	4.9	–1.9
Food, beverages, and tobacco	4.3	0.3
Natural resource–based industries	3.0	–1.3
Textile, garments, leather, and footwear	–0.6	–3.5
Other industries	5.4	0.3
All manufacturing	3.9	–0.8

Source: Weller (2000), using ECLAC's PADI data base.

a. Simple average for six countries (Argentina, Brazil, Chile, Colombia, Mexico, and Peru). Data exclude small firms and microenterprises.

Investment in the manufacturing sector followed a sequence of phases similar to the pattern for total investment.[11] In an initial phase when negative transitory factors determined the investment process, the investment-to-GDP ratio and the investment index fell. Uncertainty and inconsistencies related to macroeconomic policy and the international context led to this decline as corporate strategies reflected wait-and-see behavior. Both indexes recovered during a second phase, when some of the negative elements were reversed or weakened. Only Chile entered a third phase, in which normal long-term factors dominate investment. In the Chilean case, the indexes clearly exceeded their pre-reform levels, although this need not hold true for all countries (see table 6-9).

The manufacturing sector can play an important role in alleviating balance-of-payments constraints to growth by increasing exports in response to the signals sent by the reforms. To find out the extent to which this occurred, we need to consider what happened to the structure of manufacturing investment and whether there was a relation between those changes

11. We were able to get disaggregated information for only six of the project countries. Moreover, the data for Colombia, Mexico, and Peru only go up to 1994 or 1995, and the periodization differs slightly from that presented in table 6-6. Similarly, lack of data for the period preceding the reforms in Chile (1960–74) and Argentina (1970–89) forces us to use the initial post-reform levels as a base for the investment index. Given that investment in that period was very low, the index will tend to overestimate the impact of the reforms on investment in the following phases.

Table 6-9. Investment in Manufacturing, 1970–97

Country	Pre-reform		Phase 1		Phase 2		Phase 3	
Index of manufacturing investment								
Argentina	1970–90	n.a.	1991	100.0	1992–97ᵃ	166.0	...	...
Brazil	1970–89	100.0	1990–94	78.0	1995–97ᵃ	130.0	...	...
Chile	1960–74	n.a.	1974–85	100.0	1986–89	177.0	1990–97ᵃ	460.0
Colombia	1970–89	100.0	...	...	1990–95ᵃ	166.0	...	...
Mexico	1970–85	100.0	1986–90	67.0	1990–94ᵃ	118.0	...	...
Peru	1970–89	100.0	1990–95ᵃ	37.0	...	...	...	...
Manufacturing investment as percentage of total GDP								
Argentina	1970–90	3.3	1991	2.0	1992–97ᵃ	3.0	...	...
Brazil	1970–89	3.9	1990–94	2.0	1995–97ᵃ	3.3	...	...
Chile	1960–74	n.a.	1974–85	1.4	1986–89	2.3	1990–97ᵃ	3.8
Colombia	1970–89	2.3	...	...	1990–95ᵃ	2.2	...	...
Mexico	1970–85	1.9	1986–90	1.0	1990–94ᵃ	1.4	...	...
Peru	1970–89	4.8	1990–95ᵃ	2.6	...	...	...	...

Source: Moguillansky and Bielschowsky (2000) on the basis of project sectoral studies.
a. Data are not available for later years; periodization therefore does not necessarily indicate the end of phase.

Table 6-10. *Index of Investment and Output in Manufacturing*

Country	Investment index[a]		Output index[b]	
	Pre-reform	1990s	Pre-reform	1990s
Argentina				
Dynamic subsectors[c]	n.a.	n.a.	100	127
Others	n.a.	n.a.	100	88
Brazil				
Dynamic subsectors[c]	100	125	100	133
Others	100	97	100	117
Chile				
Dynamic subsectors[c]	100[d]	392	100[d]	185
Others	100[d]	288	100[d]	144
Colombia				
Dynamic subsectors[c]	100	198	100	162
Others	100	119	100	172
Mexico				
Dynamic subsectors[c]	100	147	100	162
Others	100	76	100	138
Peru				
Dynamic subsectors[c]	100	49	100	112
Others	100	21	100	100

Source: Project database.

a. Index of gross fixed domestic investment (100 = pre-reform period).

b. Index of GDP (100 = pre-reform period).

c. Dynamic subsectors are those that increased their participation in total manufacturing investment between the pre-reform period and the 1990s.

d. In Chile, due to lack of data, the base period is 1979–81.

and export dynamics after the reforms. Table 6-10 divides the manufacturing sector into dynamic versus nondynamic subsectors, with the former defined as subsectors that increased their participation in total manufacturing investment between the pre-reform period and the 1990s. Of the twenty-eight subsectors considered in national statistics, those categorized as dynamic ranged from a low of nine (the average for Argentina, Brazil, Mexico, and Peru) to a high of sixteen (in Chile and Colombia).

By definition, investment in the dynamic subsectors grew faster than it did in the rest of the manufacturing sector, but the differential between the dynamic and the nondynamic subsectors was considerable. In all countries except Peru, investment in the dynamic subsectors was substantially higher than in the laggards. In Peru, all investment fell in comparison with the pre-reform period. In the other cases, the increase in the dynamic subsectors ranged from 25 percent in Brazil to 292 percent in Chile. Investment in the lagging subsectors, in contrast, fell in the 1990s in comparison with the pre-reform period in Brazil and Mexico, but it rose (at a slower rate) in Chile and Colombia.

Table 6-10 further shows that the same subsectors that were dynamic in investment were also dynamic in the expansion of output. The data for Argentina fit the same pattern. What differs in the data on growth of output is the relative dynamism between fast-growing subsectors and the rest of the manufacturing sector. Brazil, Mexico, and Peru demonstrated a bigger difference between dynamic and nondynamic subsectors with respect to output than to investment. In Chile and Colombia, the relation ran in the other direction. For Argentina, of course, we cannot make such a comparison.

Thus the reforms helped some manufacturing subsectors, while others fell further behind. This was true for both investment and output. Whether the dynamic subsectors were intensive in labor, capital, or natural resources affects their potential for generating employment and improving the distribution of income. A closely related issue is the relative size of the firms in the dynamic versus the lagging subsectors.

Table 6-11 lists the subsectors that were dynamic in at least three countries and the type of firm that led the investment process in those sectors. Foodstuffs and metal products were the only subsectors that were dynamic across all the countries under consideration,[12] while pharmaceuticals and cosmetics as well as basic steel were dynamic in five countries, and beverages, plastics, and chemicals and petrochemicals were dynamic in four countries. At the other extreme, subsectors such as furniture, leather goods, and nonelectric machinery were dynamic in at most one country.

Subsidiaries of transnational corporations were important investors in dynamic subsectors, particularly in foodstuffs; pharmaceuticals, cosmetics, and miscellaneous chemicals; and transportation equipment (that is, passenger and freight vehicles). Large domestic conglomerates or firms led investment in foodstuffs, beverages, nonmetallic mineral products (cement), cellulose and paper, and metal products. The major investors in the dynamic subsectors were thus large corporations, both domestic and foreign.

The information in table 6-11 has two important shortcomings, al-

---

12. Metal products include all metal goods (such as scaffolding, pipes, nails, and screws) except machinery and equipment.

Table 6-11. *Characteristics of Dynamic Manufacturing Subsectors*

Subsector	Countries	Main investors[a]
Foodstuffs[b]	Argentina, Brazil, Chile, Colombia, Mexico, Peru	TNC, CDF
Metal products	Argentina, Brazil, Chile, Colombia, Mexico, Peru	Large and medium-size domestic firms
Pharmaceuticals, cosmetics, and miscellaneous chemicals	Argentina, Brazil, Colombia, Mexico, Peru	TNC
Basic steel	Argentina, Brazil, Chile, Colombia, Mexico	CDF
Beverages	Argentina, Chile, Colombia, Mexico	CDF, TNC
Plastics	Brazil, Chile, Colombia, Mexico	Large and medium-size domestic firms
Chemicals and petrochemicals	Argentina, Chile, Colombia, Peru	TNC
Other products of nonmetallic minerals (cement)	Chile, Colombia, Mexico	CDF
Tobacco	Argentina, Chile, Mexico	CDF, some TNC
Pulp and paper	Chile, Colombia, Peru	CDF
Transportation equipment	Argentina, Brazil, Mexico	TNC

Source: Moguillansky and Bielschowsky (2000), on the basis of project data.
a. TNC = subsidiaries of transnational corporations ; CDF = conglomerates of large domestic firms.
b. Includes "other foodstuffs," which is dynamic in four countries.

though they do not change the general conclusion. First, the data on manufacturing investment do not include *maquila* plants, which are particularly important in Mexico.[13] The Mexican apparel industry and electrical machinery and equipment (which includes electronics) both involved *maquila* assembly and both were very dynamic. The principal investors in the *maquila* industry were large and medium-size subsidiaries of foreign companies.[14]

13. This is also true in Costa Rica, which was not included in this section for lack of disaggregated investment data.
14. The average employment at a Mexican *maquila* in 1998 was around 300 people. Calculations based on data from the National Institute of Statistics, Geography, and Informatics (INEGI).

Second, the investment role of small and medium-size domestic firms may be underestimated. Investment data for those firms are particularly difficult to collect, and in the case of small firms, investment more often involves the creation of new firms than the expansion of existing units. Peres and Stumpo indicate that small and medium-size firms were important in foodstuffs, chemicals, and plastics in the six countries considered in table 6-11.[15] Nonetheless, large firms were the dominant investors, including in the majority of *maquila* activities, while smaller enterprises played a much less important role.

Among large firms, TNCs are concentrated in subsectors that are technology intensive (such as automobiles and pharmaceuticals) or marketing intensive (including brand-name foods and cleaning and hygiene products). Large domestic firms and conglomerates tend to specialize in the production of natural resource–based commodities, such as basic steel, traditional foods, cement, and cellulose and paper.[16]

Transnational corporations that invested in the region followed three types of strategies. Some investors aimed at developing an efficient platform for exporting to the United States, as was the case with FDI in the automobile industry in Mexico and the *maquila* plants in Mexico and elsewhere in the Caribbean Basin. Other TNCs sought to develop their access to natural resources, like minerals in Argentina, Peru, and Chile or oil in Argentina, Colombia, and Venezuela. For a third group, the main goal was to gain access to domestic or subregional markets, such as Mercosur or the Andean Community. This happened in tradables sectors, such as automobiles in Argentina and Brazil or agroindustry in Argentina, Brazil, and Mexico, as well as in nontradables such as banking, telecommunications, electricity, and natural gas distribution in almost all countries. What is notable about Latin America is the absence of important investments directed toward developing strategic assets, particularly technology. Although numerous joint-ventures have been forged between foreign and domestic firms, most of them have aimed at developing marketing strategies, where the domestic partners contribute mainly through opening their well-established commercialization networks to foreign products.[17]

TNCs gained ground with respect to domestic firms and conglomerates. The share of foreign firms in the sales of the 100 largest domestic manufacturing corporations in the region increased from 46 to 61 percent

15. See Peres and Stumpo (2000).
16. For a detailed account of the strategy of domestic conglomerates after the reforms, see Garrido and Peres (1998) and Peres (1998).
17. ECLAC (1998c).

in 1990–98.[18] Although the strong dynamism of the automobile industry explains most of the increased foreign presence during 1990–94, the main force behind the changes in participation in 1995–98 was the takeover of large domestic firms by foreign investors, particularly in Argentina, Brazil, and Mexico. Foreign takeovers were also significant in Chile after the sharp slowdown of growth in 1998–99. These data refer to sales, but it is likely that investment performance followed a similar path, given the great increase in foreign investment in medium-size and large countries in the region.[19] This reflects the advantages that TNCs enjoy in terms of managerial and technological capacities, opportunities for diversifying investment risk across countries, and control over oligopolistic markets, as well as their long experience operating in open markets under strong competition and uncertainty.

The reforms shaped the sectoral structure of manufacturing investment through several transmission mechanisms. Specifically, the reforms had a positive impact on subsectors with natural comparative advantages, including foodstuffs, cellulose and paper, chemicals and petrochemicals, and basic steel, and on subsectors in which the strengthening of intellectual property rights encouraged investment by foreign firms, as occurred, for example, in pharmaceuticals.[20] Trade opening had a negative impact on investment in less dynamic subsectors, such as textiles and apparel (outside the *maquila* sector) and leather goods. In these subsectors, competition from imported products accounted for the poor performance of investment and for their declining weight in total manufacturing production. This was particularly important for employment dynamics as we will see in the last section of the chapter.

Trade liberalization, however, cannot account for the dynamics of investment in all sectors. In particular, sectoral promotion policies explained the very good performance of the automobile industry and of *maquila* production of electronics, car parts, and apparel. The automobile industry continued to be protected from foreign competition and received special promotion in all producing countries in the region for most of the decade after the reforms, although promotional schemes were gradually phased out. The *maquila* plants enjoyed a tax-free regime, minimal transaction costs, and market access through subregional free trade

18. Garrido and Peres (1998) and ECLAC (2000b).

19. Although in some years the flows of investment to manufacturing fell as a percentage of the total due to the strength of foreign investment in the privatization of services, the amount of foreign investment in manufacturing grew throughout the period.

20. This factor also played an important role in the evolution of investment in the mining sector.

Table 6-12. *Index of Exports and Trade Balance according to Investment Dynamism in Manufacturing*[a]

Country	Pre-reform	Phase 1	Phase 2	Phase 3
Dynamic subsectors				
Export index				
Argentina	100.0	242.2	306.2	. . .
Brazil	100.0	194.7	258.3	. . .
Chile	. . .	100.0	168.0	350.2
Colombia	100.0	. . .	298.0	. . .
Mexico	100.0	434.5	1062.3	. . .
Peru	100.0	190.5	301.2	. . .
Trade balance as percent of total trade[b]				
Argentina	22.8	41.2	2.3	. . .
Brazil	40.9	43.6	-2.0	. . .
Chile	. . .	−13.9	0.2	−10.2
Colombia	−20.3	. . .	−14.4	. . .
Mexico	−37.8	−4.3	−5.0	. . .
Peru	4.4	2.7	−2.2	. . .
Lagging subsectors				
Export index				
Argentina	100.0	218.0	319.0	. . .
Brazil	100.0	282.3	379.1	. . .
Chile	. . .	100.0	170.6	484.7
Colombia	100.0	. . .	492.8	. . .
Mexico	100.0	370.4	826.4	. . .
Peru	100.0	196.3	280.3	. . .
Trade balance as percent of total trade[b]				
Argentina	−0.4	−0.1	-0.6	. . .
Brazil	−18.3	7.9	1.0	. . .
Chile	. . .	−77.9	−77.4	−75.3
Colombia	−70.1	. . .	−54.6	. . .
Mexico	−50.2	−24.0	−35.1	. . .
Peru	−23.4	−12.9	−34.8	. . .

Source: Adapted from Moguillansky and Bielschowsky (2000), on the basis of project data.
a. Periodization follows that of table 6-9.
b. Trade balance as a percentage of total trade is calculated as $(X - M)/(X + M)$.

agreements.[21] The recovery of domestic demand in the 1990s had a positive impact on housing and other construction, which in turn stimulated investment in metal products and cement.

21. For the countries in this study, the North American Free Trade Agreement (NAFTA) is important with respect to *maquila* and automobile exports, and the Southern Common Market (Mercosur) is important with respect to automobile exports.

Exports from sectors that were dynamic in investment grew very rapidly after the reforms, reaching levels three or four times higher than in the pre-reform period; Mexico turned in a particularly strong performance (see table 6-12). Nonetheless, exports from lagging subsectors grew even faster in all countries except Mexico and Peru. This unexpected result may be partially explained by their relatively low participation in exports before the reforms, which made it easier for them to achieve high growth rates. Chile, in particular, featured very low exports from lagging subsectors in the initial period. The difference in the growth rate of exports between dynamic and lagging subsectors also suggests that a significant part of their strong expansion was not based on the creation of new production capacity; the utilization of previously installed capacity was probably significant. Indeed, sectoral evidence at the country level shows that production capacity originally installed for the domestic market was shifted toward the external market.

Despite strong growth in exports of the dynamic subsectors, all countries show growing trade deficits or decreasing surpluses in the manufacturing sector. Such deterioration of the trade balance reflects the impact of macroeconomic policies, particularly exchange rate overvaluation, and a high income elasticity of demand for foreign products. Negative trade balances also indicate that investment was not sufficient to overcome or even significantly reduce the trade component of the external constraint on growth. Export growth was accompanied by even faster import growth, which resulted from the substitution of imports for domestic inputs following trade liberalization. A similar process took place in the larger countries with respect to capital goods.[22]

The falling share of domestic inputs in production increased the efficiency of manufacturing firms, allowing them to use better, cheaper inputs from abroad. At the same time, it also destroyed supplier chains, which may help to explain the poor investment performance of small and medium-size firms, particularly in sectors in which they were previously linked to larger firms through subcontracting. Similarly, the most dynamic exporters in the region, namely the *maquila* plants, did not foster local supplier chains; domestic production could never competitively supply more than three percent of inputs demanded by those plants.[23] The destruction of supplier chains and the inability to supply inputs to the *maquila* plants

---

22. For a detailed account, see Katz (2000, chapters 2 and 5); Reinhardt and Peres (2000); Peres (1998).
23. Buitelaar and Padilla (2000).

Table 6-13. *Labor Productivity in Manufacturing with Respect to the United States, 1970–96*

Country	1970	1980	1990	1996
Argentina	0.42	0.41	0.55	0.67
Brazil	0.28	0.26	0.29	0.37
Chile	0.25	0.24	0.23	0.20[a]
Colombia	0.29	0.25	0.37	0.34
Costa Rica	n.a.	n.a.	0.15	0.14[b]
Jamaica	0.26	0.16	0.16	0.13[b]
Mexico	0.32	0.30	0.44	0.38[c]
Peru	0.33	0.25	0.16	0.15

Source: Katz (2000), using ECLAC's PADI database.
a. Information for 1995.
b. Information for 1992.
c. Information for 1994.

provide a microeconomic explanation of why export growth did not spread to other sectors of the region's economies.

The greater competitiveness of exports in the manufacturing sector stemmed not only from investment, but also from an increase in productivity in the 1990s. Moguillansky and Bielschowsky show that dynamic subsectors experienced labor productivity growth rates above those found in the lagging subsectors in Argentina, Brazil, and Mexico.[24] Although productivity growth was weaker in the dynamic subsectors in Colombia and Chile, labor productivity at the end of the period was appreciably higher than in the pre-reform years. Even in Peru, where the indexes did not reach their previous levels, productivity grew once the initial period of decline in investment was overcome. All of this suggests that strong modernization processes are underway.

An alternative approach for evaluating the dynamism of labor productivity is to compare the relative productivity of the manufacturing sector in the project countries with that of the United States, which is a good proxy for the current technological frontier. Katz develops this indicator for eight countries[25] (see table 6-13). The region's low labor productivity is striking: in seven of the eight countries, manufacturing productivity was less than

24. Moguillansky and Bielschowsky (2000, chapter 2).
25. See Katz (2000, chapter 3). This study is based on information that includes mainly large and medium-size firms.

40 percent of the productivity of the U.S. manufacturing sector in the mid-1990s.

In the 1970s, the productivity gap widened somewhat between the project countries and the United States, while in the following decade the gap remained constant or even fell, except in Peru where it continued to widen. In the 1990s, only Argentina and Brazil displayed strong performances. Examining the period as a whole, it is important to highlight that much of the improvement in productivity can be traced to processes of modernization that unfolded as a result of the external debt crisis, before the widespread effects of the reforms were felt. Virtually all of the productivity gains that occurred in Colombia and Mexico, and half of Argentina's, took place in the 1980s. Only Brazil, which was a notorious latecomer and a cautious reformer, experienced most of the reduction in its productivity gap in the 1990s. Thus, the reforms were not the only force pressuring firms to increase efficiency; the dynamics of domestic and foreign markets were also very important.

A disaggregated analysis at the subsectoral level supports a similar conclusion about the different forces stimulating modernization. Katz describes a very heterogeneous situation across subsectors. In more than 70 percent of the subsectors that narrowed the gap in 1970–96, the shrinkage was already occurring between 1970 and 1990, that is, before the reforms could have a significant effect on the industrial structure. Production growth was instrumental in shrinking the gap. The subsectors that narrowed that gap correlated significantly with subsectors that experienced higher growth rates of production. The dynamics of the productivity gap may be explained by specific sectoral regimes that also played a role in shaping trends in manufacturing investment. A particularly important component of those regimes is the fast process of technological change that took place in many industries at the national and international levels.

The concept of the productivity gap may also be used to explore the position of small and medium-size enterprises (SMEs) relative to the larger firms and to ascertain whether the former were able to narrow their difference with respect to the latter. The productivity of SMEs in seven project countries varied between one-fourth and two-thirds of the corresponding levels for large firms in the mid-1990s.[26] Although labor productivity in

26. Peres and Stumpo (2000). Data do not include Bolivia and Jamaica. That paper defines SMEs according to the definitions used in each country, which coincides with the disaggregation of available information. The lower limit varies from 5 to 10 workers, while the upper limit reaches 499 in Brazil, 250 in Mexico, and 200 in Chile. Microenterprises (that is, firms with less than 5 or 10 workers) are not included in the analysis.

Figure 6-2. *Average Labor Productivity in Manufacturing, 1970–96*[a]

Thousands of 1980 dollars

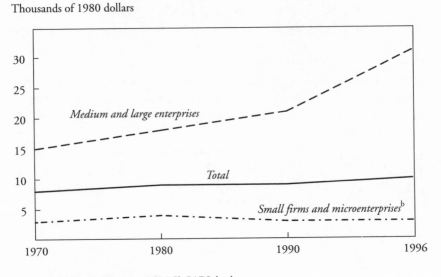

Source: Weller (2000), using ECLAC's PADI database.
a. Based on simple averages for the nine project countries.
b. Includes self-employed.

SMEs increased in all seven countries between the mid-1980s and the mid-1990s, the productivity gap narrowed in only four countries (Argentina, Brazil, Costa Rica, and Mexico), while it widened in three (Chile, Colombia, and Peru). This means not only that SME efficiency continued to lag far behind that of larger firms, but that heterogeneity across firms did not decrease.

Although data for microenterprises and informal activities are very difficult to obtain, information is available on the dynamics of labor productivity for the aggregates of large and medium-size firms, on the one hand, and small firms and microenterprises, on the other. Figure 6-2 shows that all productivity gains in manufacturing took place in the former and that the productivity gap increased over time, which is particularly troublesome given the important role these firms played in job creation.

Specialization and Polarization in Agriculture

The economic reforms had a strong impact on agriculture. Trade liberalization, privatization of state enterprises that produced agricultural inputs, and the restructuring or elimination of some of the public agrarian institutions increased heterogeneity with respect to input and product prices, the availability of services and resources, and types of producers. Some crops significantly increased their share in total production, while others lost. Productivity and foreign trade also presented a mixed performance, while the existing heterogeneity among types of producers deepened. Most countries experienced all these effects simultaneously, particularly when geographic areas specialized in activities that differed in their relative use of production factors and in the economic actors involved in production.[27]

The most important transformations in the agricultural sector resulted not only from the reforms, but also from processes that began at least a decade earlier. The most significant were the incorporation of new technologies, reduction of cultivated land, increase of land dedicated to livestock and forest plantations, and employment decline. The structure of production also changed: there was a strong development of new, highly dynamic activities linked to external markets and to the most modern agribusiness, as well as a poor performance of more traditional exports based on commodities whose profitability deteriorated because of low international prices.

The annual growth rate of agriculture and livestock was 3.5 percent in the 1970s, 2.1 percent in the 1980s, and 2.6 percent in 1990–98. These aggregate figures hide large differences among countries. In five project countries (Argentina, Bolivia, Chile, Costa Rica, and Peru), agricultural GDP grew faster in the 1990s than in the previous two decades,[28] while the trade balance improved except for Peru. In Brazil and Mexico production grew faster in the 1990s than in the previous decade, although growth rates were below those of the 1970s; the trade balance improved in the former and deteriorated in the latter. Finally, in Colombia, the agricultural growth rate was below that of the previous two decades, and the trade balance deteriorated.[29]

The structure of agricultural production is changing in favor of commercial crops with a greater elasticity of domestic and external demand. At

27. In the Andean countries, for example, new modern forms of production, which are capital-intensive and technologically sophisticated but which also make intensive use of labor (such as flowers in Colombia and Ecuador), were developed alongside natural resource exploitation and capital-intensive plantations. At the same time, there were important nuclei of peasant production, which were mainly run by the indigenous population in the Bolivian altiplano or in mountainous areas of Peru and Ecuador. This complex scenario was further complicated by the cultivation of illegal crops.

28. In both Chile and Costa Rica, growth decelerated sharply in the second half of the 1990s.

29. See Tejo (1999).

the same time, total cultivated area has stagnated or even fallen. This specialization process displayed three different patterns in the introduction and expansion of new products. In Brazil, domestic demand was the main growth factor, while in Argentina, Chile, and Costa Rica, external demand was key. Both factors operated in Mexico, albeit with varying intensity across regions of the country.

In the region as a whole, oleaginous products led expansion, followed by fruits and vegetables and planted forests.[30] Livestock grew faster than agriculture. Cereals and cane sugar were very dynamic until the first half of the 1980s, but thereafter they showed an important deceleration. Production of roots and tubers stagnated over the last quarter century, as did coffee production after the mid-1980s. As expected, the most dynamic products correspond to the most modern, capital-intensive producers in commercial agriculture. Cultivation by small producers in traditional labor-intensive agriculture has stagnated or the cultivated area has been reduced.[31]

Despite all these changes, poverty and indigence continued to present serious problems in rural areas, and in some cases poverty even increased. In addition to demographic changes, income and assets saw a greater concentration. This was especially true of land, as has historically been the case throughout the region despite policies implemented to eliminate the problem. Limitations of human, physical, and social capital as well as imperfect markets (for example, for credit, information, technology, and insurance) made it impossible or very difficult for small rural producers to shift toward products with higher demand and better prices.

Land tenure became increasingly concentrated in larger farms over the last two decades, while the number of smaller units decreased significantly. The last agricultural censuses of Bolivia and Chile, as well as studies for Argentina, Brazil, Colombia, and Mexico, show a strong decline in the number of small production units in the last two decades, a process that intensified in the 1990s. The reduction of cultivated area in Brazil and Chile was accompanied by the elimination of small units. In contrast with other regions of the world, land tenure and ownership structure are still pressing political issues in many Latin American countries. The current

30. In oleaginous products the fastest growing project countries were Argentina, Bolivia, and Brazil thanks to soybean expansion, followed by Costa Rica's production of African palm. In fruits and vegetables, most of the expansion took place in Argentina, Brazil, Chile, Costa Rica, and Mexico, whereas planted forestry increased remarkably in Argentina and Chile.

31. Dirven (1999).

concentration process is a step backward after the land reforms implemented in the 1960s and 1970s.[32]

New economic actors entered agricultural activities, particularly large TNCs in agribusiness and related marketing chains, while established firms and many family-based firms left the market. The pattern varied among specific sectors.[33] Different forces determined the new situation regarding sectors and actors, among which the most important were research and extension efforts by public and private entities and changes in international demand. For example, the expansion of soybeans was boosted by the research efforts of national agricultural technology centers in Argentina and Brazil, while the private sector was behind the introduction and expansion of sunflowers. In Chile, the private sector strongly invested in the expansion of fruit production, based on the results of a long-term public support program. Also in Chile, the national agricultural research agencies and specialized international centers obtained new high-performance varieties of cereals, while the private sector, especially international companies producing hybrid seeds, was the main force behind productivity increases in corn production.

Economic reforms, particularly trade liberalization, had an important impact on the integration of the region's agricultural sector into the international market and gave rise to new situations in the domestic markets. Domestic producers faced new competition from foreign products, some of which were strongly subsidized by the European Union and the United States. Starting in the late 1980s and continuing through the 1990s, imports of agricultural and food products increased significantly and started to compete with domestic products for the local market. Domestic producers had to specialize in activities for which they had comparative advantage, leaving other products to foreign suppliers. Consumers benefited, but producers that could not compete had to leave the market. While, this process increased efficiency, as shown by productivity growth (see figure 6-1), it also led to land concentration and polarization within the agricultural sector. The losers were not always producers without comparative advantages; overvalued domestic currencies and distortions in the international market forced out a number of competitive producers.

The share of agricultural products in the region's total exports generally fell in the 1990s. Most countries tended to compensate for low international

---

32. David and Morales (forthcoming, chapter 2).
33. Tejo (1999).

prices in their agricultural exports by increasing export volumes. In the same period, agricultural imports increased in price and volume in all countries except Argentina and Chile, where import volume increased while prices fell.

New trends in world food demand affected the ways in which agricultural and food products were produced, processed, and internationally traded. Countries that adjusted their exports toward high-quality agricultural products (for example, products that are packaged, frozen, reprocessed, or of recognized origin and that meet international sanitary regulations) could increase their share in international markets in the 1990s. Brazil, Chile, and Mexico were among the countries that benefited from such new opportunities, exporting products with higher value added and obtaining significant price increases.

Another important effect of trade liberalization on agriculture in Latin America was the strong increase of imports of chemical inputs such as pesticides, herbicides, and fertilizers. While herbicide imports were small in the 1970s and 1980s, they were a significant component of total imports in the 1990s. The increase of pesticide imports was even stronger, especially in Argentina and Bolivia. In Brazil and Mexico, local production is more developed, such that pesticides and herbicides had a relatively low share in total imports; this may hide high levels of imported chemical inputs for their production, however. This strong growth of chemical inputs widened the productivity gap between large and small producers in the region, because the latter do not have the financial resources to use those inputs intensively. Environmental deterioration may be another negative effect of this increased use of chemical inputs.

Natural Advantages and Access to Foreign Investment in Mining

Privatization, the elimination of restrictions on foreign direct investment, and the strengthening of property rights have had a strong impact on the performance of the mining sector in Latin America.[34] Accumulated capital stock and technological experience of relevant economic actors was also important. The evolution of international markets for minerals provided the context in which the various changes occurred.[35]

34. Unless otherwise indicated, the data in this section come from Moguillansky and Bielschowsky (2000, chapter 3).

35. Mining exports more than doubled in Argentina from 1990 to 1998, although they started from a very low base. Exports also increased substantially in Chile and Peru; they fell in 1998 when these countries were hit hard by the international crisis.

Table 6-14. *Investment in Mining, 1990–97*
Billions of dollars and percent

Country	Total investment	Share by country
Argentina	2.3	9.1
Brazil	4.4	17.6
Chile	15.5	61.7
Peru	2.9	11.6
Total	25.1	100.0

Source: Moguillansky and Bielschowsky (2000), on the basis of project data.

Beginning in the early 1990s, the region's mining sector experienced dynamic investment in both exploration and exploitation.[36] Investment in exploitation was heavily concentrated in Chile, with Brazil occupying a distant second place (see table 6-14). Gross fixed capital formation as a percentage of total GDP for this sector rose sharply in Chile, passing from 1 percent in 1975–79 to 4.4 percent in 1990–97, while in Brazil it fell from 0.2 percent to 0.1 percent over the same period. It remained constant at about 0.9 percent in Peru after a sharp drop in the early 1990s (see table 6-6).[37]

Trends in mining investment were determined primarily by the interaction of three factors: the evolution of the world market, new sectoral regimes, and the strategies of investing companies. Sectoral evolution was a function of the global market, which is characterized by relatively regular cycles of underinvestment and overinvestment caused by indivisibilities and projects with long maturity periods. Over the long term, growth rates of consumption and production tend to coincide.

The value of annual worldwide consumption of minerals and metals grew from $93 billion to $172 billion between 1980 and 1996. This period can be divided into two phases characterized by different dynamics. The growth rate decelerated during the 1980s in comparison with the two

36. The region as a whole increased its participation in total world exploration from 26 to 29 percent during the 1990s; investment was concentrated in Chile (51 percent) and Brazil (24 percent), with the remainder mainly in Peru (12 percent) and Argentina (10 percent).

37. The periodization used in this section and in the section on electricity and telecommunication differs from the one used in the section on manufacturing. This is due both to a lack of available quantitative information and, more fundamentally, to the fact that the principal determinant of the evolution of these sectors (namely, privatization) occurred during what was identified as the second phase in the evolution of the investment process. Therefore, it is more useful to work with a periodization that includes two stages: before and after privatization.

previous decades; it then accelerated in the late 1980s and early 1990s. Following the usual cyclical pattern, rising consumption stimulated increased supply, which was made possible by greater investments, and a decline in prices that was accentuated toward the end of the decade as a result of the international crisis.

Price reductions forced a series of technological innovations designed to reduce costs, raise productivity, and increase profits.[38] These innovations, such as mechanization, automated methods of control, robotization, new methods of processing minerals, and the use of satellites in exploration, were carried out mainly by TNC subsidiaries, particularly in iron, copper, and gold exploitation.

The growing role of TNCs was facilitated by important reforms that eliminated restrictions on foreign capital, modified the systems for granting concessions, and changed the tax regime. Chile was the first country to establish a legal framework (in 1974) that did not discriminate between national and foreign capital in the mining sector, followed by Argentina and Peru in the early 1990s and Brazil in 1995. Changes in legislation governing mining concessions sought to reduce uncertainty and risk in areas where investment costs could be recovered only in the long run. In 1980 Chile enacted so-called full legal concessions, which brought concessions exclusively within the realm of the judiciary. Expropriation would entail full indemnity calculated according to the commercial value of the concession, based on its present value. Similarly, Peru instituted a plan in 1992 which granted new concessions indefinitely.[39] Changes in tax systems tended to simplify the tax structures and in a few cases, such as Chile, to award virtually complete exemptions from income tax. In addition, several countries reduced the costs associated with payment of taxes on external remittances of capital and profits.

Chile's legislative changes involving taxation and concessions did not induce significant flows of mining investments in exploitation during the 1970s and 1980s: FDI averaged only $90 million annually in the period 1974–89; it rose to $800 million in 1990 and peaked at $1.7 billion in

38. Katz (2000, chapter 4).

39. New types of concession contracts have also been introduced in the privatization of oil and natural gas. In Argentina and Peru, privatization has been almost total, while in Bolivia and Colombia it has been only partial, and in Brazil and Mexico state monopolies are still in charge. Reforms in the way concessions are granted have been instrumental for higher FDI flows to this sector, particularly in Argentina, Bolivia, and Colombia. Moguillansky and Bielschowsky (2000, chapter 3) present a detailed analysis of the dynamics of investment in this sector.

1993–97. The state enterprise Codelco (Corporación Nacional del Cobre) was the principal investor until 1988. The change in the regulatory system permitted the acceleration of investment during the 1990s, but it had little effect until the global market began an upward trend.[40]

The principal actors in mining before the 1970s were TNC subsidiaries, although medium-size and large local companies also played a role, particularly in Peru and Brazil. The nationalizations of the 1970s strengthened the role of public enterprises, some of which remain important actors today (for example, Codelco) or did until the late 1990s (for example, CVRD, Companhia do Vale do Rio Doce, in Brazil).

The strategies and performance of public enterprises varied widely among the different countries. Codelco undertook significant processes of modernization, investment, and the forging of alliances with other firms for exploration and exploitation, all of which opened access to financing. Investment in Peru's public enterprises diminished from $259 million in 1975–79 to $27 million in 1990–92. This explains the decline in gross capital formation as a portion of total GDP in the mining sector as noted above. In Brazil, the state was the principal owner of mineral deposits until the privatization of CVRD in 1997. The decline of investment in Brazilian mining can be attributed to a lack of exploration owing to the scarcity of resources available to the public sector, restrictions on foreign investment that remained in force until 1995, and a lack of infrastructure (including energy, roads, and transportation). State investments remained stable at about $36 million in 1978–95, while national private investment was extremely unstable and foreign investment fell from $51 million in 1978–85 to $10 million in 1990–95.

In the early 1990s, foreign firms stepped up their role in the region's mining sector through privatizations in Peru and the expansion of investment into areas not allocated to Codelco in Chile, although domestic capital retained a significant presence. In Brazil, however, foreign investment did not flow heavily into the mining sector after investment liberalization because of the saturation of the global market and because the lack of exploration in previous years meant that knowledge was scarce regarding the country's mineral reserves. The latter may be the principal reason for the low level of investment in Brazilian mining, while elsewhere in the region it grew rapidly. In the second half of the 1990s, foreign investment was

---

40. In 1974–85, important investments were undertaken in exploration that laid a base for later exploitations.

substantial not only in Chile but also in Peru, where investment in mining became more dynamic in 1997–98.[41] In Argentina, foreign investment in mining jumped from only $2 million in 1992 to $316 million in 1996, suddenly ranking it among the most attractive countries in the world for mining investment.

Investments by foreign corporations and large national firms tended to be of a long-range nature and to employ cutting-edge technology. They thus contributed to technological progress in the sector. These firms had little difficulty financing their investments, and they frequently allied with one another to undertake large-scale projects. Changes in the legal framework that eliminated restrictions on contracting foreign loans, along with decreases in taxes on capital remittances and profits, provided a boost in favor of using resources from abroad. Since TNCs operate as global corporations, however, they had little incentive to establish higher value added activities within the countries where mining takes place. Mines therefore tend to function as enclaves, with scant, albeit increasing, articulation to the rest of the national economy.

The stimulation of investment in mining appears to be concentrated in relatively few countries and products. Besides the obvious fact that this reflects variation in the availability of deposits, the difference between the performance of Chile and Peru up until the mid-1990s illustrates the advantage the former enjoyed by being the first to establish a regulatory framework favorable to foreign investment, and thus to be in a position to take advantage of the change in the world market in the late 1980s.

Technological Revolution and Privatization in Electricity and Telecommunications

The electricity and telecommunications sectors underwent great changes in the 1990s. For a long time, the predominant actors in production and investment in these sectors were public firms that often failed to optimize performance, since their behavior was determined by objectives that frequently contradicted one another: generating employment, providing low-price services to low-income consumers, and subsidizing other firms at public expense. [42] This behavior was not conducive to the incorporation of

41. Expectations were also raised for important investments in so-called mega-projects, a group of large projects mainly in the fields of copper mining and natural gas, which, if realized, would represent investments of close to $5 billion.

42. Unless otherwise indicated, the data in this section come from Moguillansky and Bielschowsky (2000, chapter 4).

technological progress or to the expansion of services when public spending was curtailed. Most countries undertook privatization and established new rules of the game. These rules were directed at markets both for privatized services and for new products, particularly in telecommunications. Actions in these areas determined the level and structure of sectoral investment. New actors were incorporated through privatization and the opening to domestic and foreign investors of markets previously restricted to the state. The manner and context in which privatization occurred determined the kinds of actors that entered the market in each instance.

Chile began to privatize in the early 1980s and essentially had completed the process by the end of that decade. Privatization took place during a period of economic crisis. As Moguillanksy argues, it was accompanied by specific policies to stimulate the participation of new actors, who would be crucial to the success of the process.[43] Examples of these policies include the modernization and financial restructuring of firms prior to privatization, the enactment of new legislation regulating the service tariffs charged by firms that would be privatized, and measures to stimulate reluctant private actors to take part in the privatization process.

This policy package brought both benefits and costs. Among the most important benefits was the learning opportunity it created for local actors, who were able to develop management skills that they later used to participate effectively in similar privatizations elsewhere in the region. The costs included the low revenue obtained by the state in exchange for valuable assets and the lack of transparency that characterized the process. Participants in the privatizations were mainly domestic businesses and institutional investors, although foreign investors participated in the privatization of local telephone services. In the second half of the 1990s, foreign investors began to acquire a significant stake in electricity generation, which had been privatized in the previous decade.

Privatization spread throughout the region in the 1990s, although there were exceptions in both electricity and telecommunications. For example, the generation of electricity for public consumption remains a state monopoly in Mexico,[44] as does basic telephone service in Costa Rica. The manner in which the privatizations were carried out varied according to the circumstances of each country. "Enterprise capitalization" in Bolivia

---

43. For a more detailed analysis of the Chilean experience, see Moguillansky (1999).

44. This is not to imply that the participation of the private sector did not increase within the electricity sector. Besides generating electricity for their own use, private actors participated in the expansion of the sector through build-lease-transfer (BLT) contracts with the state, as well as through the construction of complementary works.

implied both privatization and the commitment of buyers to invest in the privatized firms.[45] Some countries attempted to introduce systems of "popular capitalism," for example by encouraging unions to acquire shares of the privatized companies. Most of the offers, however, were put out for controlling shares, which were largely acquired by international enterprises, acting alone or in partnership with local business groups. This approach avoided the fragmentation of control, and it eased the financing of the new firms by enabling them to avoid high dividends and thus to retain a greater portion of the profits, which could be reinvested. It also contributed to increased concentration.

Privatizations changed the market structure, as competition was introduced in electricity generation, long-distance telephone service, mobile telephones, and other telecommunications services. Increased competitive pressures derived not only from the introduction of more players into existing markets, but also from the creation of new markets whose products competed with those of existing markets, as in the case of satellite or mobile telephones with respect to basic telephone services. Sectoral regulations tended to prevent vertical integration of different segments of activities, as in the electrical sector in Argentina, Bolivia, and Peru. At the same time, the conditions under which privatizations were carried out and the regulatory frameworks governing privatized markets established market reserves and created entry barriers to new competitors in potentially contestable segments in the telecommunications sector. Thus, for example, long-distance telephone services were opened to competition in Chile only in 1994 and in Mexico in 1997.

In this context of heightened competition in certain segments, together with the maintenance of highly concentrated monopolistic or oligopolistic conditions in others, the regulatory systems that determined service tariffs had a powerful impact on investment performance. The regulatory agencies responsible for these sectors went through a learning process in this regard.[46] They discovered that markets with weaker regulation and higher entry barriers tended to charge higher tariffs for service and to persist in cross-subsidies.[47] In contrast, tariffs were reduced significantly in countries

45. Capitalization meant that the state kept half of the shares of the privatized company, while the remaining half was sold to investors, who acquired the controlling rights and promised to invest significant sums to capitalize the business.

46. The regulatory failures evidenced by the serious problems in the supply of electricity in Argentina and Chile in early 1999 prove that these learning processes are far from complete, even in those countries with the longest experience with privatization.

47. These subsidies occur, for example, between local and long-distance telephone or between mobile and basic service.

that established more transparent mechanisms and formulas for setting tariffs, and in sectors more open to competition. In addition to awarding periods of limited competition, countries in the region offered strong incentives for investors to participate in the electricity sector. These included the state purchase of energy in Colombia and Mexico and tariff legislation that assured levels of profitability in Bolivia, Chile, and Peru.

Evaluating the impact of the privatization processes on investment and the incorporation of technological progress in both telecommunications and electricity is difficult because of a lack of comparable information among countries, the heterogeneous paths through which the processes unfolded in the various countries, and the short time elapsed since the privatizations.

The situation is more homogeneous in the telecommunications sector. All project countries except Costa Rica had completed or were far along in the privatization process. A few TNCs, which compete with one another for global market shares, controlled or participated decisively alongside domestic groups in the privatized firms. In this context, the investment coefficient for the sector increased in most countries considered in table 6-15. These investments were also reflected in an expansion of service, as measured on the basis of total lines installed.[48] Privatizations played a crucial role in the evolution of investment, but they were not the only determinant of sectoral dynamics. Other factors that were also important include the technological dynamism of the sector at the international level, rivalry among large TNCs for new markets, the strengthening of competition pressures on firms already established in the market, and the backward initial conditions of service in the region. Companies actually exceeded their goals for the expansion of networks and services, which were negotiated during the privatization process, and investment and productivity also grew in countries that privatized late, such as Brazil, or that did not privatize at all, such as Costa Rica.

The dynamics were more uneven in the electricity sector. Costa Rica, Jamaica, and Mexico did not privatize their public enterprises, although Mexico stimulated private sector participation in financing. Argentina, Bolivia, Colombia, and Peru made significant progress toward privatization, although the state maintained an important role in investment. Chile underwent a total privatization since the 1980s. The data on the evolution of investment do not show a dynamic performance for the sector as a whole (see table 6-15), but it is important to bear in mind two relevant factors. First, in some countries, such as Argentina, the state made important in-

48. Katz (2000, chapter 4); Walter and Senén (1998).

Table 6-15. *Investment in Telecommunications and Electricity, 1980–97*
Percent of GDP

Sector and country	1980–1988	1989	1990–1995	1997
Telecommunications				
Argentina	n.a.	n.a.	0.7	n.a.
Bolivia	n.a.	n.a.	0.7	2.3
Brazil	0.4	0.6	0.6	0.8
Colombia	0.4	0.5	0.7	1.4
Chile	0.6	0.6	1.3	1.9
Mexico	n.a.	0.4	0.5	0.2
Peru	0.1	0.1	1.1	0.8
Electricity				
Argentina	1.3	0.5	0.4	0.3
Bolivia	n.a.	0.8	1.5	2.3
Brazil	1.6	1.7	1.1	0.6
Colombia	2.4	1.7	2.2	2.6
Costa Rica[a]	1.9	n.a.	1.8	2.6
Chile	1.7	2.0	1.3	2.1
Mexico	n.a.	0.6	0.6	n.a.
Peru	1.4	0.4	1.1	1.2

Source: Moguillansky and Bielschowsky (2000), on the basis of project data.
a. Includes telecommunications.

vestments before privatization, which diminished pressures on the private sector to expand immediately upon its entry into the market. Second, for those countries for which data enable us to evaluate trends in private investment (namely, Chile, Colombia, and Peru), the growth rate equaled or surpassed the corresponding levels for public investment.[49]

In both the electricity and telecommunications sectors, crucial technological advances occurred in the aftermath of privatization. Advances in the production of electricity reflected the incorporation of new processes, such as the use of combined cycle gas turbines and the adoption of new forms of strategic management. The telecommunications sector benefited from the revolution in information technologies.

49. Moguillansky and Bielschowsky (2000, chapter 4). In Chile, the private sector undertook important investments in 1989–96 that are not reflected in investment as a percentage of total GDP, owing to the decline in state investment and strong GDP growth in the period.

Privatizations were accompanied not only by the expansion of telephone networks, but also by the incorporation of new areas of activity and improved quality of service. The degree of digitalization provides an indicator of the latter; it reveals a strong absolute increase as well as a surprisingly rapid convergence toward the international frontier, as represented by levels in the United States (see table 6-16). A similar convergence is evident in the number of lines in service per employee, which is a good indicator of average labor productivity in the sector. Katz reports considerable advances in other indicators of performance, such as reductions in the number of customers lacking service and in the average daily number of service breakdowns awaiting repair. Indicators of the use of human resources in privatized companies also show substantial modernization and improvements in labor relations, including an increase in the number of professionals, a reduction in the average age and seniority of employees, decreased absenteeism, and an improvement in labor relations.[50]

The reforms involving privatization strongly affected the electricity and telecommunications sectors, even more than was the case in mining. Investment picked up, and quality and productivity quickly converged toward international levels, although the performance of telecommunications was far superior to that of electricity. Currently, their principal problem is the insufficiency of sectoral regulatory frameworks, which, together with the weakness of the regulatory agencies overseeing individual firms, often led to the establishment of barriers to entry in various segments of the market. Electricity faces an additional challenge: maintaining trends in investment and technological progress under conditions of decreased state support and tariffs established under less favorable conditions.

Increasing Heterogeneity in Sectoral Employment

At the aggregate level, as we saw in chapter 5, the reforms had a negative impact on employment creation. At the sectoral level, the impact of the reforms varied considerably, in part because they interacted with trends long underway. The long-term trend of falling employment in agriculture and expanding employment in services accelerated in the 1990s.[51] At the same time, the strong expansion of employment in the manufacturing sec-

---

50. Katz (2000, chapter 4).
51. Unless otherwise indicated, information in this section comes from Weller (2000, chapter 5).

Table 6-16. *Indicators of Quality and Productivity in Telecommunications, 1986–96*

Indicator	1986	1987	1988	1989	1990	1991	1992	1993	1994	1995	1996
Digitalization (percent)											
Latin America[a]	1.4	5.3	15.0	16.6	23.6	27.8	39.6	49.8	60.7	69.0	74.5
United States	26.0	32.0	36.0	41.0	47.0	52.7	58.7	66.0	74.1	78.4	80.5
Lines in service per employee (number)											
Argentina	70	50	55	59	62	70	90	110	150	170	296
Brazil	70	75	80	80	85	90	100	110	130	160	170
Chile	65	n.a.	n.a.	70	84	125	152	177	208	235	291
Mexico	95	90	95	100	110	120	130	150	160	170	160
Uruguay	72	77	70	59	60	65	65	70	100	110	150
Latin America[a]	72	70	73	78	86	98	110	123	139	158	185
United States	140	138	144	150	149	154	163	170	174	183	190

Source: Walter and Senén (1998); Moguillansky and Bielschowsky (2000), on the basis of project data.
a. Includes Argentina, Brazil, Chile, Colombia, Mexico, Peru, Puerto Rico, Uruguay, and Venezuela.

Table 6-17. *Employment Growth by Sector, 1990–97*[a]
Percent

Sector	Employment growth	Contribution to total
Agriculture	–0.9	–13.2
Manufacturing industry	1.1	8.5
Construction	2.7	8.8
Commerce, restaurants, and hotels	3.6	32.7
Electricity, gas and water, transportation, storage, and communications	4.9	12.0
Financial services, insurance, real estate, and business services	6.9	13.4
Social, communal, and personal services	2.7	41.7
Other	–3.1	–4.0
Total	2.0	100.0

Source: Weller (2000), on the basis of official country statistics.
a. Annual weighted averages for the nine project countries.

tor, which came to a halt in the early 1980s and then resumed at the end of that decade, appears to have come to an end.[52]

Between 1990 and 1997, agricultural employment fell by an annual average of 0.9 percent in the nine project countries (see table 6-17). In three countries where total employment in the sector decreased (Brazil, Chile, and Costa Rica), both family and commercial agriculture performed poorly (see table 6-18). Demand for labor in the more dynamic activities was not strong enough to offset the loss of employment in the less dynamic ones.[53] The family-based rural economy, for its part, did not even generate enough jobs to cover its natural population growth. In countries where total employment in the sector increased (Mexico and Peru), it expanded in all the main categories, namely, wage earners, self-employed workers,

52. Reinhardt and Peres (2000) show that agriculture reduced its share in total employment from 41 percent in 1970 to 24 percent in 1995–97, while total industry, which includes manufacturing and construction, reduced its share from 23 percent to 21 percent. The share of services increased from 36 percent to 55 percent in the same period.

53. This was not the situation in the 1980s. In Chile and Costa Rica, for example, nontraditional agricultural exports contributed to the strong growth in employment in the middle of that decade (Gómez and Echeñique, 1998; Weller, 1996).

Table 6-18. *Change in Agricultural Employment by Occupational Category,*
1988–97
Percent

Country (period)	Wage earners	Self-employed	Nonwage workers	Total agricultural employment[a]
Brazil (1992–97)	−2.6	−0.8	−2.8	−1.9
Chile (1990–96)	−0.8	1.3	−8.5	−0.8
Colombia (1988–95)	n.a.	n.a.	n.a.	−1.3
Costa Rica (1990–96)[b]	0.1	−1.1	−7.4	−1.1
Mexico (1991–97)	5.7	2.7	3.0	1.6
Peru (1994–97)[b]	8.5	8.2	10.5	9.4

Source: Weller (2000), on the basis of project data.
a. Includes other non-specified employment.
b. Self-employed workers include employers.

and nonwage workers. In Peru, the exceptional growth of the rural work force is explained by increased security in rural areas.[54]

These situations were influenced by the demographics of each country and by job opportunities in agriculture and in the rest of the economy, both urban and rural. In fact, by the mid-1990s more than 20 percent of the total agricultural labor force lived in urban areas.[55] At the same time, rural residents were increasingly employed in nonagricultural jobs, which currently represent more than 30 percent of rural residents' principal employment and more than 40 percent of their incomes.

Employment dynamics across agricultural activities varied according to their labor intensity. The reduction of import tariffs, the elimination of production or import monopolies, and the overvaluation of national currencies resulted in a greater supply of more diversified and less expensive agricultural equipment. Counteracting lower prices, the cost of credit to the agricultural sector increased (previously it was heavily subsidized in most countries), and its availability decreased when targeted credit lines were eliminated. Producers with access to credit were therefore the main beneficiaries of the fall in machinery prices. They substituted equipment for unskilled (sometimes temporary) labor, thereby keeping a substantially

54. The data on Mexico are of doubtful quality owing to measurement problems. Consequently, caution should be used in drawing conclusions from them.
55. As defined by the population census in each country (see Dirven, 1999).

Table 6-19. *Change in Manufacturing Employment, 1990–97*
Percent

Country	Annual growth rate
Argentina (urban total)	−2.2
Bolivia (provincial capitals)	8.8
Brazil[a]	0.3
Chile	2.2
Colombia[b]	−0.9
Costa Rica	0.6
Jamaica[b]	1.1
Mexico[b]	4.3
Peru (Lima)	−0.1
Total[c]	1.2

Source: Weller (2000), on the basis of household surveys.
a. Data for 1992–97.
b. Data for 1991–97.
c. Weighted average.

smaller, but more stable and highly skilled, work force. The reduction of labor demand is reflected in the evolution of wages. For the three project countries for which information is available (Chile, Costa Rica, and Mexico), agricultural wages fell in relation to the average wage in the economy.

Manufacturing employment increased in Latin America as a whole in the 1990s, with an annual growth rate of 1.1 percent (see table 6-17). The project countries demonstrate a sharp contrast between situations in which manufacturing employment was stagnant or falling (Argentina, Brazil, Colombia, and Peru) and those in which it increased substantially (Mexico and Bolivia) (see table 6-19). Weller shows that in countries where employment grew slowly or fell, average labor productivity increased; the converse was the case for countries where employment grew.[56] This evolution was the result of the interaction of forces related to dynamics of manufacturing employment in large versus smaller firms and to changes in the subsectoral structure of manufacturing.

Microenterprises and small firms provided strong employment growth. For the six project countries included in table 6-20, their job creation record was much better than that of large enterprises and better than the manufac-

56. Weller (2000, chapter 5).

Table 6-20. *Change in Manufacturing Employment by Size of Firm, 1990s*
Percent

| Country (period) | Wage earners | | | | | |
	Micro-enter-prises	Small enter-prises	Medium-size and large enter-prises	Un-specified	Other	Total
Change in employment						
Argentina (1991–97)	0.2	0.6	–1.0	–13.6	–2.6	–2.1
Bolivia (1989–96)	14.3	16.8	5.9	n.a.	16.8	13.3
Brazil (1993–96)	8.8	4.5	–2.5	–11.1	1.1	–0.7
Chile (1990–96)	3.0	3.7	–1.9	0.3	2.4	3.1
Costa Rica (1990–96)	7.4	7.3	–0.3	23.4	–1.3	0.5
Mexico (1991–97)	12.2	1.7	4.3	–16.3	4.9	4.3
Contribution to total employment change						
Argentina (1991–97)	1.1	8.1	–11.6	–71.4	–26.2	–100.0
Bolivia (1989–96)	11.6	13.8	9.6	n.a.	65.0	100.0
Brazil (1993–96)	106.1	53.6	–265.0	–17.7	23.1	–100.0
Chile (1990–96)	27.6	122.8	–67.8	1.1	16.3	100.0
Costa Rica (1990–96)	118.0	42.8	–34.4	34.9	–61.3	100.0
Mexico (1991–97)	26.4	6.7	42.2	–3.7	28.4	100.0

Source: Weller (2000), on the basis of household surveys.
Note: The definition of groups of enterprises varies by country. Microenterprises always contain up to 5 workers. Small enterprises contain 6 to 9 in Costa Rica, 10 or under in Brazil, 49 or under in Chile, and 50 or under in Argentina, Mexico, and Peru.

turing total in most countries.[57] Indeed, they created enough jobs to offset the decline in larger firms. Argentina, Brazil, and Chile experienced a large decline in manufacturing employment in medium-size and large firms, while only in Bolivia and Mexico did employment in larger firms grow. In the case of Mexico, larger firms accounted for 42 percent of net new job creation.

The characteristics of job creation in Mexico differed from those of other project countries, except Costa Rica.[58] Labor-intensive sectors rap-

57. Periodization in table 6-20 differs slightly from that in table 6-19 because of different availability of disaggregated data..
58. Similar processes are taking place in other Central American and Caribbean countries as well (Buitelaar, Padilla, and Urrutia, 1999).

idly increased their share of total manufacturing employment, which grew substantially. Jobs also grew strongly in metal products, automobiles, and the *maquila* plants. Employment in *maquila* plants, whose output consists mainly of car parts, electrical and electronic products, and garments came to account for more than one million jobs and about one-fourth of all manufacturing employment in the country. Integration into the North American economic space began before the reforms, but the reforms accelerated the process. As a result, Mexico's employment pattern approximated the expectations described at the beginning of this chapter.

At the subsectoral level, data for employment in medium-size and large firms show that two simultaneous processes were at work. First, labor-intensive subsectors lost share relative to more capital-intensive ones. Highly labor-intensive sectors such as textiles, garments, leather products, and footwear continued to lose ground within manufacturing in the 1990s (see table 6-8), while the capital-intensive production of natural resource–based commodities kept the important share it won in the 1970s and 1980s.[59] Although some relatively labor-intensive subsectors were dynamic (for example, metal products), the changes in the production structure of the sector had a negative impact on job creation. Thus, if the sectoral composition of manufacturing output had not changed between 1990 and 1996, employment in the medium-size and large firms would have fallen by only 0.4 percent instead of 0.8 percent, as a simple average for the six projects countries shown in table 6-8. Second, within subsectors, incorporation of technical progress resulted in layoffs or less employment creation than usual, even in sectors with strong increases in output (such as automobiles).

Wages in manufacturing increased in relation to the average wages in the total economy in only three project countries (Chile, Costa Rica, and Mexico), while they fell in four (Bolivia, Brazil, Colombia, and Jamaica). As discussed in chapter 5 for the economies as a whole, this pattern suggests that there was no trade-off between the evolution of wages and the dynamics of sectoral employment. Nor was there always a direct relation between wages and labor productivity. In Brazil, sharp sectoral employment reduction implied increased productivity; this was accompanied by a fall in relative wages. Labor productivity growth thus resulted more from layoffs rather than from an upgrading of the labor force.

Finally, in almost all project countries, the wage gap between formal and informal firms increased in favor of the former throughout the 1990s. This is consistent with the concentration of productivity gains in the larger

59. Katz (2000, chapter 2).

firms, and it shows that segmentation between firms of different sizes included all variables: investment, productivity, and wages. Microenterprises were the main providers of jobs, but they could only offer low-productivity, relatively low-paid employment. Even the fast-growing *maquila* plants in Mexico paid wages 30 percent below the average for manufacturing in the mid-1990s.[60] Growth of labor demand in countries with important *maquila* operations could not offset their large supply of unskilled labor.

The most dynamic employers were in the services, which explain more than 95 percent of new net job creation (see table 6-17). The services sector is highly heterogeneous, but two general situations can be identified. First, commerce, restaurants and hotels, together with social, communal, and personal services, accounted for 74 percent of all jobs created in the region. Second, financial services, insurance, real estate, and business services experienced even faster growth, as did electricity, natural gas and water, in addition to transportation, storage, and communications. Their small share in total employment, however, meant that these categories contributed only 26 percent of new jobs.

Each of these branches of the services sector is internally diverse in terms of the qualifications of those working there. In commerce, restaurant, and hotel activities, the informal nature of much retail trade contrasts sharply with the expansion of large modern supermarkets. Similar diversity is found in communal, social, and personal services and in financial services, insurance, real estate, and business services. The former manifests a clear polarization between the demand for more highly qualified labor in health and education, on the one hand, and employment in domestic service, on the other. In the latter, financial activities and insurance contrast with business services, which include security, maintenance, and cleaning.

The economic reforms played an important role in the growth of employment in services, as well as in the polarization that took place within the sector. Although the privatization of electricity and telecommunications was immediately followed by significant layoffs in most countries, it led to the modernization and expansion of those services, which account for their job creation. Similarly, trade liberalization led to the expansion of services related to export-import processes, while financial liberalization led to the introduction of new financial services and to new employment. Finally, pressures to reduce costs led to the outsourcing of service activities

60. Buitelaar and Padilla (2000).

previously undertaken within manufacturing firms, which account for the strong development of business services.

These sectoral and microeconomic impacts of the reforms ran parallel to macroeconomic impacts. Moderate economic growth, in the context of a growing economically active population, implied a supply push for job creation that resulted in the strong expansion of employment in the informal sector. As was the case in manufacturing, some very dynamic job creators in the services offered low-paid jobs. In particular, wages in commerce, restaurants, and hotels, which accounted for 33 percent of net job creation, fell in relation to the average wage in the economy in five out of seven project countries.

Conclusions

The sectoral and microeconomic analyses complement the results on growth and employment presented in the previous two chapters. Behind aggregate figures showing moderate growth of GDP, investment, and employment, we found substantial heterogeneity with respect to patterns across sectors and types of firms. Capital formation was concentrated in a relatively small number of subsectors, giving rise to processes of specialization that coincided with a strong export orientation in many, but not all, cases. Nonetheless, production for the domestic market was not neglected: the poor performance of sectors such as clothing and footwear was offset by the excellent performance in foodstuffs.

Large firms were the most important investors, although smaller companies had a minor presence in some activities where investment grew rapidly. Among big firms, TNC subsidiaries gained ground vis-à-vis large domestic conglomerates. These subsidiaries were responsible for much of the investment growth, not only in the most dynamic areas of manufacturing, but also in mining and telecommunications. Privatizations, liberalization of regulations that prevented foreign firms from investing in many sectors, and the globalization of important industries combined to strengthen the position of foreign corporations.

As with investment, technological progress was not distributed homogeneously among sectors and firms. Manufacturing subsectors in which investment grew most rapidly generally showed a sharp increase in productivity and, in many cases, closed the productivity gap with respect to the United States. This was partly a continuation of adjustment processes begun during or even before the crisis of the 1980s. Although the gap between the productivity of large firms and that of small and medium-size enterprises narrowed in some countries, performance continued to be extremely dissimilar. Modernization processes, like investment, occurred mainly among larger firms.

The importance of external factors in the incorporation of new technologies increased in tandem with the investment process. The growing significance of imported capital goods, the substitution of foreign for domestic inputs, and the construction of technologically advanced plants by foreign firms all resulted in a greater presence of foreign components in the region's national innovation systems. At the same time, the state reduced its involvement in technological efforts, but private actors have not always stepped in to fill the void.[61]

Trade liberalization and privatization were the reforms that had the greatest impact at the sectoral and microeconomic levels. Trade liberalization put pressure on firms to increase competitiveness by substituting imported for national inputs. It also facilitated subregional integration processes that opened markets for manufacturing subsectors in which investment and the incorporation of technical progress were most dynamic. Privatization, meanwhile, was instrumental in stimulating the mining, electricity, and telecommunications sectors, especially when it coincided with a favorable international environment or took place in sectors experiencing accelerated technological change.

Despite many positive developments, important problems remain, including growing manufacturing trade deficits; the enclave nature of large mining firms; uncertainty about future investments in the electricity sector once the currently installed capacity is fully utilized and service tariffs are set under market conditions; and poor regulation plus high barriers to entry for new competition in both electricity and telecommunications.

At a more general level, the reforms did not solve, and quite probably increased, two problems: investment continued to be concentrated among large enterprises that have not shown the capacity to develop backward and forward linkages with smaller firms, and supplier chains were destroyed by the quest for competitiveness through increasing imported inputs. Both processes led to specialization and higher efficiency, but they also led to polarization among actors and the persistence of the external constraint on growth.

Moreover, the reforms did not deliver the expected employment growth in the tradables sectors. Commercial agriculture and formal sector manu-

61. Katz (2000, chapter 6).

facturing firms underwent an important process of modernization, which implied a more intensive use of capital. This negatively affected job creation in those sectors where output grew most strongly, such as natural resource–based commodities and the automobile industry. Changes also occurred across sectors, as well as within sectors. Specifically, activities that have traditionally produced the largest volume of employment, such as textiles and garments, declined across the board. Only the *maquila* assembly plants, operating under conditions that differ from those of the rest of the economy, provided the strong growth in highly labor-intensive activities that the reforms were expected to produce.

Slow growth in labor-intensive tradables had a number of causes. First, the contradiction between the reforms, which sought to move toward an export-led growth model, and macroeconomic policies, which led to overvalued exchange rates, sent producers ambiguous signals that hindered investment in tradables sectors. This contradiction led to crises that produced a high degree of instability in GDP growth and thereby had a negative effect on investment. Second, assumptions made about the region's comparative advantage were wrong, at least for the level of generalization to which they applied. The regional experience and international comparisons have shown that the main advantage of Latin America in general, and of the South American countries in particular, lies in natural resources rather than in unskilled labor. This factor was compounded by changes in the relative prices of factors of production, which occurred when trade liberalization sharply reduced the relative cost of capital goods.

The services absorbed much of the residual labor not employed by manufacturing and agriculture. In the process, polarization increased between activities that had been rapidly modernized and traditional ones that employed a low-skill work force. The residual labor tended to be employed by the latter, leading to slow growth in the overall productivity of the sector. Microenterprises offered the greatest number of jobs, with most of them operating on an informal basis. The low rate of job creation by large, modern firms that offered higher wages led to a wider wage gap. Poor employment performance in the tradables sectors has thus been accompanied by increasing heterogeneity and polarization in the labor market.

7 | A Policy Agenda for the Next Decade

This final chapter of the book first summarizes what the empirical research says about the recent trajectories of the nine economies we have studied, focusing on how the reforms have changed these economies at the aggregate, sectoral, and microeconomic levels. We also attempt to determine the direction in which they seem to be heading in order to explain the reasons for undertaking the second task of the chapter: to propose a set of policy recommendations on how to improve the performance of the nine economies as they move into the new century. While we agree with many of the basic orientations that have emerged in the last ten to fifteen years, the reforms and the policies that have accompanied them can work much better. This is particularly the case with respect to employment and equity, but growth also needs to be more dynamic.

The Reforms and Their Impact

All nine project countries effected major changes in development strategy and public policies. A set of "first generation" reforms—import liberalization, domestic financial liberalization, capital account opening, privatization, and tax reform—was adopted to open the economies and to increase the role of market forces. In addition, macroeconomic policies became more equilibrated, and social expenditure increased substantially. Despite the generally similar policy trends, however, countries differed considerably in the extent to which they implemented the reforms and the style in which they were introduced. The reforms were instituted to varying degrees in the nine countries because of differences in initial conditions, especially inflation rates, past growth performance, and economic distortions. Countries with especially negative initial conditions—namely, Argentina, Bolivia, Chile, and Peru—turned out to be aggressive reformers. Presumably thinking they had little to lose and much to gain, they implemented many reforms in rapid order. Other countries, which had done well in previous periods and wanted to preserve certain elements in their societies and economies, became cautious reformers. This group—including Brazil, Colombia, Costa Rica, Jamaica, and Mexico—adopted a more gradual, selective approach to the reforms.

The reform results were neither as positive as supporters predicted nor as negative as opponents feared. Indeed, the reforms per se seem to have had a surprisingly small impact at the aggregate level, based on calculations using regional averages. It is only when we move to the country, sectoral, and microeconomic levels that the magnitude of the changes begins to become apparent. The principal aggregate level results can be summarized in five points.

—Growth recovered with respect to the 1980s, but there was no generalized surge (or decline) in output; many countries grew below their rates in the 1950–80 base period. Econometric evidence suggests that the impact of the reforms was positive, but small.

—Exports increased substantially, but imports grew even faster, leading to enlarged trade deficits.

—Investment and productivity recovered the ground that was lost in the 1980s, but no big gains occurred. As with growth, the reforms played a positive, but minor, role.

—Employment lagged behind the modest growth rates, and the quality of new jobs presented serious problems. The reforms appear to have played a negative role with respect to the quantitative aspects of job creation, but once again it was small.

—Inequality increased slightly, although serious measurement problems prevent a precise analysis of distribution trends. The reforms played a small, negative role, as with employment.

The biggest policy changes in a generation thus resulted in fairly modest changes in performance at the aggregate level. The propositions set out in chapter 1 provide elements for solving this puzzle. First, the reforms worked slowly, especially with respect to investment, because of the great uncertainty they generated; this was frequently exacerbated by macroeconomic instability. Uncertainty gave rise to three phases in the post-reform investment process: an initial decline, a recovery, and—only after the transitory factors that produced the first two phases had dissipated—a consolidation to normal levels. Second, the reforms and policies were frequently inconsistent, which increased the uncertainty that investors had to face. Third, international variables, especially volatile capital flows, contributed to both inconsistency and uncertainty. Fourth, different actors (that is, countries and firms) had different capacities to respond to the reforms; only a few could move quickly to take advantage of new opportunities, which contributed to slow change and inequality. Fifth, the reforms were incomplete and need complementary policies to make them function properly. Only now are most countries beginning to implement a "second generation" of reforms that involve improvement of regulation, public administration, the judiciary, and particularly education.

Proponents of the reforms expected that growth, employment, and equity outcomes would demonstrate a consistent, positive relation as a result of the policy changes. The reforms were expected to increase the efficiency of the economies and provide incentives for more investment. Investment and increased productivity would raise growth rates. In turn, higher growth would lead to more employment, especially for unskilled labor, and ultimately result in increased equity. Table 7-1 provides a very rough set of qualitative indicators that summarize performance results in comparison to these expectations.

Of the nine countries in the project, only Chile has come near to fulfilling the broad expectations held out for the reforms. It is essential to point out, however, that the Chilean economy went through multiple crises in the first decade after the initiation of the reforms. Significant policy adjustments were made starting in the mid-1980s, and these were deepened after the resumption of democratic rule in 1990, leading to the performance described in the table. What has Chile achieved? In quantitative terms, it has greatly increased investment and productivity with respect to its own past and to the rest of the region in the present. It has also kept its external accounts in order through an emphasis on exports and high domestic savings. These factors led to rapid and stable growth (until the crisis

Table 7-1. *Relation between Reforms and Outcomes in the 1990s*

Country	Reforms[a]	Invest-ment[b]	Produc-tivity[c]	Growth[d]	Employ-ment[e]	Equity[f]
Argentina	Aggressive	=	+	+	−	−
Bolivia	Aggressive	+	−	+	+	−
Brazil	Cautious	−	−	−	−	=
Chile	Aggressive	+	+	+	+	+
Colombia	Cautious	+	−	−	−	−
Costa Rica	Cautious	+	−	−	+	+
Jamaica	Cautious	n.a.	n.a.	−	=	n.a.
Mexico	Cautious	=	−	−	+	−
Peru	Aggressive	=	+	+	−	+

a. Reforms: for definition, see chapter 3.

b. Investment: + means that a country had a higher investment coefficient in the 1990s than in the base period (1950–80); − means that it had a lower coefficient; = means there was little change (see chapter 4).

c. Productivity: + means that growth of total factor productivity was higher in the 1990s than in the base period (1950–80); − means that it was lower; = means there was little change (see chapter 4).

d. Growth: + means that a country grew faster in the 1990s than in the base period (1950–80); − means that it grew more slowly (see chapter 4).

e. Employment: + means that the country ranked high on the labor market index; − means than it ranked low; = means that there was little change (see chapter 5, first three elements of the index only).

f. Equity: + means that primary income distribution in the latest available year was more equal than the pre-reform period; − means that it was less equal; = means that there was little change (see chapter 5).

of the late 1990s revealed some previously ignored weaknesses on the external front and with respect to macroeconomic consistency). With GDP growth averaging about 7 percent per year for nearly fifteen years, employment creation was strong and poverty alleviation was notable. Household income concentration remained stubbornly high, but primary distribution became somewhat more equal and social services expanded. In qualitative terms, innovative macroeconomic policies were geared to maintaining stability and restraining volatility. Equally important, incentives were provided to the private sector to stimulate the investments that were needed to continue the economic expansion.

The experiences of the other eight project countries are a mix of partial successes and pending challenges. They can be divided into three groups, based on the nature of their achievements and the problems they still face. First, Argentina, Bolivia, and Peru also improved their growth records in the 1990s in comparison with their past performance. Like Chile, they were all aggressive reformers that initially faced overwhelming problems including hyperinflation, poor economic performance, highly distorted economies, and serious problems of governability. All this represented enormous opportunities for improvement once new policies—both reforms and macroeconomic stabilization—were implemented and gained credibility. High GDP growth was achieved through a combination of factor accumulation or strong productivity growth. Nonetheless, all three economies are still fragile, and the societies have serious social problems, especially unemployment in Argentina and poverty in Bolivia and Peru.

A second group had less success in matching its past growth performance, but was nonetheless highly successful regarding exports and employment. The primary example is Mexico, closely followed by Costa Rica. Both countries were able to break into the markets of the industrialized countries, particularly the United States. Their higher participation in those markets was achieved mainly through labor-intensive exports from the *maquila* (in-bond) plants, which are part of the production chains that integrate the northern part of the hemisphere. Costa Rica and Mexico generated a substantial amount of employment through these exports. Real wages rose rapidly in Mexico until the peso crisis in 1994–95, but they have been stagnant since them. In Costa Rica, wages are among the most dynamic found in the project countries. Both countries turned in surprisingly strong performances in the face of the international financial crisis that buffeted the region in the late 1990s, based largely on the strength of the U.S. economy. On the social front, the improvement of basic services, together with relatively better initial conditions, allowed Costa Rica to deal with issues of equity more successfully than Mexico.

The remaining countries are mainly characterized by the multifaceted challenges they face. Brazil, Colombia, and Jamaica make up this group, although the lack of information on Jamaica makes it very difficult to judge what is happening there. Brazil and Colombia were strong performers in an earlier period; they have undertaken significant reforms without yet consolidating a new model to replace the one that served them well in the past. Serious ongoing macroeconomic problems, including fiscal deficits, external deficits, and high interest rates, have made the private sector very reluctant to participate in moving the economies forward. Low growth rates have begun to increase unemployment and other social problems, which undermine the governments' ability to find solutions to the challenges they face.

The type of aggregate analysis that is possible at the regional and country levels leaves many unanswerable questions. Moving to the sectoral and microeconomic levels provides additional insights and offers leverage to draw conclusions about probable future trends. It also offers a contrast to the aggregate analysis, since here we find evidence of stronger impact of the reforms. Beginning with the sectoral level, two reforms—namely, trade liberalization and privatization—had an important impact on investment, productivity, and employment.

—Investment was concentrated in a relatively small number of sectors. Only one sector (telecommunications) saw dynamic investment in all countries, and only one country (Chile) increased investment in all major sectors. Manufacturing investment was particularly dynamic in some capital-intensive subsectors (for example, cement, steel, petrochemicals, and chemicals). Nonetheless, investment coefficients in manufacturing as a whole were, at best, slightly higher than in the pre-reform period.

—Productivity gains were more evenly spread across broad sectors, but heterogeneity increased within sectors, for example, between commercial and family agriculture. Likewise, within manufacturing, some subsectors performed very well but others lagged behind. Despite productivity growth in manufacturing as a whole, the productivity gap vis-à-vis the United States did not narrow in the 1990s.

—Trade liberalization led to two different patterns of export growth in the 1990s: integration into the North American market through manufactured exports in Mexico, Central America, and the Caribbean versus a strong concentration in natural resource–based commodities in South America. The difference was due to trade arrangements such as the North American Free Trade Agreement (NAFTA) and the Caribbean Basin Initiative. To a lesser extent, subregional trade agreements in South America have also been instrumental in fostering manufactured exports. Strong local supplier linkages have not accompanied export growth in either of the two patterns: the *maquila* plants use few domestic inputs, and modernization of commodity production led to higher imports of capital goods.

—Privatization was instrumental to investment recovery and to modernization when other necessary conditions were also present. It fostered investment in certain tradables (for example, mining and natural gas), although linkages with the rest of the economy continued to be weak. In nontradables, the biggest increases in investment were in telecommunications; results were mixed in electricity. Privatization alone did not guarantee efficient performance. Strengthening property rights proved to be an important factor for attracting foreign investment in mining, while increasing competitive pressures were necessary to ensure efficient market outcomes in the services sectors, like telecommunications.

—When the concentration of growth in capital-intensive activities created few jobs, services became the residual source of employment. Services had a heterogeneous performance: high-quality jobs were created in telecommunications, banking, and finance, but the bulk was in low-skill services. Overall, employment generation was jointly determined by secular trends and the impact of the reforms. Agriculture continued its long-term decline in total employment, and manufacturing generally lost share, except for the *maquila*.

The old-style "triple alliance" among transnational corporations (TNCs), large domestic firms, and the state has broken down.[1] The state privatized most of its firms, and local capital lost out to TNCs in the late 1990s. TNCs are less exposed to strategic uncertainty about opening new markets and using new technologies than are large domestic firms. They also have access to international finance under better conditions than even the largest domestic firms. The reforms that had the most important impact at the microeconomic level were privatization and the greater welcome for foreign direct investment.

—Large corporations led the investment process, and TNCs gained share in sales among the larger firms. Restructuring of corporate ownership was increasingly important in the second half of the 1990s. Nonetheless, the large firms contributed relatively little to the generation of employment since they tended to be highly capital-intensive.

—Despite the common perception that small and medium-size enterprises (SMEs) have done extremely poorly, they maintained their share in total production and employment. The fact that they did not grow rapidly, however, had negative implications for job creation.

—In the manufacturing sector, most new jobs were created by small firms and microenterprises. These were the only firms that increased employment in countries like Argentina, Brazil, Chile, and Costa Rica, where they accounted for more that 100 percent of the net job creation, because larger firms posted a net job loss as a result of the downsizing that accompanied modernization. Only in Mexico were large manufacturing firms more dynamic than smaller ones; the *maquila* played a very positive role in this outcome.

1. Evans (1979).

—Although the labor productivity of larger companies is three or four times higher than that of SMEs, the latter increased their efficiency and in some countries even narrowed the gap. Nonetheless, the productivity gap widened between large and medium-size firms, on the one hand, and small firms and microenterprises, on the other. Thus a large share of job creation took place in firms whose efficiency declined or at best stagnated.

—Wage differentials between larger firms and microenterprises increased, particularly in the second half of the 1990s. This is consistent with a widening productivity gap between the two groups of firms. All else equal, this wage differential contributed to increased inequality.

By the end of the 1990s, regional economies had more or less recovered what they had lost during the 1980s in terms of investment and productivity levels.[2] The new investments were more efficient than the ones they replaced, but they were highly concentrated in a few sectors, namely, natural resources, resource-based manufactured products, automobiles, and the *maquila*. Many subsectors in these industries are growing slowly in the world market, face falling terms of trade, or are technologically mature. Moreover, the expected rates of return on these investments are likely to be lower than before the reforms were introduced, due to greater competition and less state support. Labor productivity also returned to its pre-crisis levels, but this implies that the gap in Latin America and the Caribbean with respect to the member countries of the Organization for Economic Cooperation and Development (OECD) and the newly industrializing economies of East Asia increased. While a number of individual sectors did very well, their dynamism was not transmitted to the economies as a whole. This was partly due to weak or nonexistent supplier relations.

These weak domestic supplier networks have both advantages and disadvantages. Weaker links may be an advantage for exporting firms because their competitiveness increases when they are able to select the most efficient source of inputs, irrespective of domestic or foreign origin. When imported inputs grow as fast as total exports, however, trade surpluses in exporting activities are not sufficient to compensate for deficits in other sectors. The opportunity for technological progress is lost since it tends to concentrate in the user-supplier interface, and employment creation is weakened because of the destruction or non-creation of domestic suppliers.

---

2. It is important to recall that we are using simple averages to prevent Brazil and Mexico from overwhelming our results. Weighted averages would show that investment has yet to return to the 1980 peak.

Given this constellation of factors, a significant increase in growth rates in the next decade cannot be taken for granted. Lacking strong growth, unemployment rates are likely to remain high, which will exacerbate social problems and hinder attempts to lower the very high rates of inequality that characterize the region. External vulnerability, which has probably risen because of increased globalization together with trade and financial liberalization, makes solutions more complex. This outlook surely justifies the consideration of policy changes to improve expected outcomes. Or, as one ECLAC economist has put it, there is a need "to reform the reforms."[3]

Recommendations to Improve the Outlook for the Region

A first principle in establishing a policy agenda for the future—one that was frequently violated during the first round of reforms—is to avoid across-the-board policy recommendations. Latin American and Caribbean countries are currently in very diverse situations with respect to the reforms themselves and to other structural and policy variables. What will work for one is not necessarily appropriate for another. Nonetheless, the experiences of the nine project countries provide both positive and negative lessons. A good source of lessons for the future is what has and has not worked in the past.

Another principle—also frequently violated in the first round—is to obtain the necessary information and to engage in the appropriate analysis before making irreversible policy decisions. Many of the theoretical propositions underlying the first round of reforms were based on different types of economies than existed in Latin America, and the necessary preconditions, including those pertaining to the international economy, did not hold. It was not surprising that many of the predictions turned out to be erroneous, especially those for employment, but also for investment and growth. The analysis must include the individual country, sectoral, and microeconomic levels rather than vague generalities about the region as a whole. One of the most important examples of the need for information on which to base rational decisionmaking is in the area of labor reform. Beyond general considerations about the advantages of more efficient labor markets, we do not know what to expect from that reform in terms of growth and employment.

3. Ffrench-Davis (1999).

Policymakers must be specific about what they hope to achieve from a new round of reforms or policy changes. It is very difficult to judge the success or failure of the reforms or other policies without a benchmark of the results they are expected to produce. This has been a problem in writing this book, but much more important, it is also a problem for governments themselves and for the policy debate within the political system and with civil society. Of course, we are not advocating comprehensive, detailed forecasting and planning, but without identifying specific targets for new reforms, it is very difficult to monitor their performance.

The ten to fifteen years of reforms in the region have led to significant accomplishments, but much remains to be done and many problems still exist. One influential set of proposals recommends further reforms; it calls for a deepening of first generation reforms complemented by a second generation of reforms, particularly in the field of education.[4] Our view is that the vast majority of benefits that can be obtained from first generation reforms have already materialized. Decreasing returns would quickly set in from deepening those same reforms, although some individual countries, particularly the late reformers, may indeed require more first generation reforms. Furthermore, in the case of large, federal countries, first generation reforms may still have a role to play at the state or local levels. Finally, some "hot issues" (for example, the possible privatization of firms like Petrobras, Pemex, and Codelco) involve political decisions that go beyond the scope of this book.

We agree with the growing consensus that another generation of reforms is needed.[5] Our agenda, however, is broader than that of most others. Our policy discussion is organized around three central issues: the need to engage in competitiveness policies and investment promotion to increase growth, to undertake a major offensive in the social area, and to maintain and improve macroeconomic stability. We also discuss two issues that cross the three topic areas: the need for closer relations between the public and private sectors and for policies to deal with external vulnerability. We focus the recommendations at an intermediate level: more than a list of topics, but less than detailed programmatic prescriptions.[6]

---

4. IDB (1997).

5. See, for example, IDB (1997); Burki and Perry (1998); Birdsall, Graham, and Sabot (1998).

6. A more detailed, and much broader, set of policy recommendations, which is consistent with those proposed here, is found in ECLAC (2000a). An earlier version of the main arguments was presented in Ocampo (1998).

Policies to Increase Growth

The Latin American and Caribbean economies need to grow faster and increase their competitiveness to improve their integration into the world market through higher value added exports. The two tasks are closely related: the core of a policy to achieve faster growth is to create better conditions for increasing productivity and investment. Higher productivity leads to cost reductions and higher profitability rates, which attracts more investment. At the same time, increases in investment are usually accompanied by the incorporation of new machinery and equipment, which embody technological advances and lead to higher productivity and more competitiveness.

While most analysts agree with these objectives, they differ on the means to achieve them. Many would say that markets can handle these issues by themselves. In particular, they would argue that the reforms have strengthened competition in the countries of the region, having thus already generated the necessary incentive for higher productivity and more investment. We disagree because we do not believe that markets operate perfectly, always producing the most efficient outcome.

More investment is needed in all countries, but this alone is insufficient; the region also needs more efficient allocation of investment. The reforms have corrected the major distortions that led to inefficient investment, but they did not generate the incentives necessary to achieve faster capital accumulation. Investment depends on expected rates of return, which can be affected through prices, costs, and the management of uncertainty. Since little can be done regarding prices, we focus on the other two elements. Progress in correcting market failures to increase competitiveness will benefit the investment process through lower costs for technology, more skilled human resources, better access to and lower cost of credit, and more modern infrastructure. Further reduction of costs could be obtained through generalized tax reductions. Such an alternative, however, would run counter to the need for greater social spending as we will discuss in the following section. Although it is impossible to eliminate the uncertainty inherent in market economies, it is possible to reduce the uncertainty caused by pendular swings in policy and unexpected policy shifts. We return to this issue when we present our proposals regarding macroeconomic policies, which have to be consistent with the policy package to increase growth.

Reduction of costs and uncertainty will benefit investment irrespective of its origin, but a particular way of stimulating investment is to design policies to attract foreign direct investment (FDI). This was a major component of the first generation reforms, and one of the successes of those reforms was the dramatic increase of FDI in total capital inflows in the 1990s. The majority of that investment, however, went to purchase existing assets, either through privatization of public firms or takeovers of private corporations. What is needed in the coming years is to design policies to attract more greenfield investment, for which several international experiences (for example, Ireland, Scotland, or Singapore) provide useful lessons regarding both business facilitation measures and FDI targeting.

Given the increasingly important role of TNCs in the region and in the world market, we also need to foster strategic joint ventures between local business and leading global players. Changes in corporate governance regimes, particularly strengthening minority shareholders' rights, have elsewhere proved to be an efficient means to prevent TNCs from insisting on majority or total ownership in joint ventures. This would open space for local business in modern sectors, because foreign partners are likely to participate as minority shareholders only if their rights are adequately protected.

Since TNCs also play a crucial role in world exports, policies to attract foreign direct investment would simultaneously have a positive impact on the region's export performance, both in volume and composition. To make sure that domestic producers also benefit from increasing access to world markets, it is necessary to reduce transaction costs of foreign trade operations, ensure their access to credit under competitive conditions, and reduce the cost of information. All of this, of course, must be done within the framework of the new international trading system.

These suggestions for increasing investment would have a positive impact on competitiveness, but direct measures are also needed. Correction of market failures and reduction of transaction costs are the key components of our proposals to foster competitiveness.

Concentrated markets do not necessarily lead to inefficient outcomes, when businesses operate under the pressure of strong rivalry among domestic firms or external competition. Competition, however, cannot be taken for granted. Even in tradables, unfair practices may arise. Competition policies should be aimed at preventing or eliminating such practices. In sectors where competition cannot work (for example, natural monopolies), regulation is the answer.

Privatization of public services (utilities) has made it imperative to introduce or modernize regulatory regimes in the region, because competition cannot always produce efficient market outcomes in this sector. Although conditions vary across sectors and countries, the region should work on establishing sectorwide regulatory frameworks. As is the case with competition policy, regulation should aim at preventing unfair business practices (for example, abuse of market power), although the only efficient alternative in some cases may involve actions that affect the market structure (for example, preventing or eliminating inefficient vertical integration).

Major factor markets (namely, technology, skilled labor, and capital) usually operate quite inefficiently. Policy proposals in these areas have long formed part of the academic and policymaking debate in the region. A detailed consideration of each proposal is beyond the scope of our analysis, but we want to highlight a few issues we consider particularly important. With respect to technology, Latin America should focus its limited resources on diffusion and adaptation of technology rather than on innovation per se. Stronger linkages between users and suppliers are particularly important, since this is the area where adaptation is most central. In human resource development, improving the educational stock will take at least a generation, so we need to focus simultaneously on short-term measures. Training should receive a special emphasis; the most useful training programs are those that combine school with apprenticeship. Finally, reducing capital market failures implies at least two different strategies according to potential beneficiaries. For larger firms, the main element is the development of domestic sources of long-term finance, while for smaller firms, the most important step would be improvement of access through second-tier development banks.

Smaller firms need special support to be able to access factor markets. While the costs of using the market (for example, those of applying for a loan) are relevant for all kinds of firms, they are particularly burdensome in relative terms for the smallest companies. The reduction of costs for small firms is most efficient when these firms are clustered in particular regions or sectors. Interaction, either through subcontracting between large and small firms or horizontal linkages among small firms themselves, can provide the basis not only for accessing factor markets but also for jointly developing new activities and markets. The problems that the absorption of these transaction costs puts on microenterprises—as opposed to small and medium-size firms—go beyond credit market failures and are considered in the next section.

A Social Offensive

Important problems remain with respect to growth, investment, and productivity, but progress has been made in these areas. Problems involving employment and equity, in contrast, have been exacerbated. Employment creation has been slow, and job quality has deteriorated. Inequality has probably increased. The proposals for increasing growth are likely to have a positive impact on employment and equity. Indeed, achieving high, stable growth rates is a necessary prerequisite for lowering unemployment and inequality, but growth alone is not enough. We recommend that governments assign the highest priority to these issues.

Employment is the place to start. Even if investment grows rapidly in the region, our research has shown that the likely investors would be large firms. With the exception of the *maquila*, these are not in labor-intensive activities. At the same time, the public sector, which has traditionally provided a large number of high quality jobs in the region, is actually reducing its work force. We must therefore look elsewhere for job creation. At this point in time in Latin America, most jobs in both urban and rural areas are in small firms and especially in microenterprises, so this group of firms merits special attention. Experiences with the *maquila* plants provide one source of lessons, but this would not be enough, particularly for the South American countries. Labor-intensive activities, such as housing and infrastructure construction, should be encouraged by public policy.

Transaction costs are especially burdensome for small firms, as mentioned above. Moreover, an inefficient and costly supply of public goods and services has a particularly negative impact on small production units. Consideration should therefore be given to widespread deregulation for this type of firm. Experiences in export processing zones in Latin America and Asia suggest that the reduction of regulation and controls can lead to rapid creation of new firms and employment opportunities, without a deterioration of work conditions. Indeed, since these are formal sector jobs, workers moving from the informal sector are likely to experience an improvement in well-being. Policymakers should consider extending such arrangements to the domestic economies, perhaps combined with tax incentives as in the enterprise zones in the major cities in the United States.

In any case, it is necessary to find ways to provide services and public goods to small production units. Cluster solutions may reduce costs and open alternatives for microenterprises as well as for small firms. Credit operations are particularly costly when negotiations must be carried out with a great many small units; various international examples show that a collective approach to credit for microenterprises has produced very positive results (for example, the Banco del Sol in Bolivia). This approach has also proved useful for small agricultural producers.

An alternative suggestion on how to increase job opportunities is through flexibilization of the labor market more generally. Our view is that labor markets are already much more flexible than usually perceived. We are also concerned about jumping into drastic reform without adequate information on the likely consequences, with respect to both new jobs and the quality of existing jobs. A generic solution is particularly inappropriate given the extreme differences among labor markets in the region.

Policymakers would be better advised to think about ways to improve the functioning of labor markets rather than to concentrate exclusively on flexibilization. However, if a particular government decides that it wants to move forward on flexibilization per se, it would be essential to simultaneously guarantee access to unemployment insurance and to make benefits portable to smooth the transition between jobs. An additional policy that would make labor markets function better is to increase information available to workers and firms in order to reduce search periods and frictional unemployment. Clearly these measures will not eliminate structural unemployment, so they need to be combined with job creation policies as mentioned earlier.

The second main element of the social offensive has to do with greater, more efficient social expenditure. After the contraction of social spending during the crisis years of the 1980s, all countries in the region increased such outlays in the 1990s and some did so dramatically. The funds for increased social spending come from one or more of three sources: faster GDP growth, an increase in public expenditure as a percentage of GDP, and an increase in the share of social spending in total public expenditure. For countries with a low share of public expenditure in GDP, it would be desirable to raise the share to increase social services further. Others will likely need to rely on one of the other two mechanisms. With respect to the share of social spending in total public expenditure, however, a number of countries are close to the maximum that is politically viable. This leaves three alternatives: more efficient use of existing resources, an increase in total public expenditure, which would require an increase in revenues, or greater participation by the private sector. All three have their problems; which alternative is more attractive would vary from country to country, depending on local circumstances and public preferences.

Improving and expanding access to education must receive priority among social services. Education expenditure has the double advantage of simultaneously contributing to competitiveness and greater equality, although this is a relatively long-run process. A large share of Latin America's distribution problems, as well as of its productivity problems, comes from its large stock of unskilled labor, which in turn derives from many years of inadequate education. High priority must be assigned to overcoming the legacy of this education gap. This subject has been widely studied, but many controversies and implementation issues remain. How to improve quality is the main issue for primary education. At the secondary level, the issue is expansion of coverage and access, while at the university level, access and relevance of areas of specialization are paramount. Dramatically increasing the share of entrants to the labor market who have secondary education would simultaneously contribute to the solution of both economic and social problems in the region.

Increasing and improving social expenditure will not do much good if it is then cut when a crisis arises. This was the prevalent pattern in the 1980s, and since social expenditure is strongly procyclical, the threat of future cuts remains. Governments should make sure that social spending is protected when hard times come. The long-term social losses through crises are often never recovered. Children who leave school may never return; workers who lose their jobs may lose invaluable experience if they have trouble returning to work later; families who lose their homes may have difficulties for many years. Those who benefit from the later economic recovery are unlikely to be the same ones who lost as a result of the crisis.

Macroeconomic Policy

It is essential to achieve greater competitiveness and social progress without undermining the macroeconomic stability that has been achieved at great cost over the last decade. This is not just because macroeconomic stability has proved valuable for other reasons; without stability it is impossible to advance either in competitiveness or on social issues. Thus there can be no trade-off between stability and the other two goals. The question is how to finance those elements of the two agendas that depend on the public sector. This requires a reassignment of resources in government budgets if no new resources are forthcoming.

The macroeconomic agenda can be divided into traditional and new topics. Traditional issues include fiscal, monetary, and exchange rate policies aimed primarily at stabilizing inflation. These have been remarkably successful over the last decade, although with variations across the region. In all nine project countries, inflation has been brought down significantly; average inflation rates are now in the single digits. The main variation in policies has had to do with the role assigned to the exchange rate. In several cases it has been the main instrument for stabilization, displacing fiscal and monetary policy.

The main trouble spot in the traditional macroeconomic area has to do with a resurgence of fiscal deficits. To some extent, this is the result of the cyclical downturn at the end of the decade, but the reforms themselves also contributed. One of the inconsistency syndromes identified in chapter 3 suggested that the reforms conflicted with attempts at fiscal consolidation by cutting tax rates, lowering tariffs, and earmarking revenues for states and municipalities. Given the variations across countries in terms of the share of GDP controlled by the state, individual governments must decide whether deficit reduction should be accomplished by increasing revenues or cutting expenditure.

Two new topics are also on the agenda in the macroeconomic sphere. One has to do with growth and its finance; the other relates to the issue of volatility. Although the public sector has generally abandoned the role of producing goods (with the important exception of some key natural resource firms), it retains the function of providing an adequate context for growth. This involves not only stabilization, but also the promotion of savings and finance for growth. We have already discussed the need to develop capital markets as an intermediary between savings and investment; here the topic is savings.

Clearly, the government must make its own contribution to savings; hence the emphasis on fiscal consolidation. It must also seek policies to promote savings in the private sector. One policy that has become prominent among the project countries is the introduction of private pension schemes to complement or replace the old public social security systems. While these policies may promote savings in the long run, experience shows that they mainly substitute private for public savings in the short run. Thus other savings promotion policies are required; other ECLAC publications have suggested the usefulness of prior savings for home purchase and some kinds of tax incentives. Nonetheless, higher growth rates themselves will continue to be the main determinant of higher savings.

The volatility issue has several components. First, fiscal and regulatory policies should seek to avoid boom-bust cycles. Governments have much more policy space during booms. It is then that they must act to mitigate downswings, since they have fewer options during a crisis. Macroeconomic policy should be strongly counter-cyclical. Two important instruments are stabilization funds for public sector income (that is, putting aside revenues during boom periods to be drawn on when revenues fall) and social spending. Another innovative proposal consists of the use of counter-cyclical financial regulation (for example, flexible capital adequacy requirements for banks). But the increasing integration of Latin American and Caribbean economies into the world market makes macroeconomic policy much more complex, since a substantial part of volatility is imported via terms-of-trade fluctuations and especially financial flows. Additional instruments are needed to deal with the new situation.

A particular variant concerns another of the inconsistency syndromes identified in chapter 3. Trade liberalization combined with capital account opening, in the presence of international liquidity, leads to capital surges that inflate the value of the local currency. This can occur with any type of exchange rate regime, but it is especially associated with attempts to halt inflation via an exchange rate anchor. Overvaluation of the local currency, in turn, leads to large trade and current account deficits, which can result in foreign exchange and banking crises. Such crises have proved to be very expensive (fiscal costs up to 20 percent of GDP in some of the project countries), and they undermine progress in growth and the social area as well.

Governments must seek ways to dampen imported volatility as well as that originating in the domestic economy. Policies that have proved helpful in some countries could be studied for possible use elsewhere. These include commodity stabilization funds to mitigate cycles caused by terms-of-trade fluctuations and controls on short-term capital flows to limit the impact of swings in international finance. Adequate prudential regulation for the banking system is a complementary requirement to avoid the transmission of external volatility to the domestic financial system and thus to the rest of the domestic economy.

Cross-Cutting Issues: Public-Private Relations and International Economic Management

The three areas discussed above should constitute the main focus of government policy in the coming years. Two additional topics condition regional governments' ability to make progress on competitiveness and growth, the social offensive, and macroeconomic stability. These are the need to foster cooperation between the public and private sectors and to encourage more efficient management of international economic relations.

The new economic model in Latin America and the Caribbean features a substantially stronger role for the private sector than was the case in the earlier postwar period. It is therefore essential for the government and private actors to work together more closely. The risky environment created by globalization, combined with the opening of regional economies, requires such collaboration to strengthen the competitive position of Latin American countries. At the same time, the lower volume of resources at the disposal of the public sector means that more activities must be carried out in collaboration. What is still being worked out is the nature of the relationship. There will clearly be variation among countries, given their different histories and capacities, but some elements are common to all cases.

First, the new relationship does not imply the elimination of the economic role of the state; rather the state will be smaller and more efficient but will still play a very important role. Second, some aspects of the relationship will be conflictual insofar as the state must regulate private sector activities when the absence of competition prevents markets from producing efficient outcomes (for example, natural monopolies) or which could endanger the rest of the economy if not managed properly (for example, the financial sector). Third, other activities will be shared under mutually supportive arrangements, such as the provision of infrastructure or some aspects of social services. New institutions that bring together the government, entrepreneurs, and labor may be useful for implementing policy cooperation. Fourth, the term private sector does not refer exclusively to for-profit institutions. Nongovernmental organizations (NGOs) may also play an important role, especially in the social sectors or in the promotion of microenterprises. Fifth, exactly where the boundaries between public and private sector responsibilities will be drawn will largely depend on the willingness of each society to pay for state services. If the fiscal compromise provides for a low resource base, fewer services can be offered. Finally, whatever the nature of the relationship that is ultimately chosen, it is essential that it be transparent and open to all. This is necessary for avoiding an increase in corruption that could destroy the legitimacy of the entire system, as has happened in some other regions and in some instances in Latin America itself.

The other set of issues that affects all policy areas involves the international economy into which the region is increasingly integrated. Globalization provides both challenges and opportunities. While the terms of trade continue to pose problems for Latin American economies, and shifts in international demand can also play havoc at times, financial flows have been the most problematic aspect of the international environment in the last two decades. After abandoning the region during much of the 1980s, external finance returned with a vengeance in the early 1990s, only to partially withdraw again. Short-term flows were particularly volatile; they destabilized macroeconomic balances on various occasions through their impact on different variables, especially the exchange rate. This would imply lower growth rates in the future because uncertainty may hamper investment.

Since Latin America is not the only region where such volatility has caused problems, the topic has been put on the international agenda, but few concrete results have emerged thus far. The so-called new financial architecture remains to be created, and industrialized countries continue to manage their economies in ways that serve their own interests but that can undermine growth and cause other problems in developing countries. An important aspect of the problem is that the developing countries have very little voice in decisions about international economic management.

Several policy recommendations flow from this situation. First, Latin American governments have to put policies in place that will protect them from international volatility without returning to the closed economies of the past. The controls on capital inflows and commodity reserve funds mentioned above are examples of such policies. Second, the new regional integration schemes may provide a partial buffer against international volatility. As with domestic policies, the new type of regional integration (namely, the so-called open regionalism) is concerned with retaining its links with the rest of the world economy, rather than being an extension of closed economies as was the case in the first round of integration in the 1960s. Finally, Latin American countries, whether individually or as members of subregional groupings, should seek increased negotiating power in international decisionmaking. A combination of the three approaches is probably necessary to facilitate the objectives—specifically, increased economic growth with greater equity—that most governments of the region have espoused.

Concluding Comments

The agenda set out in the previous section is not a new one. On the contrary, our aim was to combine into a coherent package a number of policy recommendations that have been under discussion for some time now. Many analysts who agree with the basic thrust of the reforms also believe that markets alone cannot resolve the problems that remain, not to mention the new ones that have emerged. While faster growth is needed, growth alone cannot provide a better quality of life for the population of the region. Additional measures must be taken, both to foster growth itself and to promote employment and equity.

We realize that this policy package is expensive and that all policies suggested probably cannot be implemented simultaneously, especially given the priority that governments today assign to macroeconomic stability. The relative weight each government gives to individual measures will depend on individual country conditions, which differ considerably. Countries with acute social problems would probably pay special attention to proposals in that area, while others, where those problems are less severe, could assign more resources to improve competitiveness. Although we recognize this dilemma, it cannot be resolved at the abstract level.

A consensus is currently building around these issues in most of the governments of the region. Implementation has thus become the new priority. Policymakers have gone through a learning process with respect to the reforms. Implementation and monitoring have improved, and of course they have been easier for latecomers, but implementation failures are still widespread in all countries. With the partial exception of the macroeconomic area, the institutions responsible for implementing the policies discussed above are weak with respect to both human and financial resources. Fragmented decisionmaking compounds the difficulties.

Institution building through private-public partnerships is central to future progress. Latin America has made headway in this field, but achieving better results requires resources and consistency. Although policy design can always be improved, we think that the marginal benefits of looking for new policy instruments are smaller than those that can be reaped from better implementation of certain well-known, and even well-tested, instruments. Macroeconomic stabilization and the first generation of reforms were timely and critical in the late 1980s and early 1990s; now is the time for action on growth, competitiveness, employment, and equity. More effort is also needed in the macroeconomic area itself. Almost two decades of reforms and macroeconomic achievements have provided important lessons that, if heeded, would allow Latin American and Caribbean countries to avoid mistakes and, above all, to benefit from past experience to get better results.

Latin America is clearly a different place than it was fifteen or twenty years ago. One way of characterizing the change is that the region is now an integral part of a single global economy. The reforms have been an important element in the transformation, although far from the only one. At the most general level, the reforms have had three results. They have solved some longstanding problems, such as cases of excessive protectionism and inefficient public utilities. They have opened up unexpected possibilities, of which the most dramatic is perhaps the export potential demonstrated by Mexico and some Central American and Caribbean countries. But they have also created new problems and exacerbated certain old ones. Employment is probably the most serious, especially given the implications for equity. The urgency of this agenda means that the region cannot afford further delay in responding to the new challenges or tackling the new problems.

References

Aghion, Philippe and Peter Howitt. 1998. *Endogenous Growth Theory*. MIT Press.

Altimir, Oscar. 1996. "Economic Development and Social Equity: A Latin American Perspective." *Journal of Interamerican Studies and World Affairs* 38(2-3): 47–73.

Altimir, Oscar and Luis Beccaria. 1999. "El mercado de trabajo bajo el nuevo régimen económico en Argentina." Serie Reformas Económicas 28. Santiago: ECLAC.

América Economía. 1999. *Latin America's 500 Largest Companies*. (July).

Balassa, Bela and others. 1986. *Toward Renewed Economic Growth in Latin America*. Washington: Institute for International Economics.

Barro, Robert and Xavier Sala-i-Martin. 1995. *Economic Growth*. Macmillan.

Berry, Albert, ed. 1998. *Poverty, Economic Reform, and Income Distribution in Latin America*. Boulder, CO: Lynne Rienner.

Bhagwati, Jagdish N. 1978. *Foreign Trade Regimes and Economic Development: Anatomy and Consequences of Exchange Control Regimes*. Cambridge, MA: Ballinger.

———. 1998. "The Capital Myth." *Foreign Affairs* 77(3): 7–12.

Birdsall, Nancy, Carol Graham, and Richard H. Sabot, eds. 1998. *Beyond Tradeoffs: Market Reform and Equitable Growth in Latin America*. Washington: Inter-American Development Bank and Brookings.

Birdsall, Nancy and Richard H. Sabot, eds. 1996. *Opportunity Foregone: Education in Brazil*. Johns Hopkins University Press.

BIS (Bank for International Settlements). 1999. *Annual Report, 1998–99*. Basle.

Borensztein, Eduardo, José de Gregorio, and Jong-Wha Lee. 1995. "How Does Foreign Direct Investment Affect Economic Growth?" Working Paper 5057. Cambridge, MA: National Bureau of Economic Research.

Buitelaar, Rudolf M. and Ramón Padilla. 2000. "Maquila, Economic Reforms, and Corporate Strategy." *World Development* 28(9) (forthcoming).

225

Buitelaar, Rudolf M., Ramon Padilla, and Ruth Urrutia. 1999. "The In-Bond Assembly Industry and Technical Change." *CEPAL Review* 67 (April):137–56.

Bulmer-Thomas, Victor, ed. 1996. *The New Economic Model in Latin America and its Impact on Income Distribution and Poverty.* New York: St. Martins Press.

Burki, Shahid Javed and Guillermo E. Perry. 1997. *The Long March: A Reform Agenda for Latin America and the Caribbean in the Next Decade.* Washington: World Bank Latin American and Caribbean Studies.

———. 1998. *Beyond the Washington Consensus: Institutions Matter.* Washington: World Bank Latin American and Caribbean Studies.

Calvo, Guillermo. 1986. "Incredible Reforms." University of Pennsylvania, Department of Economics.

Cárdenas, Enrique, José Antonio Ocampo, and Rosemary Thorp, eds. Forthcoming. *Industrialization and the State in Latin America: The Black Legend and the Post-War Years.* Macmillan.

Corbo, Vittorio and Stanley Fischer. 1994. "Lessons from the Chilean Stabilization and Recovery." In *The Chilean Economy: Policy Lessons and Challenges*, edited by Barry P. Bosworth, Rudiger Dornbusch, and Raúl Labán, 29–80. Brookings.

Cominetti, Rossella and Emanuela di Gropello. 1995. *El gasto social en América Latina: un examen cuantitativo y cualitativo.* Cuadernos de la CEPAL 73. Santiago: ECLAC.

Cominetti, Rossella and Gonzalo Ruiz. 1998. *Evolución del gasto público social en América Latina, 1980-1995.* Cuadernos de la CEPAL 80. Santiago: ECLAC.

David, Beatriz and César Morales, eds. Forthcoming. *¿Desarrollo rural en América Latina y el Caribe: la construcción de un nuevo modelo?* Santiago: ECLAC.

De Gregorio, José and Jong-Wha Lee. 1999. "Economic Growth in Latin America: Sources and Prospects." Paper presented at annual meeting of Latin America and Caribbean Economics Association (LACEA), Santiago, Chile.

Di Gropello, Emanuela and Rossella Cominetti, eds. 1998. *La decentralización de la educación y la salud.* Santiago: ECLAC.

Dirven, Martine. 1999. "El papel de los agentes en las políticas agrícolas: intenciones y realidad." *Revista de la CEPAL* 68 (August): 171–86.

Drazen, Allan. 1997. "Policy Signaling in the Open Economy: A Re-examination." Working Paper 5892. Cambridge, MA: National Bureau of Economic Research.

Duryea, Suzanne and Miguel Székely. 1998. "Labor Markets in Latin America: A Supply-Side Story." Working Paper 374. Washington: Inter-American Development Bank, Office of the Chief Economist.

Easterly, William, Norman Loayza, and Peter Montiel. 1997. "Has Latin America's Post-Reform Growth Been Disappointing?" *Journal of International Economics* 43(3/4): 287–311.

ECLAC (Economic Commission for Latin America and the Caribbean). 1996. *Strengthening Development: The Interplay of Macro and Microeconomics.* Santiago.

———. 1997. *The Equity Gap: Latin America, the Caribbean, and the Social Summit.* Santiago.

———. 1998a. *América Latina y el Caribe: políticas para mejorar la inserción en la economía mundial.* Santiago: ECLAC/Fondo de Cultura Económica (originally published in 1995).

———. 1998b. *The Fiscal Covenant: Strengths, Weaknesses, Challenges.* Santiago.

———. 1998c. *Foreign Direct Investment in Latin America and the Caribbean, 1998.* Santiago.

———. 1999a. *Economic Survey of Latin America and the Caribbean, 1998–99.* Santiago.

———. 1999b. *Latin America and the Caribbean in the World Economy, 1998.* Santiago.

————. 1999c. *Social Panorama of Latin America, 1998*. Santiago.

————. 1999d. *Statistical Yearbook for Latin America and the Caribbean, 1998*. Santiago.

————. 2000a. *Equity, Development, and Citizenship*. Santiago.

————. 2000b. *Foreign Direct Investment in Latin America and the Caribbean, 2000*. Santiago.

ECLAC/UNESCO. 1992. *Education and Knowledge: Basic Pillars of Changing Production Patterns with Social Equity*. Santiago.

ECLAC/World Bank. 1999. *TradeCAN: Database and Software for a Competitiveness Analysis of Nations. User Guide*, 1999 ed. Washington: World Bank.

Edwards, Sebastian. 1995. *Crisis and Reform in Latin America: From Despair to Hope*. Oxford University Press.

Edwards, Sebastian and Nora Claudia Lustig, eds. 1997. *Labor Markets in Latin America: Combining Social Protection with Market Flexibility*. Brookings.

Escaith, Hubert and Samuel Morley. Forthcoming. "The Impact of Reforms on Growth in Latin America and the Caribbean: An Econometric Estimation." Santiago: ECLAC.

Evans, Peters. 1979. *Dependent Development: The Alliance of Multinational, State, and Local Capital*. Princeton University Press.

Fernández Arias, Eduardo and Peter Montiel. 1997. "Reform and Growth in Latin America: All Pain, No Gain?" Working Paper 351. Washington: Inter-American Development Bank, Office of the Chief Economist.

Ffrench-Davis, Ricardo. 1999. *Reforming the Reforms in Latin America: Macroeconomics, Trade, Finance*. Macmillan.

Ffrench-Davis, Ricardo and Helmut Reisen, eds. 1998. *Capital Flows and Investment Performance: Lessons from Latin America*. Paris: OECD Development Centre/ECLAC.

Ganuza, Enrique, Arturo León, and Pablo Sauma, eds. 1999. *Gasto público en servicios sociales básicos en América Latina y el Caribe*. Santiago: UNDP/ECLAC/UNICEF.

García, Pablo, Patricio Meller, and Andrea Repetto. 1996. "Las exportaciones como motor de crecimiento: la evidencia chilena." In *El modelo exportador chileno: crecimiento y equidad*, edited by Patricio Meller, 19–42. Santiago: CIEPLAN.

García-Huidobro, Guillermo. 1999. "La capacidad generadora de empleo productivo de la economía chilena." Serie Reformas Económicas 31. Santiago: ECLAC.

Garrido, Celso and Wilson Peres. 1998. "Big Latin American Industrial Companies and Groups." *CEPAL Review* 66 (December): 129–50.

Gibney, Frank and others. 1995. "Letters to the Editor. Asia's Growth: Miracle or Myth?" *Foreign Affairs* 72(2): 170–77.

Goldsmith, Raymond W. 1951. "A Perpetual Inventory of National Wealth." *Studies in Income and Wealth* 14: 5–61.

Gómez, Sergio and Sergio Echeñique. 1998. *La agricultura chilena: las dos caras de la modernización*. Santiago: Latin American Faculty of Social Sciences (FLACSO) and Agraria.

Government of Argentina. 1999. *El impacto redistributivo del gasto público en los sectores sociales*. Documento de Trabajo GP/08. Buenos Aires: Dirección Nacional de Programación del Gasto Social, Ministerio de Economía y Obras y Servicios Públicos.

Government of Chile. 1996. *Balance de 6 años de las políticas sociales 1990–96*. Santiago: Ministerio de Planificación y Coordinación.

Government of Chile. 1998. *Distribución e impacto distributivo del gasto social en los hogares 1996*. Santiago: Ministerio de Planificación y Coordinación.

Griffith-Jones, Stephany. 1998. *Global Capital Flows*. Macmillan.

————. 2000. "International Capital Flows to Latin America." Serie Reformas Económicas 55. Santiago: ECLAC.

Griliches, Zvi. 1998. "Productivity: Measurement Problems." In *The New Palgrave: A Dictionary of Economics*, 4 vols., edited by John Eatwell, Murray Milgate, and Peter Newman, 1010–13. Macmillan.

Hofman, André. 2000. "Economic Growth and Performance in Latin America." Serie Reformas Económicas 53. Santiago: ECLAC.

IDB (Inter-American Development Bank). 1993. *Economic and Social Progress in Latin America, 1993 Report.* Johns Hopkins University Press.

————. 1996. *Economic and Social Progress in Latin America, 1996 Report.* Johns Hopkins University Press.

————. 1997. *Economic and Social Progress in Latin America, 1997 Report: Latin America after a Decade of Reforms.* Johns Hopkins University Press.

————. 1998a. *Economic and Social Progress in Latin America, 1998–1999 Report: Facing Up to Inequality in Latin America.* Johns Hopkins University Press.

————. 1998b. "Employment in Latin America: What Is the Problem and How to Address It?" Document prepared for IDB meeting in Cartagena de las Indias.

ILO (International Labour Organization). 1999. *Panorama Laboral de América Latina y el Caribe, 1999.* Lima: ILO Regional Office.

IMF (International Monetary Fund). 2000. *International Financial Statistics Yearbook, 2000.* Washington.

IPEA. 1999. "A mensuração do impacto redistributivo do gasto social: un estudo para região metropolitana de São Paulo." Gasto Social. *IPEA debate* 1(1). Brasilia.

Katz, Jorge. 2000. *Reformas estructurales, productividad y conducta tecnológica en América Latina.* Santiago: ECLAC/Fondo de Cultura Económica (forthcoming).

King, Damien. 2000. "The Evolution of Structural Adjustment and Stabilization in Jamaica." Serie Reformas Económicas 65. Santiago: ECLAC (forthcoming).

King, Damien and Sudhanshu Handa. 2000. "Changes in the Distribution of Income and the New Economic Model in Jamaica." Serie Reformas Económicas 57. Santiago: ECLAC.

Krueger, Anne O. 1978. *Foreign Trade Regimes and Economic Development: Liberalization Attempts and Consequences.* Cambridge, MA: Ballinger.

————. 1981–83. *Trade and Employment in Developing Countries.* 3 vols. University of Chicago Press.

Krugman, Paul. 1994. "The Myth of Asia's Miracle." *Foreign Affairs* 73(6): 62–78.

Kuwayama, Mikio, ed. 1999. *Nuevas políticas comerciales en América Latina y Asia: algunos casos nacionales.* Santiago: ECLAC.

Kuznets, Simon. 1955. "Economic Growth and Income Inequality." *American Economic Review* 45(1): 1–28.

Larrañaga, Osvaldo. 1999. "Distribución de ingresos y crecimiento económico en Chile." Serie Reformas Económicas 35. Santiago: ECLAC.

Londoño, Juan Luis and Miguel Székely. 1997. "Persistent Poverty and Excess Inequality: Latin America, 1970–1995." Working Paper 357. Washington: Inter-American Development Bank, Office of the Chief Economist.

López, Julio. 1999. "Evolución reciente del empleo en México." Serie Reformas Económicas 29. Santiago: ECLAC.

Lora, Eduardo. 1997. "A Decade of Structural Reforms in Latin America: What Has Been Reformed and How to Measure It." Document presented to the Annual Meeting of the Board of Governors of the Inter-American Development Bank, Barcelona, Spain.

Lora, Eduardo and Felipe Barrera. 1997. "A Decade of Structural Reform in Latin America: Growth, Productivity and Investment Are Not What They Used to Be." Working Paper 350. Washington: Inter-American Development Bank, Office of the Chief Economist.

Lora, Eduardo and Mauricio Olivera. 1998. "Macro Policy and Employment Problems in Latin America." Working Paper 372. Washington: Inter-American Development Bank, Office of the Chief Economist.

Márquez, Gustavo and Carmen Pagés. 1998. "Trade and Employment Evidence from Latin America and the Caribbean." Working Paper 366. Washington: Inter-American Development Bank, Office of the Chief Economist.

Moguillansky, Graciela. 1999. *La inversión en Chile: ¿el fin de un ciclo en expansión?* Santiago: ECLAC/Fondo de Cultura Económica.

Moguillansky, Graciela and Ricardo Bielschowsky. 2000. *La inversión en un proceso de cambio estructural: América Latina en los noventa.* Santiago: ECLAC/Fondo de Cultura Económica (forthcoming).

Montiel, Nancy. 1999. "Costa Rica: Reformas económicas, sectores dinámicos y calidad de los empleos." Serie Reformas Económicas 26. Santiago: ECLAC.

Morley, Samuel. 1995. *Poverty and Inequality in Latin America: The Impact of Adjustment and Recovery in the 1980s.* Johns Hopkins University Press.

———. 2000. *El problema de la distribución del ingreso en América Latina.* Santiago: ECLAC/Fondo de Cultura Económica (forthcoming).

Morley, Samuel A., Roberto Machado, and Stefano Pettinato. 1999. "Indexes of Structural Reform in Latin America." Serie Reformas Económicas 12. Santiago: ECLAC.

Mostajo, Rossana. 2000. "Gasto social y distribución del ingreso: caracterización e impacto redistributivo en países seleccionados de América Latina y el Caribe." Serie Reformas Económicas 69. Santiago: ECLAC (forthcoming).

Ocampo, José Antonio. 1998. "Beyond the Washington Consensus: An ECLAC Perspective." *CEPAL Review* 66 (December): 7–28.

Oman, Charles. 1994. *Globalisation and Regionalisation: The Challenge for Developing Countries.* Paris: OECD, Development Centre.

Paunovic, Igor. 2000. "Growth and Reforms in Latin America and the Caribbean in the 1990s." Serie Reformas Económicas 70. Santiago: ECLAC (forthcoming).

Peres, Wilson, ed. 1998. *Grandes empresas y grupos industriales latinoamericanos. Expansión y desafíos en la era de la apertura y la globalización.* Mexico: Siglo XXI.

Peres, Wilson and Giovanni Stumpo. 2000. "Small and Medium-sized Manufacturing Enterprises in Latin America and the Caribbean under the New Economic Model." *World Development* 28(9) (forthcoming).

Persson, Torsten. 1988. "Credibility of Macroeconomic Policy: An Introduction and Broad Survey." *European Economic Review* 32: 519–32.

Persson, Torsten and Guido Tabellini. 1989. *Macroeconomic Policy, Credibility and Politics.* London: Harwood.

Radelet, Steven and Jeffrey Sachs. 1998. "The Onset of the East Asian Crisis." Working Paper 6680. Cambridge, MA: National Bureau of Economic Research.

Ramírez, Juan Mauricio and Liliana Núñez. 1999. "Reformas estructurales, inversión y crecimiento: Colombia durante los años noventa." Serie Reformas Económicas 45. Santiago: ECLAC.

Reinhardt, Nola and Wilson Peres. 2000. "Latin America's New Economic Model: Micro Responses and Economic Restructuring." *World Development* 28(9) (forthcoming).

Robbins, Donald. 1996. "HOS Hits Facts: Facts Win: Evidence on Trade and Wages in the Developing World." Harvard Institute for International Development.

Rodrik, Dani. 1989. "Promises, Promises: Credible Policy Reform via Signaling." *The Economic Journal* 99: 756–72.

———. 1996. "Understanding Economic Policy Reform." *Journal of Economic Literature* 34 (March): 9–41.

———. 1998. "Who Needs Capital Account Convertibility?" In *Should the IMF Pursue Capital-Account Convertibility?*, Stanley Fischer and others, 55–65. Essays in International Finance 207. Princeton University.

———. 1999. *The New Global Economy and Developing Countries: Making Openness Work.* Policy Essay 24. Washington: Overseas Development Council.

Rogoff, Kenneth. 1987. "Reputational Constraints on Monetary Policy." *Carnegie-Rochester Conference Series on Public Policy* 26: 141–81.

Rostow, Walt W. 1995. "Letters to the Editor." *Foreign Affairs* 74(1): 183–84.

Saavedra Chanduví, Jaime and Juan José Díaz. 1999. "Desigualdad del ingreso y del gasto en el Perú antes y después de las reformas estructurales." Serie Reformas Económicas 34. Santiago: ECLAC.

Servén, Luis and Andrés Solimano. 1993. " Economic Adjustment and Investment Performance in Developing Countries: The Experience of the 1980s." In *Striving for Growth after Adjustment. The Role of Capital Formation*, edited by Luis Servén and Andrés Solimano, 149–79. Washington: World Bank.

Spilimbergo, Antonio, Juan Luis Londoño, and Miguel Székely. 1997. "Income Distribution, Factor Endowments, and Trade Openness." Working Paper 356. Washington: Inter-American Development Bank, Office of the Chief Economist.

Stallings, Barbara. 1992. "International Influence on Economic Policy: Debt, Stabilization, and Structural Reform." In *The Politics of Economic Adjustment*, edited by Stephan Haggard and Robert R. Kaufman, 41–88. Princeton University Press.

———, ed. 1995. *Global Change, Regional Response: The New International Context of Development.* Cambridge University Press.

Stallings, Barbara, Nancy Birdsall, and Julie Clugage. 2000. "Growth and Inequality: Do Regional Patterns Redeem Kuznets?" In *Distributive Justice and Economic Development: The Experience of Chile and Developing Countries,* edited by Andrés Solimano, Eduardo Aninat, and Nancy Birdsall, 48–111. University of Michigan Press.

Tejo, Pedro. 1999. *El modelo agrícola de América Latina en las últimas décadas: una síntesis.* Santiago: ECLAC, Agricultural Development Unit.

Tokman, Victor E. 1994. *Generación de empleo en un nuevo contexto estructural.* Lima: ILO Regional Office.

Turner, Louis and Michael Hodges. 1992. *Global Shakeout: World Market Competition—the Challenge for Business and Government.* London: Century Business.

Tussie, Diana. 1997. "Trade Policy within the Context of the World Trade Organization." *CEPAL Review* 62 (August): 121–37.

United Nations. 1999. *World Economic and Social Survey, 1999*. New York: Department of Economic and Social Affairs.

Vélez, Carlos E. 1996. *Gasto social y desigualdad: logros y extravíos. Estudio de la incidencia del gasto público social en Colombia*. Santafé de Bogotá: Departamento Nacional de Planeación.

Villasuso, Juan Manuel. 2000. "Reformas estructurales y política económica en Costa Rica." Serie Reformas Económicas 64. Santiago: ECLAC (forthcoming).

Vos, Rob and others, eds. Forthcoming. *Balance of Payments Liberalization in Latin America and the Caribbean: Effects on Employment, Inequality, and Poverty*.

Walter, Jorge and Cecilia Senén G. 1998. "La privatización de las telecomunicaciones en latinoamérica y el caso argentino: balance de un período de transición." Santiago: ECLAC.

Weller, Jürgen. 1996. "Efectos del ajuste estructural en el empleo y los ingresos agropecuarios, con énfasis en las exportaciones no tradicionales: los casos de Costa Rica y Honduras." In *Apertura comercial en Centroamérica: nuevos retos para la agricultura*, edited by Helmut Nuhn and Andreas Stamm, 195–224. San José, Costa Rica: Departamento Ecuménico de Investigaciones.

———. 2000. *Reformas económicas, crecimiento y empleo: los mercados de trabajo en América Latina durante los años noventa*. Santiago: ECLAC/Fondo de Cultura Económica (forthcoming).

Williamson, John, ed. 1990. *Latin American Adjustment: How Much Has Happened?* Washington: Institute for International Economics.

———. 1993. "Democracy and the Washington Consensus." *World Development* 21(8): 1329–36.

World Bank. 1991. *World Development Report, 1991*. Oxford University Press.

———. 1993. *The East Asian Miracle: Economic Growth and Public Policy*. Oxford University Press.

———. 1995a. *Bureaucrats in Business*. Oxford University Press.

———. 1995b. *Labor and Economic Reforms in Latin America and the Caribbean: Regional Perspectives on World Development Report 1995*. Washington: World Bank.

———. 1995c. *World Development Report, 1995*. Oxford University Press.

———. 2000. *World Development Report, 2000*. Oxford University Press.

WTO (World Trade Organization). 1998. *Annual Report, 1998*. 2 vols. Geneva.

Additional Project Publications

This book synthesizes the main results of the project, "Growth, Employment, and Equity," which was conducted by the Economic Commission for Latin America and the Caribbean (ECLAC). The project also produced a large number of more specific studies listed below.

The first five titles analyze the impact of the reforms with respect to the topics of investment, technical change, employment, equity, and the agricultural sector, drawing on material from some or all of the nine project countries. Nine edited volumes present papers on various topics related to the reforms and their impact in the individual project countries. And last, there are two series of working papers, both of which can be found on the ECLAC website (www.eclac.cl): the ECLAC Working Paper Series on Economic Reforms, which examines the major components of the reforms in each individual country, and the ECLAC Working Paper Series on Environment and Development, a special set of studies on the relation between the reforms and the environment.

Comparative Topic Volumes

Beatriz David and César Morales, eds. Forthcoming. *Desarrollo rural en América Latina y el Caribe. ¿La construcción de un nuevo modelo?* Santiago: ECLAC.

Jorge Katz. 2000. *Reformas estructurales, productividad y conducta tecnológica en América Latina*. Santiago: ECLAC/Fondo de Cultura Económica. An English version will be published by ECLAC.

Graciela Moguillansky and Ricardo Bielschowsky. 2000. *La inversión en un proceso de cambio estructural: América Latina en los noventa*. Santiago: ECLAC/Fondo de Cultura Económica. An English version will be published by ECLAC.

Samuel Morley. 2000. *El problema de la distribución del ingreso en América Latina*. Santiago: ECLAC/Fondo de Cultura Económica. An English version will be published by ECLAC.

Jürgen Weller. 2000. *Reformas económicas, crecimiento y empleo: los mercados de trabajo en América Latina durante los años noventa*. Santiago: ECLAC/Fondo de Cultura Económica. An English version will be published by ECLAC.

Country Volumes

Eduardo Antelo and Luis Carlos Jemio, eds. 2000. *Quince años de reformas estructurales en Bolivia: sus impactos sobre inversión, crecimiento, empleo y equidad*. La Paz: CEPAL/Universidad Católica Boliviana.

Renato Baumann, ed. 1999. *Brasil: uma década em transição*. Rio de Janeiro: CEPAL/Editora Campus.

Fernando Clavijo, ed. 2000. *Las reformas económicas en México en los últimos veinte años*. México: CEPAL/Fondo de Cultura Económica.

Juan José Echavarría, ed. 2000. *La crisis y la industrialización*. Santafé de Bogotá: CEPAL/Ediciones Tercer Mundo.

Ricardo Ffrench-Davis and Osvaldo Rosales, eds. 2000. *Reformas, crecimiento y equidad: Chile desde 1973*. Santiago: CEPAL.

Daniel Heymann and Bernardo Kosakoff, eds. 2000. *Desempeño económico en un contexto de reformas: la Argentina en los noventa*. Buenos Aires: CEPAL/EUDEBA.

Damien King, ed. 2000. *Reform and Crisis in Jamaica*. Kingston: Ian Randle Publishers.

Alberto Pasco-Font and Jaime Saavedra, eds. 2000. *Perú: balance de una década de reformas estructurales*. Lima: CEPAL/GRADE.

Anabelle Ulate, ed. 2000. *Crecimiento, empleo y equidad: los desafíos de las reformas económicas de finales del siglo XX en Costa Rica*. San José: CEPAL/Editorial de la Universidad de Costa Rica.

Working Papers (ECLAC, Serie Reformas Económicas)

1. Graciela Moguillansky. "La gestión privada y la inversión en el sector eléctrico chileno." September 1997.

2. Graciela Moguillansky. "Chile: las reformas estructurales y la inversión privada en áreas de infraestructura." November 1997.

3. Graciela Moguillansky. "Chile: las inversiones en el sector minero 1980-2000." July 1998.

4. Graciela Moguillansky. "Las reformas del sector de telecomunicaciones en Chile y el comportamiento de la inversión." August 1998.

5. Carlos Adrián Romero. "Regulación e inversiones en el sector eléctrico argentino." September 1998.

6. Ricardo Delgado. "Inversiones en infraestructura vial: la experiencia argentina." October 1998.

7. Nicolás Gadano. "Determinantes de la inversión en el sector petróleo y gas de la Argentina." October 1998.

8. Omar Chisari y Martín Rodríguez. "Algunos determinantes de la inversión en sectores de infraestructura en la Argentina." November 1998.

9. Marcelo Celani. "Determinantes de la inversión en telecomunicaciones en Argentina." November 1998.

10. Jurgen Weller. "Los retos de la institucionalidad laboral en el marco de la transformación de la modalidad de desarrollo en América Latina." November 1998.

11. Jurgen Weller. "Los mercados laborales en América Latina: su evolución en el largo plazo y sus tendencias recientes." December 1998.

12. Samuel Morley, Roberto Machado, and Stefano Pettinato. "Indexes of Structural Reform in Latin America." January 1999.

13. Jorge Katz. "Reformas estructurales y comportamiento tecnológico: reflexiones en torno a las fuentes y naturaleza del cambio tecnológico en América Latina en los años noventa." February 1999.

14. Jorge Katz. "Cambios estructurales y evolución de la productividad laboral en la industria latinoamericana en el período 1970–1996." February 1999.

15. Gover Barja. "Inversión y productividad en la industria boliviana de la electricidad." February 1999.

16. Gover Barja. "Inversión y productividad en la industria boliviana de telecomunicaciones." February 1999.

17. Rebeca Escobar de Medécigo. "El cambio estructural de las telecomunicaciones y la inversión: el caso de México." February 1999.

18. Víctor Rodríguez Padilla. "Impacto de la reforma económica sobre las inversiones de la industria eléctrica en México: el regreso del capital privado como palanca de desarrollo." February 1999.

19. Ramón Carlos Torres Flores. "México: Impacto de las reformas estructurales en la formación de capital del sector petrolero." April 1999.

20. Isaac Scheinvar. "Las carreteras y el sistema portuario frente a las reformas económicas en México." April 1999.

21. Daniel Bitrán B. "México: Inversiones en el sector agua, alcantarillado y saneamiento." April 1999.

22. Humberto Campodónico. "La inversión en el sector telecomunicaciones del Perú en el período 1994–2000." May 1999.

23. Humberto Campodónico. "La inversión en el sector petrolero peruano en el período 1993–2000." May 1999.

24. Humberto Campodónico. "Las reformas estructurales en el sector minero peruano y las características de la inversión 1992–2008." May 1999.

25. Humberto Campodónico. "Las reformas estructurales del sector eléctrico peruano y las características de la inversión 1992–2000." May 1999.

26. Nancy Montiel. "Costa Rica: Reformas económicas, sectores dinámicos y calidad de los empleos." May 1999.

27. Jaime Saavedra. "La dinámica del mercado de trabajo en el Perú antes y después de las reformas estructurales." May 1999.

28. Oscar Altimir y Luis Beccaria. "El mercado de trabajo bajo el nuevo régimen económico en Argentina." July 1999.

29. Julio López. "Evolución reciente del empleo en México." July 1999.

30. José Marcio Camargo y Marcelo Neri. "Emprego e productividade no Brasil na década de noventa." July 1999.

31. Guillermo García-Huidobro. "La capacidad generadora de empleo productivo de la economía chilena." July 1999.

32. Emilio Morgado. "Las reformas laborales y su impacto en el funcionamiento del mercado de trabajo en Chile." July 1999.

33. Luis Carlos Jemio. "Reformas, crecimiento, progreso técnico y empleo en Bolivia." July 1999.

34. Jaime Saavedra y Juan José Díaz. "Desigualdad del ingreso y del gasto en el Perú antes y después de las reformas estructurales." July 1999.

35. Osvaldo Larrañaga. "Distribución de ingresos y crecimiento económico en Chile." July 1999.

36. Mauricio Cárdenas and Raquel Bernal. "Changes in the Distribution of Income and the New Economic Model in Colombia." November 1999.

37. Juan Diego Trejos. "Reformas económicas y distribución del ingreso en Costa Rica." November 1999.

38. Luis Carlos Jemio. "Reformas, políticas sociales y equidad en Bolivia." November 1999.

39. Marcelo Neri and José Marcio Camargo. "Structural reforms, macroeconomic fluctuations and income distribution in Brazil." November 1999.

40. Oscar Altimir and Luis Beccaria. "Distribución del ingreso en la Argentina." November 1999.

41. Roberto Bisang and Georgina Gómez. "Las inversiones en la industria argentina en la década de los noventa." November 1999.

42. Gover Barja Daza. "Las reformas estructurales bolivianas y su impacto sobre inversiones." November 1999.

43. Diego Montenegro Ernst and Alvaro Guzmán Bowles. "Inversión y productividad en el sector agrícola-agroindustrial boliviano: caso de la agricultura comercial período 1985–1998." November 1999.

44. Ricardo Bielschowsky. "Investimentos na indústria brasileira depois da abertura e do real: o mini-ciclo de modernizações, 1995–1997." November 1999.

45. Juan Mauricio Ramírez and Liliana Núñez. "Reformas estructurales, inversión y crecimiento: Colombia durante los años noventa." November 1999.

46. Francisco Silva Torrealba. "La inversión en el sector agroindustrial chileno." November 1999.

47. Juan Carlos Moreno-Brid. "Reformas macroeconómicas e inversión manufacturera en México." December 1999.

48. Luis Abugattás. "Estabilización macroeconómica, reforma estructural y comportamiento industrial: la experiencia peruana." December 1999.

49. Gerardo Mendiola. "México: Empresas maquiladoras de exportación en los noventa." December 1999.

50. Virginia Moori-Koening. "Reformas económicas y la inversión en el sector minero argentino." December 1999.

51. Israel Fainboim and Carlos Jorge Rodríguez. "El desarrollo de la infraestructura en Colombia en la década de los noventa." March 2000.

52. José Antonio Cordero P. "El crecimiento económico y la inversión: el caso de Costa Rica." March 2000.

53. Jorge Katz, Jaime Cáceres and Kattia Cárdenas. "Instituciones y tecnología en el desarrollo evolutivo de la industria minera chilena." March 2000.

54. André Hofman. "Economic Growth and Performance in Latin America." March 2000.

55. Stephany Griffith-Jones. "International Capital Flows to Latin America." March 2000.

56. Max Spoor. "Two Decades of Adjustment and Agricultural Development in Latin America and the Caribbean." March 2000.

57. Damien King and Sudhanshu Handa. "Changes in the Distribution of Income and the New Economic Model in Jamaica." March 2000.

58. Rodolfo de la Torre. "La distribución factorial del ingreso en el nuevo modelo económico en México." March 2000.

59. Juan Mauricio Ramírez and Liliana Núñez. "Reformas, crecimiento, progreso técnico y empleo en Colombia." March 2000.

60. Dillon Alleyne. "Employment, Growth, and Reforms in Jamaica." 2000.

61. Daniel Heymann. "Políticas de reforma y comportamiento macroeconómico: la Argentina en los noventa." 2000.

62. Eduardo Antelo. "Políticas de estabilización y de reformas estructurales en Bolivia a partir de 1985." 2000.

63. Rubens Penha Cysne. "Aspectos macro e microeconômico das reformas brasileiras." 2000.

64. Juan Manuel Villasuso. "Reformas estructurales y política económica en Costa Rica." 2000.

65. Damien King. "The Evolution of Structural Adjustment and Stabilization Policy in Jamaica." 2000.

66. Alberto Pasco-Font. "Políticas de estabilización y reformas estructurales: Perú." 2000.

67. Fernando Clavijo. "Reformas estructurales y política macroeconómica: el caso de México 1982–1998." 2000.

68. Juan José Echavarría. "Reformas estructurales y política económica: Colombia durante los años noventa." 2000.

69. Rossana Mostajo. "Gasto social y distribución del ingreso: caracterización e impacto redistributivo en países seleccionados de América Latina y el Caribe." 2000.

70. Igor Paunovic. "Growth and Reforms in Latin America and the Caribbean in the 1990s." 2000.

Working Papers (ECLAC, Serie Medio Ambiente y Desarrollo)

19. Marianne Schaper. "Impactos ambientales de los cambios en la estructura exportadora de los países de América Latina y el Caribe: 1980-1995." December 1999.

20. Guillermo Acuña. "Reformas macroeconómicas en América Latina y el Caribe: Su impacto en los marcos regulatorios e institucionales ambientales de nueve estudios de caso." 2000.

21. Claudia Schatán. "Contaminación industrial en los países latinoamericanos pre y post reforma económica." 2000.

22. Claudio Ferraz and Carlos E.F. Young. "Trade Liberalization and Industrial Pollution in Brazil." 2000.

23. Fidel Aroche Reyes. "Reformas estructurales y composición de las emisiones contaminantes industriales. Resultados para México." 2000.

24. Alberto Pasco-Font. "El impacto del Programa de Estabilización y las reformas estructurales sobre el desempeño ambiental de la minería de cobre en el Perú: 1990–1997." 2000.

25. Hernán Durán. "El impacto de las reformas económicas y ambientales sobre el desempeño de la minería del cobre en Chile: 1970–1998." 2000.

Index

ECONOMIC COMMISSION FOR LATIN AMERICA AND THE CARIBBEAN

ECLAC is one of five United Nations regional commissions. All Latin American and Caribbean countries are members, as are a number of developed nations in America and Europe with strong historical, cultural, and economic ties to the region. Since its founding in 1948, ECLAC has promoted economic and social development and cooperation between nations through training courses, technical assistance, and policy-oriented research projects. As well as providing general economic analysis, these projects also address the particular problems of individual Latin American and Caribbean countries. In recent years, ECLAC has focused its efforts on the challenges faced by the region in achieving sustained (and environmentally sustainable) growth among pluralist democracies. These democracies face very real demands as they find ways to develop their economies in order to benefit the majority of the population. As a result, ECLAC's main focus has been on helping countries improve economic growth and social equity simultaneously. ECLAC, with headquarters in Santiago, Chile, has two subregional offices in Mexico and in Trinidad and Tobago, together with national offices in Argentina, Brazil, Colombia, Uruguay, and the United States.